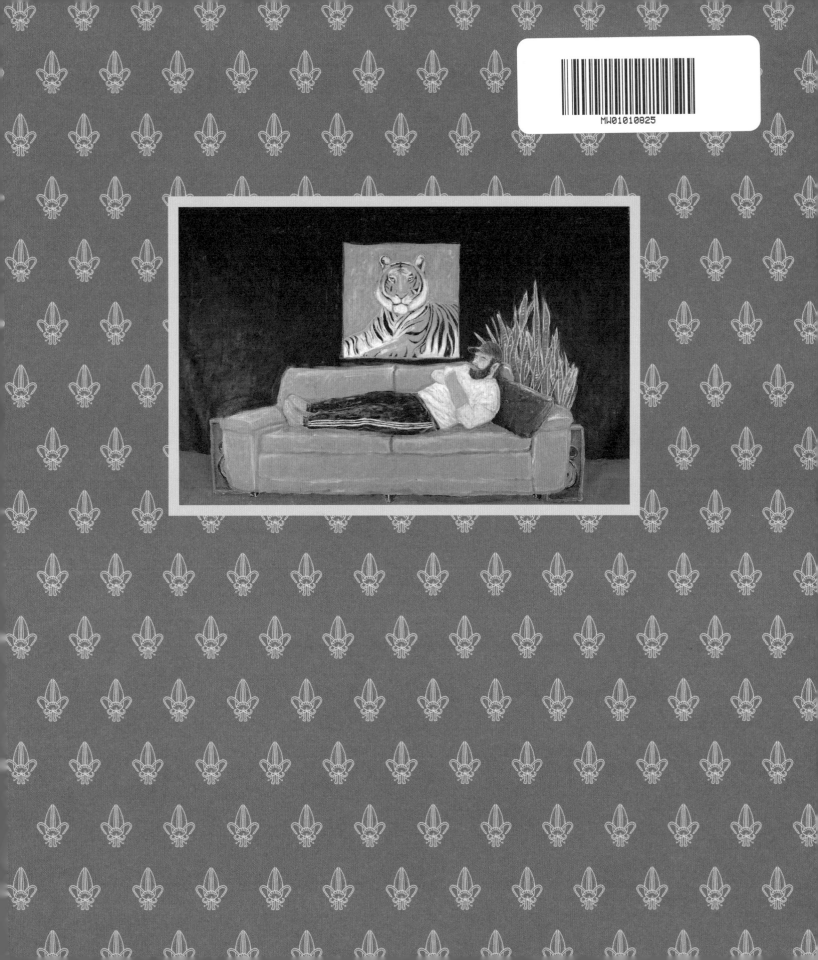

ALSO BY FRÉDÉRIC MORIN, DAVID McMILLAN, AND MEREDITH ERICKSON

The Art of Living According to Joe Beef: A Cookbook of Sorts

JOE ⚜ BEEF

Surviving the Apocalypse

JOE ⚜ BEEF

Surviving the Apocalypse

⤙⤙⤙ ANOTHER COOKBOOK OF SORTS ⤚⤚⤚

FRÉDÉRIC MORIN, DAVID McMILLAN, and MEREDITH ERICKSON

Photographs by Jennifer May

appetite
by RANDOM HOUSE

This book is dedicated in loving memory
to Anthony Bourdain and John Bil,
qui dort dîne.

—F&D&M

Appetite by Random House® and colophon are registered trademarks of
Penguin Random House LLC.

Library and Archives Canada Cataloguing in Publication is available upon request.

ISBN: 978-0-14-753079-0
eBook ISBN: 978-0-14-753080-6

Book design by Cassandra J. Pappas
Jacket photograph by Jennifer May
Jacket design by Stephanie Ross
Copyediting and recipe testing by Kendra McKnight
Food styling by Jennifer May, Meredith Erickson, Frédéric Morin, Marco Frappier,
and David McMillan
Printed and bound in China

Published in Canada by Appetite by Random House®,
a division of Penguin Random House Canada Limited.

www.penguinrandomhouse.ca

10 9 8 7 6 5 4 3 2 1

appetite
by RANDOM HOUSE

Penguin
Random
House

Left column (partial, cut off)

es — E, MA — 3 chq
lish, MA
DM 16$
y (RI),
de — 12$
repoix — /6
iges, QC — 20$/39
rdiques — 14$
sh — 12$
ontecarlo 12$
'Alsacienne 10$
oishe's pickle
2.50
ique 11$
sabayon
u miel — 12$
pour 2 — 15$
lle rum-raisin
10$
x Chèvre 10$
andez-nous!

Center column

Patras, Roditis, Tetramythos '15 GR 40$
Muscadet Sèrre & Maine 'fief du Breil', Jo Landron '13 55$
Bourgogne Aligoté, Pierre Morey '00 60$
Alsace Pinot Blanc 'Barriques', A. Ostertag '14 FR 55$
Arbois Chardonnay 'follasses' M. Gahier '14 FR 65$
Ontario Riesling, Norman Hardie '14 ONT 65$
Vinho Verde, Loureiro 'Aphros' '14 Port 105$
Beaujolais Blanc, Domaine du Gaget '14 65$
Lisboa Vital Casal Figueira '15 Port 75$
Roussette de Savoie 'Son Altesse' Ch. de Mérande '15 75$
Mosel Riesling Spätlese, Hofgut Falkenstein '15 70$
Venezia Giulia, Malvasia, Edi Kante '13 85$
Collio Friulano, Gianni & Giorgio Venica '14 80$
Irouleguy 'Hegoxuri', Arretxea '12 FR 95$
Penedès 'Sasso', Finca Parera '14 Esp. 95$
Etna Bianco, 'Aurora' I Vigneri '15 It 90$
Chablis 'Croix aux Moines', Pommier '14 85$
Crête Assyrtiko, Economou '13 Grèce 90$
Alsace Grand Cru 'Kirchberg de Barr', Willm '10 95$
Saumur blanc, Chateau Yvonne '14 FR 95$
VDF Maconnais 'D14', Alexandre Jouveaux '14 125$
Jasnières 'Bistrologie', J.P. Robinot '13 125$
Saint Romain, Sarnin Berrux '13 FR 130$
Reuilly, Pinot gris, Les Poète, Guillaume Sorbe '14 135$
Alsace, Burg, Marcel Deiss '09 FR 130$
Beaune 'En Lulune' Genot Boulanger '12 140$
Ladoix 'le Clou', Prieuré Roch '11 170$
Chassagne Montrachet 1er cru Caillerets, Morey-Coffinet '12 235$
Puligny Montrachet Corvée des Vignes, J. Chavy '13 195$
Chablis 1er cru Beauroy, Philippe Pacalet '09 220$
Corton Charlemagne Grand Cru, P. Javillier '12 370$
Chateau Grillet, Neyret Gachet '04 FR 315$

Right column (partial, cut off)

Beaujo
Puglia
Bairra
VDF Lo
Rosso
VDP C
Venezia
hen
Bourg
Côte
Langh
Toscar
Faugè
Naoù
Côte
Dogli
Sour
es Cat
once
El Do
Savoie,
Etna
Bourgo
Vignet
Jasnie
VDF S

Contents

———

Prologue

I love restaurants. Everything about them. Always have.

A restaurant is both a superficial and deeply profound experience. Restaurants can leave an existential mark on your life, though you're essentially just sitting down to eat food and drink booze.

A restaurant is built on a foundation of broken hearts, failed relationships, trips to the hardware store, the clinic, extended credit, and the goodwill of people who care about you. Writing a book and building a restaurant are deeply personal acts. They require everything of you, your passion and your spirit. You can meander in fits and starts for months, years even, down the wrong path, all to get to the right one. Books and restaurants, the best ones in my estimation, are built on unworkable rewrites and failed ideas, and let me tell you: that body count is high.

Writing a book or opening a restaurant can make you lose your mind.

Until you haven't.

And then it clicks. And *that's* Day 1. *That's* where you start.

Building and then maintaining a restaurant is about loyalty. And this is why Joe Beef thrives. Because it is a deeply personal restaurant. That is not to say the food made in this tiny French restaurant isn't technically on point (it is) or that the old cottage influence of Maine or Gaspé won't fill you with nostalgia (it will), or that the care of the staff doesn't enchant you (it does).

The attraction to Joe Beef is due to its authenticity. You cannot bullshit people with an inauthentic voice or cooking. Well, you can. But it won't last.

"Deeply personal" is the beginning and the end of Fred and David's playbook.

The point of a prologue is to make overarching sense of the chapters, to lay out the sequence of what you're about to read. To pop the hood and preview what's inside. But I'm not going to do that. Because this book is simply about *where we are now*.

"Surviving the Apocalypse" was a theme we dreamt up in 2014. We're well aware there have been a few instances (some extreme weather, more-than-extreme election[s]) over the last couple of years when it seemed survivalism and talk of impending doom had jumped the shark. The cars were packed and the hazmat suits taped shut. The zeitgeist seemed to be closing in on us. Maybe the world was *actually* going to end. But this book was never about the headline.

This book is about how to build things for yourself.

This book is about how to make it on your own.

We don't expect anyone to build a trout pond that doesn't work, like our pond at Joe Beef. Or to create your own makeshift cellar to house thirty-one bunker-friendly foods (though it would be prudent). But maybe you'll write a poem about the Laurentians. Or make wine in a YETI cooler. Or cook up a pot-au-feu in the autumn for your girlfriend, and then a baby for the spring.

We set out to write a book about shutting out the noise, because that was the problem in our own lives. We vowed there would be fewer recipes than in our first book (*The Art of Living According to Joe Beef,* henceforth referred to as Book One), because recipes are time-consuming to write, but . . . we found inspiration in our weird theme and are giving you even more this time around (158!). So, the joke's on us.

After twelve years of Joe Beef, and seven years after our first book, we think you know us by now. And so, in the pages to come, you'll find good ideas, less-good ideas, and other ramblings. You'll find etiquette on how children should behave at dinner, quick tricks for cheat sauces, a chapter devoted to the weird and wonderful Quebec tradition of celebrating Christmas in July, a recipe for soap, and a towering cake made of rum balls.

I waitressed at Joe Beef on Day 1. We never thought we would make it to Week 2.

We never imagined people could love the restaurant as much as they do.

We never dreamt of writing a book.

We never thought anyone other than maybe our moms would buy the book.

And we definitely didn't think we would have the opportunity for a second.

With gratitude and tremendous love, this book is dedicated to our city of Montreal.

—M.E.
October 24, 2017

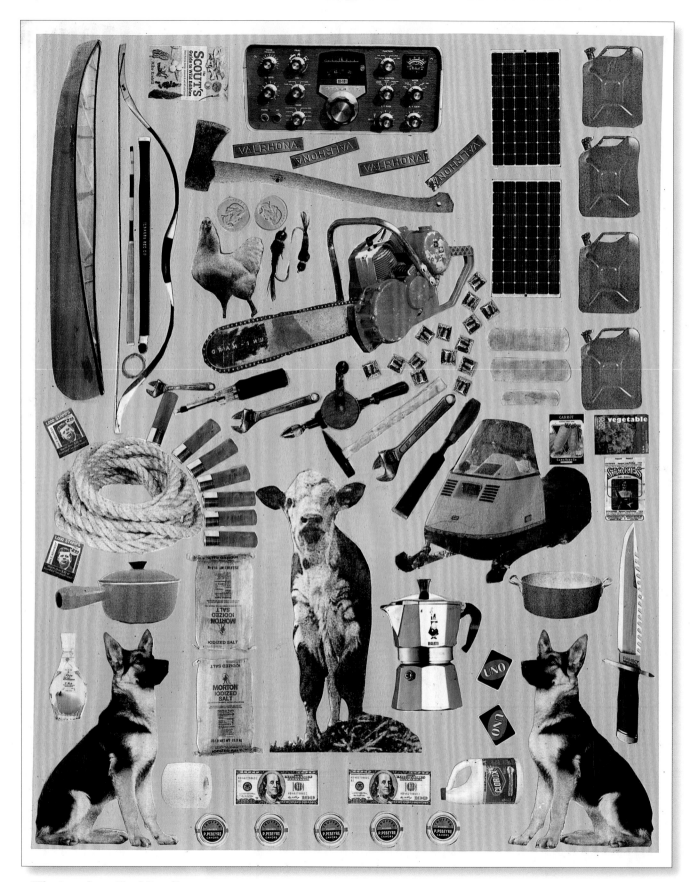

"The Apocalypse Mood Board"

Notes on Instruments and Ingredients

Bamboo-handle skimmer Get a medium hemispheric sieve with a bamboo handle; pick the one with fine mesh, it is really handy. You can find sieves in Chinatown.

Butter We use unsalted in the restaurant, cultured unsalted butter.

Cooking wine Buy good wine, made respectfully and cleanly, but don't break the bank.

Deep-frying thermometer

Dutch oven An oval Staub or Le Creuset fits an entire rabbit, pot-au-feu, braised leeks, or deer necks and only looks better over the years. A real must for this book (and your concrete bunker).

Fine-mesh sieve or strainer You'll never get bored of using this.

Frying food A French fry is a French fry is a French fry. We give no alternative to frying; oven roasting is a different game and panfrying, although misperceived as "healthier," is a messy and greasy affair. We could never in good conscience advise frying on the stove, as we have friends who are firemen and that's their main day-to-day housecall. Buy a small and cheap fryer, then fill it with lard or beef fat or whatever you decide.

Grams For cures, pastry, and precision, grams is where it's at. If you work with curing salt, cheese-making salts, or others, buy a digital pocket scale.

Instant-read digital thermometer

Knives The dimensions of your toolbox are inversely proportional to the size of your skill set. When you're older and perhaps better, you should use one or two knives: a small paring knife and a medium chef's knife.

Meat thermometer We strongly encourage this purchase.

Milk It's full-fat, homogenized milk—that's it.

Oil Grapeseed oil until they prove otherwise! For cooking and vinaigrettes.

Salt You do what you want for finishing salt, but for sausages and cooking we use kosher salt, for salt crust it is pickling salt.

One

Surviving the Apocalypse

W e're not *completely* serious when we say that zombies are coming. But we do feel we're living out the end of something. So, what is this apocalypse?

The apocalypse is on Instagram. It's self-praise. It's the obsession of the self. The glorification of the superficial.

It's the constant noise distracting us from creating anything real. It's Facebook ads we're afraid of.

It's climate change. It's the lack of jobs.

It's the overzealous adoration for food culture without the most basic understanding of where food comes from. The restaurant world is *Spinal Tap*-ing itself: the austerity of dining rooms, the tiring philosophizing about food. The stories told and the lies believed would make even a WWE fan cringe. We're living that out now, and we would rather think for ourselves and not drink the Kool-Aid (even if it is flavored with foraged berries).

We didn't think we'd ever have partners. Or kids. Fred and David *definitely* did not think there would be six kids between them. "Something happens to a man when less than three years go by and he now has three little wards to care for," David says. "An internal switch flips; there's a heightened awareness about everything. We used to drink and eat

with reckless abandon. And drive in the same manner. Now, we're willing to crowbar any idiot with a souped-up Honda Civic who seems to reenact all the installments of *The Fast and the Furious*. In fact, sometimes when we're at the park watching our kids play while scanning for predators, we start to fantasize about catching a criminal, who we stuff into a hockey bag, load into the trunk of our car, and dump in a cornfield so far north, they would never make the walk home. As a colorful Mafia character once told us, "A man has a lot of time to reflect on his mistakes when he is in a hockey bag in the trunk of a car."

But that's an aside. Point is: we have become obsessed not only with our own survival but that of our families. And when the apocalypse, or the nuclear winter hits, we don't want to just survive: we want to live it out in full Burgundy style. What do we mean by that? We mean not just camping food. When the year-long winter settles, and the mood turns sour in the lead-lined bunker, nothing warms the soul like a VGE consommé in a can topped with your own truffles and mutant duck fatty liver (a scene straight out of a Bruegel).

Living in the woods, albeit romantic at times, requires the skill to fight away any threats to your confits. Luckily at Joe Beef, we can count on some of the best pugilists in the world to teach us the right way to choke a cattle thief. It also requires that you know how to cook the basics well. Jobless or alone, cooking will always be a savior, regardless of doomsday.

Some people walk into Joe Beef looking for Eleven Madison Park, and when they arrive, we can see the disappointment in their eyes. Here, good wine is served in $1 glasses. Yes, we have a double rib steak of grass-fed prime beef for $120 on the menu and piles of truffles on everything when in season. You can sit alone in the corner of the garden with a Thierry Allemand Cornas to go with that rabbit in a mustard sauce that's been covered in lobster. Or you can order a Coke, a pork sausage, and a salad from our garden. And that's fine. That's it, that's who we are. There will always be a bottle of Muscadet on the list for $30 and we serve Molson Ex in cans.

Joe Beef is its own disarming ecosystem, an incubator for survivalists. If you come in from the alley or if you're seated outside, you'll see the trout pond, a row garden, a hoarder's shed, a brick oven, and an Old Town vintage canoe hanging from the ceiling. The canoe—more useful than any "art"—will actually get you to an island (because, as everyone knows, zombies can't swim).

Unbeknownst to us, a few years ago we made it onto an award list endorsed by a fancy Italian bottled water. We have worked all of our lives to *not* be on this list. Our careers have in some ways been dedicated against such lists. There is something

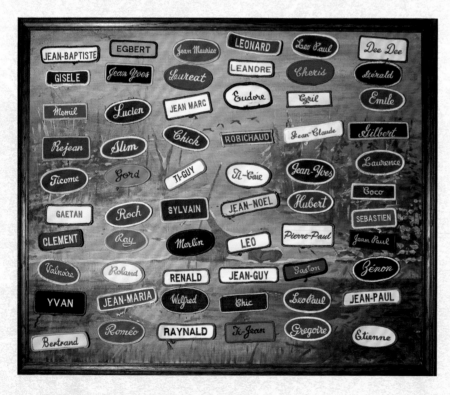

to be said for putting the blinders on and focusing on real things around you. Although all this restaurant talk often feels like sand in our gears, we do love what we do. We are hosts, whether it be underground, in the cabin, the workshop, and, *bien entendu,* the restaurant. We care about your comfort.

Although dictatorial at times on wines, we are happy to quench your thirst and send you home in a cab. If your back hurts, we will get you a pillow. If you're allergic, we won't kill you, not because that might inconvenience fellow diners around you but because we actually care.

The golden road to your own Walden Pond isn't paved with Top 50 lists and hashtags: it's about the

land, your own ambitions, and the people around you. Just remember to get there in style, and always ask yourself: What would Martha Stewart or Norm Abram do?

—M.E.

O Spirit of the mountain that speaks to us tonight,
Your voice is sad, yet still recalls past visions of delight,
When 'mid the grand old Laurentides, old when the earth was new,
With flying feet we followed the moose and caribou.

And backward rush sweet memories, like fragments of a dream,
We hear the dip of paddle blades, the ripple of the stream,
The mad, mad rush of frightened wings from brake and covert start,
The breathing of the woodland, the throb of nature's heart . . .

But Spirit of the Northland! let the winter breezes blow,
And cover every giant crag with rifts of driving snow.
Freeze every leaping torrent, bind all the crystal lakes,
Tell us of fiercer pleasures when the Storm King awakes.

—"Memories," poet unknown, taken from
The Habitant and Other French Canadian Poems

Smallmouth Bass in Birch Bark

Serves 4

~~

You will need

Metal wire

Coals

Grill

Pliers

In the event of the great cataclysm or grand-mal zombie apocalypse, one thing is for sure: there will still be smallmouth bass in our Laurentian lakes. Less pedigreed as an eating fish than its cousins the trout or walleye, the bass is an angler's joy because it puts up a fight. David can often be found in his boat on "Secret Lake," three daughters in tow. We really like early-spring bass and late-fall bass. Hot-lake summer bass are soupy with less impact on taste. Steam roasting the bass in cedar and wet birch bark is fun to prepare with the kids. Dave says, "My oldest daughter, Dylan, suggested we cook the bass in compost leaves in October, and while the end result wasn't flavorful enough, I liked the path she was on. Lake-cold cheap canned beer with bass is best. I like filling regular hamburger buns or sliced white bread with bass meat too, maybe frying and serving with hot sauce (see the photograph on page 14). My kids like it with honey Dijon." It's very acceptable to eat bass for breakfast with a side of bacon and eggs for those early-dawn catches. Better yet, a canoe lunch with said sandwich, a G and T with cedar gin (see page 15), and Cardinal Peaches (page 9) for dessert.

Birch bark, enough to wrap 2 fish

4 small cedar branches

7 ounces (200 g) wild mushrooms (bolets, chanterelles, or whatever you can forage), cleaned by hand, coarsely chopped

2 whole bass (around 1½ pounds each), scaled, gills removed, gutted

2 tablespoons (30 g) unsalted butter

Kosher salt

A few handfuls of fresh wild thyme

10 to 20 Labrador tea leaves

I. About the bark: Take the birch bark off a recently fallen log, not any live tree. To do this, make a shallow slit that cuts only through the outer layer. From there the bark should peel easily. Warming the bark makes it more pliable. If you are having trouble working with it, place it near the fire,

being careful to just warm it up, not burn it.

2. Soak the cedar branches in water. Birch bark is naturally water-repellent, but give it a brief soak anyway and rinse to remove any dirt and small insects.

3. Sauté the mushrooms in a small pan for about 2 minutes in butter, just until they start to soften, but do not cook fully. Season lightly and set aside to cool.

4. Season the fish liberally, inside and out. Fill the cavity of the fish with the mushrooms, then stuff in the wild thyme and tea leaves. Lay the birch bark out in slightly overlapping layers, making a sheet that is about three times the width of the fish by one and a half times the length. Place a piece of bark (roughly 3 × 6 inches; 8 cm ×

15 cm) perpendicular to these layers, with 4 inches (10 cm) or so sticking out the end. Place a few small cedar branches down the middle of the birch bark and lay the stuffed fish on top. Lay more cedar on top of the fish, fold the perpendicular end pieces to cover the head and tail, and then roll the whole thing to form a closed package. You may require a few extra pieces of birch bark here and there, depending on the size and quality of what you have gathered. No matter how patchwork, it is important to have a nicely closed package. Wrap with metal wire to secure and snip the remaining end.

5. To cook: Start a fire with a nice amount of coals. (If you are making this at home, a medium-hot grill or 400°F [200°C] oven can be used—cooking time will be similarly vague.) Place

the fish parcels a good 4 to 5 inches (10 cm to 13 cm) above the coals and turn regularly. Keep some cold water nearby, and brush the outside as you turn it to keep the bark from going up in flames (if you don't have a brush handy, cedar branches work well). Cooking time varies depending on the size of the fish and the heat of the fire, but expect about 30 minutes. Remove from the heat and let sit for 5 to 10 minutes.

6. Snip the wire to cut the parcel open, peel back the layers, and serve. The fish should separate easily from the bones. If you find it's not cooked enough, close the parcel back up if possible, and return to the heat. Otherwise return to the heat with the parcel open, and carefully flip the fish after 5 minutes or so.

𝕹ote If you find yourself without metal wire, long strands of birch bark, small vines, et cetera, can be used to secure the fish parcel. . . . Whatever you use is likely to be singed off, but as you start cooking the bundle, the bark will glue itself together somewhat. We're mostly working with things you find in the woods, so use this recipe as a guide and do what makes sense. The end goal is to have a fish filled with mushrooms, steamed with wild herbs, enclosed in a package made of cedar and birch bark. Not every measurement will be exact.

Cardinal Peaches

Serves 4

You will need

Fine-mesh sieve

There is something refreshingly carefree about giving a grandiose name to a dish made from canned and frozen food.

You may approach this dish a few ways: it's a good occasion to hit the small-batch canned peach section at your local yuppie grocer, or you can put up your own freestone peaches at the peak of the season, and pick your own raspberries wearing vintage summer attire.

One 6 oz. (170 g) can Carnation extra thick cream or 1 small jar clotted cream

½ cup (120 g) fresh quark cheese

1 teaspoon Amaretto liqueur

¾ cup (150 g) sugar

2 pints fresh raspberries

1 teaspoon fresh lemon juice

8 peach halves

Papineau or shortbread cookies

1. In a small bowl, combine the cream, quark, Amaretto, and ¼ cup (50 g) of the sugar, mixing well. Refrigerate.

2. Bring the raspberries, lemon juice, and the remaining ½ cup (100 g) sugar to a slow simmer. Cook for 5 minutes and proceed to strain the coulis through the sieve, while pushing with the back of a spoon to extract every last drop. Refrigerate.

3. In pretty milk glass cups, dollop a few spoons of the cream-quark mix, top with 2 peach halves and raspberry coulis, then serve with the cookies.

L'Absorbine Junior

When we were kids, playing on outdoor rinks and building snow forts, if we ever complained of aches or pains . . . or really, even when we didn't complain . . . out would come *l'Absorbine Jr.:* a tall, slim bottle of absinthe-green liquid that smelled of rubbing alcohol and wintergreen. Wintergreen is an evergreen found all over Quebec and broadly, North America. Our local First Nation Iroquois have been using its oil for back pain, headaches, fever, and arthritis for centuries.

Wintergreen strongly evokes one of two things: the beautiful Laurentian woods, their shaded patches of decaying bark and needles where wild mushrooms and said wintergreen abound, or, sharing a tepid subway bench with a muscularly ailing stranger. If the latter is the case, I suggest a glass of wine, but the addition of a few leaves, steeped in gin, used in turn in this somewhat loose interpretation of a French 75 is also very delicious.

If you lack the fresh leaves, don't even try to use the extract; it's allegedly toxic in certain doses and society ain't getting less litigious! Instead, crush a Necco Wafer pink sugar mint. They are available in the creases of old couches and candy stores.

---

1 teaspoon lemon juice

1 sugar cube

½ ounce (15 ml) wintergreen and spearmint cordial

1 glass of dry sparkling wine

1 cherry

1. In a nice old cup, pour the lemon juice and cordial over the sugar and mix with a wooden stick.

2. Pour the sparkling wine to top and give it a stir.

3. Garnish with the cherry.

CAIRNCLIFF

David's Secret Lake

T oday, no parent in their right mind would let a long-haired forty-something vegetarian teacher take five boys to his off-the-grid cottage for four days. But in 1988, a high school teacher named Bob Hartley brought me and four friends to "Secret Lake" in a milk truck. His truck was usually a chase vehicle for cyclists, so you could also eat in it and sleep in it. And we did exactly that.

Mr. Hartley brought six giant loaves of sourdough bread, a massive jar of Hellmann's mayonnaise, tomatoes, and a block of sharp Québécois Perron Cheddar. That was the Secret Lake sandwich, and we ate it for breakfast, lunch, and dinner.

I bought my own cabin there a few years back—a jewel of the Laurentians, it is boat in and out only. No road, no public sewer, completely off the grid. The landscape is best described as End Times. The lake's shores are lined with rudimentary crumbling boathouses. The people? A *Jurassic Park* gin-and-tonic drinking mix of Anglos, Francos, Germans.

I can't tell you the real name of Secret Lake because the first rule of Secret Lake is there is no Secret Lake. I would be shunned by the community.

The goal of the Secret Lake cabin is to go solar and be completely self-reliant: there's something to be said about having all my amenities from home but not paying a dime for it. If you're going to grow stuff—and you should—grow edible stuff, à la *Northern Gardener:* sweet potatoes, kale, borage, Roman chamomile.

Success means different things to different people. Success for me has never been a home, a car, or material possessions. It's just swimming in a lake every day.

—D.M.

The drink of choice at the Secret Lake is this cedar gin:

→ Equal parts cottage gin and tonic water (cottage gin is that gin that's been sitting on your cottage bar for years until you decide suddenly to make gin cocktails one night because friends who drink gin are over or you've run out of everything else)

→ 2 short cedar twigs

Making Soap

Makes 4 bars of soap,
approximately 3½ × 2 inches
(9 cm × 5 cm) each

You will need

Rubber gloves

Very large cook pot

Very long spoon to stir

Glass measuring cup
(for measuring the lye and fat)

Soap molds of your choice
(madeleine molds are a nice option)

Instant-read thermometer (optional)

pH meter (optional)

With all three restaurants and our own growing expectations, a handyman at Joe Beef was needed. Enter Pat the Gardener (aka Patrick Thibault). From welding to garbage management, to gardening and aquaculture, to fermentation and woodworking, to general upkeep and therapist, Pat is it. He works days, running between all three restaurants and Rona, our local hardware store. Behind every foraging excursion in the woods and every small goat-farm sourcing visit, there are also ten trips in a beat-up car to the local cash-and-carry.

The cash-and-carry's role in the birth and coming of age of small restaurants is underappreciated: brown paper, staff-meal corn dogs, and mop buckets don't make those Top 50 lists. But a huge part of *cuisine du marché* rests on being able and allowed to change your mind about what to cook as the seasons ease in and out, and when you run out of love for an item, the cash-and-carry can also be an unspoken catalyst of true market cuisine.

We have a smoker and wood-burning oven that produces a lot of ashes daily. Knowing that rainwater and ashes can create lye, we wanted to add to the cyclical nature of our garden and create something new. This is our soap recipe.

¾ cup (180 ml) concentrated brown lye water (see Note)

2 cups (475 ml) melted beef fat

2 to 4 drops essential oil(s) of your choice (we used citronella and geranium)

1. Wearing rubber gloves, mix the concentrated brown lye water and the fat, stirring thoroughly with a very long spoon, and allow the chemical reaction to gradually take place over 30 minutes to 3 hours—the minimum soap mixture temperature is 125°F (52°C) for 100 percent beef fat.

Disclaimer: Pat the gardener isn't wearing gloves. Tsk tsk. Don't try this at home.

2. Still wearing gloves, verify the soap mixture is warm enough and that it is ready to be poured into the molds using one (or both) of the following test methods:

Test Method One: Use a spoon to lift a little of the soap mixture about 1 inch (2.5 cm) above the top surface of the mixture, and then allow one drop to fall back onto the top of the mixture. If the surface of the mixture supports the drop for a moment, then the soap is done.

Test Method Two: Try to draw a medium-thick line in the top of the soap mixture with the front tip of your spoon. If you can see the line, then the soap is done.

3. Add the essential oils of choice.

4. Pour the soap into the soap molds and let the soap rest in a cold, dark place for 7 days.

5. After a week, remove the soap from the molds. Let the soap bars air-dry for 2 to 6 weeks in a warm, dry, but also dark space.

Note Making lye (images 1, 2, 3, 4): Ten cups (4 liters) of tightly packed cold ashes will yield 1 gallon of average-strength brown lye water. It's up to you what essential oils you use. Remember, it's the end of the world now, so carefully choose your fragrance and that of your intended partner.

Porter Rabbit Stew

Serves one family over 2 days

Once the nuclear winter has settled—or Ebola, or the oil crisis—we will be enjoying this delicious dinner and thinking of you. Survival skills don't come easy, but for us, with a stint in the Scouts and research on Cabelas.com, we are ready. Seriously though, the old fur trappers kept a simple larder of salt, pepper, flour, a few roots, and salt lard. They trapped, sold the furs, and kept the meat. And they ate well; maybe not this exact dish, but pretty close.

½ pound (225 g) Cedar Salt Lard (The Cellar, page 5)

1 tablespoon rendered lard

1 rabbit 2 to 2½ pounds (about 1 kg), cut into eighths by you (or your butcher)

1 or 2 Hardtack, aka Prison Bread (The Cellar, page 7), per person

2 small white onions

1 large carrot

1 small turnip

One 14.9-ounce bottle or can (440 ml) stout or porter beer

1 cup (240 ml) water

1 whole head garlic

1 small cedar branch (like a sprig of rosemary)

¼ cup (57 g) unsalted butter

2 tablespoons Herbes Salées (The Cellar, page 7)

I. Preheat the oven to 350°F (180°C). Over medium heat—either stove top or fire pit—warm up a Dutch oven.

2. Sear the salt pork in the lard until crisp, about 5 minutes.

3. Add the rabbit, bread, and then the vegetables, cutting them roughly over the top with a jackknife. Pour the beer and water into the mix and add the garlic and cedar.

4. Bring to a simmer, reduce the heat, cover, and transfer to the oven. Braise for 2 hours, or until the hardtacks are tender and the rabbit falls off the bone.

5. Swirl in the butter and season to taste with the Herbes Salées.

Though now rare, woven rabbit-skin was once common among Indians from Mexico to northern Canada. Generally used as a robe, which might be a blanket or a wrap, sometimes it was made into a coat or hooded jacket. The old skill is still practised occasionally, as shown in these photographs at Fort Hope in northern Ontario taken last winter.

RABBIT SKIN ROBE

Photographs by A. B. McIVOR

First step in making a robe is trapping and skinning the fur-bearer. In Canada it is the varying hare, or so-called snowshoe rabbit, for years the chief source of food in much of the bush country.

Long strips are cut spirally round the pelt to get the greatest length. The strips, about one inch wide (narrower or wider depending on what is being made), are rolled on a thin rod of about half-inch diameter.

When pulled off the rod, the twist brings all the fur outside and natural shrinkage is sufficient to hold the twist in the skin. The strips are joined in lengths with twine—in earlier times with sinew or babiche.

A frame is set up and a strip of the twisted skin is lashed along the top and sides, making the framework for the robe. A pile of boughs is used as a mat to keep the feet of the weaver off the snow.

The actual weaving is begun. Techniques vary in different parts of the country but this Cree method is a kind of netting. The finished netting sets firmly and would not easily unravel.

The partly finished robe, which is extremely warm and light in weight, though apt to shed hair. Sometimes the skin robes are put between two layers of fabric and stitched through to form a quilt.

The finished robe, cut free from the frame at the sides. This is a small blanket, for which 85 skins were used. Robes for use in extreme cold or outdoors would be woven more closely and need a greater number of skins.

The rarely made rabbit coats are worn only by small children these days. Formerly a new jacket was made every year, though older people might make one last for three or four years—still warm but somewhat hairless.

Pot-au-Feu D'hiver (Winter)

Serves 4 with leftovers

Unless you live on some vegan moon of Venus, you've probably heard about bone broth. From leaky gut to stiff skin, this concoction will surely help cure one of the most unbearable ailments—hunger.

We sing the praises of L'Express in Montreal quite a bit—see the Oeuf en Gelée (page 57) in Book One—and their pot-au-feu is an absolute Montreal classic. This pot-au-feu is often on the JB menu in snow season, and the Pot-au-Feu D'été (Summer) recipe (page 22) arrives promptly with warmer winds. This recipe doesn't involve poultry, but you can adjust the times and add a few drumsticks or even a Lyonnais cooking sausage.

1½ pounds (675 g) beef brisket

2 pieces (1 pound/454 g) bone-in beef short ribs

1 whole veal tongue

Two 1-pound (450 g) flat-iron steaks

4 white onions, each studded with 1 clove

1 head garlic, cleaned

1 bouquet garni: 6 fresh thyme sprigs, 1 tablespoon black peppercorns, 4 fresh flat-leaf parsley sprigs wrapped tightly in the reserved leek greens and tied with butcher's twine

⅛ to ¼ cup (30 to 60 ml) Kikkoman or other naturally brewed soy sauce

Salt and white pepper

2 tablespoons apple cider vinegar

4 marrow bones, 2 inches (5 cm) tall

1 large carrot, cut into 4 pieces

1 rutabaga, peeled and cut into 4 pieces

4 small white turnips

1 leek white, greens reserved for the bouquet garni

To serve

Minced fresh flat-leaf parsley

Baguette

Dijon mustard

Gherkins

Coarse sea salt

Pepper mill and peppercorns

1. Preheat the oven to 300°F (150°C).

2. Like most of our recipes, this one starts with a large Dutch oven—not a shameless plug for Le Creuset, we swear; we just seriously appreciate the brand's ability to distribute heat evenly and maintain a solid seal! So, place the brisket, short ribs, tongue, flat-iron steak, onion, garlic, and bouquet garni in a large Le Creuset.

3. Add ¼ cup (60 ml) soy sauce then enough water to barely cover. Add 2 generous pinches salt and the vinegar. Cover and transfer to the oven.

4. After 2 hours, retrieve the pot and add the bones, carrot, rutabaga, turnips, and leek white. Add a little more water to cover, but not drown, the veggies. Cover and return to the oven for another 1½ hours.

5. Check the pot-au-feu for doneness: When you touch the meat, there should be little or no resistance; it should yield to a gentle touch from your finger without bouncing back. Using a skimmer or a slotted spoon, gently transfer each ingredient to a clean sheet pan, being careful to maintain its structural integrity. Cover the pan with plastic wrap.

6. Give the remaining broth a good boil, skimming off any impurity that threatens to betray your reputation as a champion meat-liquor maker. Season with salt and white pepper to taste, adding a splash of soy sauce as you see fit.

7. Divide the pot-au-feu ingredients equally among shallow bowls, discarding the bouquet garni. Ladle some broth into each bowl and sprinkle each with parsley. Serve with the baguette, mustard, and gherkins, with salt and pepper on the side and a jug of the remaining hot broth. Provide soup- and marrow spoons.

Pot-au-Feu D'été (Summer)

Serves 4 with leftovers

Top two things that will bring a look of true disgust to a child's face: seeing their parents perform sexual acts on each other (or their neighbors) and . . . savory meat jelly. If you made too much pot-au-feu, and you are over thirty, eat it cold, like a salad, with some of the jelly. Just be careful not to do it in front of the kids.

To the master pot-au-feu recipe (page 21), you are adding

1 tablespoon powdered gelatin per 2 cups cooking liquid

3 tablespoons apple cider vinegar instead of 2

For the vinaigrette

½ cup (75 g) chopped gherkins

½ cup (75 g) pickled white onions, chopped

½ cup (120 ml) Dijon mustard

½ cup (75 g) capers

½ cup (120 ml) olive oil

¼ cup (60 ml) apple cider vinegar

¼ cup (60 ml) honey

1 bunch each fresh flat-leaf parsley, chervil, and tarragon

Salt and pepper

I. Make the Pot-au-Feu (page 21).

2. When the cooked broth is still hot (step 6), measure it in order to calculate the gelatin you need (1 tablespoon per 2 cups liquid). Bloom the gelatin in cold water according to the instructions on the packet, then mix the water and gelatin into the scalding broth. Season, keeping in mind that foods eaten cold need to be seasoned more aggressively. Cover and refrigerate overnight.

3. Make the vinaigrette: In a bowl, mix together all the ingredients, seasoning with salt and pepper to taste. If you feel the need to loosen it, go ahead, with a splash of vinegar and oil, but do check the taste. Set aside.

4. When ready to serve, cut the meats into thin slices and the veggies in smaller wedges. Arrange on each plate and squeeze some of the set jelly over each, then drizzle the vinaigrette in an artful way that clearly communicates your level of sophistication to your guests.

Note This pot-au-feu is designed to be eaten cold, so plan to make your pot-au-feu one day ahead or morning of.

VGE Consommé

Serves 2

A soul-warming preamble to a main course of cyanide capsules or before going for a stroll into the plague-ravaged suburbs. Seriously, as far as cottage/survival food goes this soup hands down beats mountain-house freeze-dried chili and a glass of Tang. Take it at face value, a bit like a joke, or read into it and realize that some great stuff ends up in cans: sweetbreads, morels, terrines, rich molasses, sailor's loaves, truffles, and foie gras. As for the VGE soup, it's now a classic, a soup that Paul Bocuse created for then président de la république Valerie Giscard d'Estaing. It's a deep broth, laced with root vegetables and sherry, but most importantly, truffles and foie gras. It is cooked under a dome of puff pastry, but due to the limited means of your bunker, we skipped that step.

---

1 can of broth, beef or chicken

A few roots, diced

1 small can of foie gras

1 small jar of truffles, summer, winter, or trims

A dash of sherry

Some chervil

1. On whatever source of heat, warm the consommé and simmer a few tablespoons of diced roots in it.

2. In two cups, place some foie gras, truffles, a dash of sherry, and some chopped chervil. Pour the piping hot broth over.

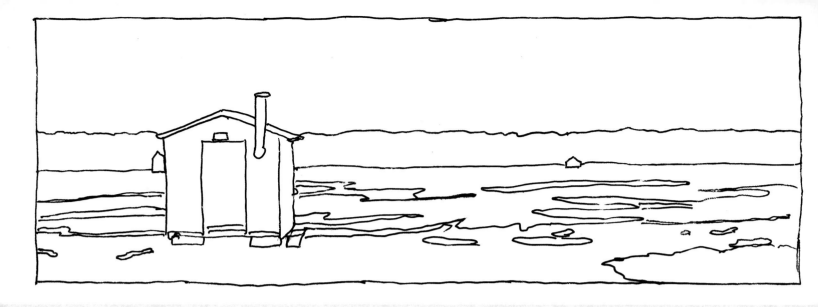

Cooking with Tea / Seasoning During the Apocalypse

It is not human to live throughout the war without the shield of liquor. Indeed, should we ever run out of wine, open the vault doors and may the wolves, corpses, and plagues take life from our feeble bodies!

In Book One, we talked about seasoning, under the Big Mac Theory (page 169). But, we realize now, there was a majestic omission. When seasoning, we always consider sweet, salty, the acid, umami, and bitterness, and spiciness sometimes fits in there as well. In the noble tradition of French cooking, where carefully sourced protein is cooked simply with nothing else but salt, pepper, and wine, it's mind-boggling how a dish can attain such depth with so few layers and techniques. Could it be that the naturally occurring tannins in grape skins also perform a role?

Cooking in a kitchen in a country far away from vineyards is different from the French ability to use abundant and affordable wine in every dish. It's not easy to purchase those naturally occurring tannins at a fair price. Then pair this with the religious authority that stirred every pot in Quebec's kitchens, disapproving of wine altogether. Cooks, unbowed, found ingenious ways to give an edge to their sauces, stews, and pan juices, like adding a splash of steeped Five Roses tea.

3. Measure out the plum purée. For every cup of purée, stir in ¾ cup (150 g) sugar and the juice of ½ lemon.

4. Return the mixture to the pot and cook over low heat, stirring constantly, until a candy thermometer reads 220°F (105°C), or what's daintily referred to as the pearl stage. Transfer immediately to clean sterilized jars and seal according to the rules of jam canning.

Cellared Russet Apples

Apples rot the way a Twitter post goes viral: one takes the rot from another and gives it to a bunch. A traditional way to keep apples is to wrap them individually in newspaper and store them apart. First, choose a variety that is known to store well or that is delicious even when a bit soft. The Golden Russet or, as it's known overseas, Reinette du Canada, is a very sweet and mealy apple, the best kind for a tarte Tatin or to roast alongside a duck. These apples will keep their shape.

Hardtack, aka Prison Bread

Makes about 20 crackers

You will not enjoy these plain. Hardtack is, nonetheless, very useful if you find a stash of it while stranded in your hunting cabin or lower bunk. It provides sustenance and is good crumbled over a stew (for example, Porter Rabbit Stew, page 18) or into boiling milk with honey and cinnamon.

---

4 cups (600 g) whole wheat flour
2 teaspoons salt
2 teaspoons baking powder
1⅓ cups (320 ml) water

1. Preheat the oven to 350°F (180°C).

2. In a large bowl, combine the dry ingredients, then stir in the water and knead for a few seconds until well incorporated.

3. On a floured surface, roll out the dough to ¼-inch (6-mm) thickness, then cut it into rectangles the size of playing cards. Poke the dough all over with a fork at regular intervals.

4. Transfer to a parchment-lined baking sheet and bake for 30 minutes before turning the hardtack over and baking for another 20 minutes.

5. Let dry at room temperature for a few days before storing in an airtight container forever.

Smoked Confit Gizzards

Makes three 1-quart (1-l) widemouthed mason jars

You will need
Smoker with a nice, cool and mellow smoke

1 cup Confit Salt (The Cellar, page 9)
3 pounds (1.4 kg) duck gizzards (chicken gizzards also work, but will cook faster)
2 pounds (900 g) duck fat

1. Mix the confit salt with the gizzards. Cover and refrigerate for 3 hours.

2. Rinse the gizzards in a colander, pat dry, and smoke them for 1 hour.

3. Preheat the oven to 300°F (150°C).

4. Melt the duck fat in a Dutch oven over medium heat. Place the gizzards in the Dutch oven and cover, then cook gently (only an occasional bubble should be rising up in the melted fat) in the oven for 2 hours. After 2 hours, retrieve a gizzard and cut it open—it should be firm, not juicy.

5. We suggest a glass dish with a lid for storage: pack the gizzards tightly, cover with just enough fat to cover them fully, and refrigerate. When the fat has set, pour in another layer of warmed fat to cover any bits of gizzard poking out. Don't forget—apocalypse or not—that duck fat is gold, so you should reserve! It will crisp potatoes and sear a salmon like nothing else.

Plum Jelly

Yield here is based on ratio (see below)

Whenever we can get our hands on Damson plums, we make this jelly. The plums are so delicious but tiny, and all that pitting makes you wish you had a whole Scout jamboree busy at it. But it's worth it. Obviously, this is an amazing accompaniment to goat's cheese, as well as to roast pork or Pickled Pork Butt ('The Cellar,' page 8).

1. Pit the plums, and simmer them in a heavy-bottomed pot for 30 minutes, stirring constantly to avoid any scorching!

2. Purée the plums right in the pot using a

Pickled Eggs and Pickled Tongues

Makes 8 pickled eggs or 6 pickled pig tongues

This brine recipe works for both the eggs and the tongues.

8 eggs, boiled for 7 minutes with a spoonful of baking soda, cooled then peeled
OR
6 pig's tongues, boiled in water with a pinch of curing salt, 1 tablespoon black peppercorns, and 1 garlic clove, for 1 hour, then cooled in the cooking broth and peeled
3 cups (750 ml) white vinegar
½ cup (100 g) sugar
1 tablespoon green peppercorns
1 tablespoon mustard seeds
8 pearl onions, peeled

1. Place the eggs or the tongues in a sanitized mason jar large enough to accommodate them.

2. Combine the rest of the ingredients in a saucepan and heat them over high heat. Bring to a boil, and pour into the jar to cover. Let the liquid cool, then cover and refrigerate for 1 week before eating. These will keep refrigerated for 2 months.

Herbes Salées

Makes 3 cups (tightly packed)

Taken from the Acadians, the OGs of survivalism, this is an herb salt that goes well with the Porter Rabbit Stew (page 18) and the Deer Beer Belly (page 167).

1 bunch each fresh flat-leaf parsley, chervil, and lovage
1 bunch scallions
1 cup sea asparagus aka sea beans aka salicornia
1 carrot, coarsely chopped
1 parsnip, peeled and coarsely chopped
10 ounces (300 g) pickling salt

1. Wash and dry the herbs, scallions, and sea asparagus. Combine them with the carrot and parsnip in the bowl of a food processor and pulse until finely chopped.

2. Transfer to a bowl and stir in the salt. Store in sterilized jars and refrigerate. Wait 1 month before using. These Herbes Salées will keep for 3 to 6 months refrigerated.

Dried Verbena

In the depths of March's darkness, when light therapy, SSRIs, and a trip to Florida have failed to raise you from the dead of winter, it's nigh impossible to imagine that a few months away lie tractor-loads of fresh produce. Amid the bounty, year after year, we get bucket-loads of lemon verbena, which—oddly—appear only at Montreal's Jean-Talon Market and nowhere else. Fresh, it's excellent for flavoring milk-based desserts (Igloo Mousse [or Winter Milk Jellies], page 38) or fruit, particularly peaches; but it's best brewed as a quick herbal tea, with a bit of honey and a few drops of apple cider vinegar. Chilled over ice, it's kind of like an Amish Gatorade!

Clear Fruit Spirits/Cordials

Spirits, or eaux-de-vies, are distilled from a fermentation of ripe, sweet fruits as opposed to cordials, which are a maceration of fruits or aromatics in strong alcohol and sugar.

Clear spirits of pear, yellow plum, and apricot top our spirits list. The alcohol vapors are carrying the fruits' ripeness and smell; it's summer. These bottles are best sampled in moderation, then forgotten for a while. They are awesome over ice in summer and at cellar temperature in winter; they will tastefully sanitize a cut and find a use in any backcountry childbirth. For the cordials we use Everclear grain alcohol, 40%, with the exception of the melon, which uses 94%. This neutral white alcohol is available everywhere.

Base Cordial Syrup

Equal parts liquid glucose, sugar, and water

Bring to a boil.

Crab Apple Cordial

Makes 1 quart (1 l)
(takes 2 months)

2 pounds (900 g) hard, fragrant crab apples
4 cups (1 l) 40% Everclear neutral white alcohol
One 8-inch (20-cm) cinnamon stick
(or equivalent length in smaller pieces)
1 cup (240 ml) Base Cordial Syrup
(recipe above)
Gold flakes

1. Place the crab apples in a jar and top with the alcohol and cinnamon. Store in a cool, dark place for 2 months. Strain and stir in the syrup.

2. Transfer to a bottle and add some superfluous yet pretty gold flakes.

Wintergreen and Spearmint Cordial

Makes 1 quart (1 l)
(takes 1 month)

¼ cup (40 g) fresh wintergreen
1 nice bunch fresh spearmint
1 peppermint tea teabag
2 cups (500 ml) 40% Everclear neutral white alcohol
1½ cups (300 ml) Base Cordial Syrup
A few drops of natural green coloring, for vanity

1. Combine the wintergreen, spearmint, teabag, and alcohol in a glass jar. Let it macerate in a cool, dark place, for 1 month.

2. Filter through a paper filter and add the syrup and green coloring. Mix well and transfer to a nice old bottle reserved for this purpose.

Toasted Hazelnut Cordial

Makes 1 quart (1 l)
(takes 1 month)

2 cups (250 g) toasted hazelnuts, skins rubbed off and discarded
1 whole vanilla bean
1 cup (80 g) espresso beans
2 cups (500 ml) 40% Everclear neutral white alcohol
1 cup (240 ml) Base Cordial Syrup

1. Combine the hazelnuts, vanilla bean, and espresso beans with the alcohol. Let macerate in a cool, dark place for 1 month.

2. Filter through a paper filter and add the syrup.

Melon Liqueur

Makes 1 pint (½ l)
(takes 1 month)

1 about-to-rot small muskmelon
2 cups (500 ml) or bit more of 94% Everclear neutral white alcohol
1 cup (240 ml) Base Cordial Syrup

1. Peel and seed the melon, then place it in a jar. Pour the alcohol into the jar—you may need a little more to cover the fruit. Close the jar lightly and let macerate in a cool, dark place for 1 month, shaking occasionally.

2. Filter through multiple layers of cheesecloth, squeezing the juice out. Add the syrup, stir, and store in a nice bottle. You can add syrup to taste, but too much and it will bubble.

Canned Bread
(Coureur des bois)

Makes 8 aluminum cans of bread

You will need
8 food-grade 2½-inch-wide cans

⅓ cup (50 g) spelt flour
⅓ cup (50 g) whole wheat flour
3 cups (400 g) all-purpose flour
½ teaspoon (2 g) instant yeast
1¾ cups (400 ml) lukewarm water
1 tablespoon molasses
1½ teaspoons salt
¾ cup (125 g) dates, roughly chopped
8 bacon slices

1. In a large bowl, stir all the ingredients (except the dates and bacon) together. Let the dough ferment for 2 hours or so, folding the dough over itself every 45 minutes, in order to develop the gluten. At the last fold, add the dates and give the dough a good knead. Refrigerate overnight.

2. Preheat the oven to 450°F (230°C). Generously grease the cans and line them with a band of parchment paper.

3. Divide the dough into 8 equal pieces and shape into balls. Lay a slice of bacon in the bottom of each can. Next, place the bread dough on top of the bacon. Let it proof until doubled in size.

4. Place on a sheet pan. Bake top side up for 25 to 30 minutes, until golden brown and the bread feels light.

4

THE CELLAR

—✺—

Items in the cellar are listed from left to right. Because it's the end of the world, you can play a bit faster and loose with these recipes. We are by no means the icons of canning, so if this method intrigues you beyond our items, we suggest *Blue Ribbon Canning,* a comprehensive guide to preserves. And hey, it's endorsed by Vanna White.

Note that the cellar's entire contents are not listed in full. And that all cordials, liquors, and syrups will last up to one year; pickled fruit/veg up to six months; meats up to three months.

Save your ashes for corn nixtilization and soap making.

We also suggest: Champagne, one elegant Champagne saber, condoms, one hidden pack of cigarettes, a ham radio, ½ bottle of red wine, a garden's worth of seeds, a machete, one slingshot, one gold bullion, 12-gauge slugs, dried ramen, a tarp, coconut fat, vitamins, one MarkTen tobacco can, Vieille Prune brandy, cans of cassoulet, an ax, bleach, one suture kit, a hand-cranked nut mill, and the list provided by Dr. Cernovitch on page 32.

Although living in a cellar you should can or freeze according to stringent laws of hygiene and common sense!

1. Base Cordial Syrup
1a. Clear Fruit Spirits/Cordials
1b. Crab Apple Cordial
1c. Wintergreen and Spearmint Cordial
1d. Toasted Hazelnut Cordial
2. Melon Liqueur
3. Canned Bread (Coureur des bois)
4. Chien Chaud Spice
5. Cedar Salt Lard
6. Crab Apple Syrup
7. La Bomba
8. Pickled Eggs and Pickled Tongues
9. Plum Jelly
10. Herbes Salées
11. Cellared Russet Apples
12. Hardtack, aka Prison Bread
13. Dried Verbena
14. Smoked Confit Gizzards
15. Pickled Pork Butt
16. Bark, Root, and Twig Beer
17. Beef Jerky
18. Growing Endives and Endive Salad
19. Jambe de Boeuf au Bouillon de Ginseng
20. Maple Syrup
21. Confit Salt
22. Smoked Apple Cider Vinegar
23. Pickled Deer Necks
24. Acorns and Black Walnuts
25. Potatoes Stored in Sand
26. Sauerkraut
27. Ham Hocks
28. Clear spirit in recycled magnums
29. Solar-generated power
30. Lead-lined reinforced subterranean bunker

Chaga Stock

Makes 4 quarts

Chaga holds court on the higher shelves of modern health food stores. It also grows on one out of every fortieth birch tree in northern Quebec and tastes quite good in a broth. This is a quick and multiuse staple to have on hand.

½ pound (250 mg) fresh chaga mushrooms, properly identified and cleaned

4 quarts (4 l) water

1 large carrot

1 small white onion

½ pound (250 g) pork belly skin (ask your butcher)

1 juniper berry or tiny juniper stem

10 black peppercorns

1. In an appropriate pot—we like the Vision cookware in our photo—combine the mushrooms and water and bring to a slow boil over medium heat, skimming any impurities from the surface of the liquid.

2. Add the carrot and onion. Roll the pork belly skin with the juniper and peppercorns inside.

3. Maintain a pleasant gentle simmer and cook until the skin is tender, about 2 hours. Strain and freeze in small portions. This stock will keep for up to 3 months.

Crispy Frog Legs

Serves 4

~~~

You will need

Deep-frying thermometer

Deep fryer or heavy-bottomed pot with tall sides

The main indication of End Times in movies is when it starts to rain frogs. Whatever happens, we'll be up North where frogs already reign abundant. Here is our simple French way to cook their little legs.

20 pairs of frog legs

1 tablespoon fresh lemon juice

2 teaspoons salt, plus a pinch for seasoning the legs and more for final seasoning

Neutral oil for frying

2 cups (250 g) all-purpose flour

1 teaspoon garlic powder

1 teaspoon ground white pepper

1 teaspoon mustard powder

Pinch of cayenne pepper

2 cups (500 ml) whole milk whisked with 4 large egg yolks

3 cups (210 g) panko bread crumbs, pulsed in the food processor until fine (a few pulses at most)

12 garlic scapes

To serve (optional)

Your favorite aioli

A few lemon wedges

Red wine sauce of your choice

I. Place the frog legs under running water in a strainer and give them a good rinse. Pat dry and toss in a bowl with the lemon juice and a pinch of salt.

2. Preheat a good 2 inches (5 cm) of oil in a fryer or heavy-bottomed pot to 350°F (180°C).

3. In a shallow bowl, combine the flour, garlic powder, white pepper, salt, mustard powder, and cayenne. Mix well.

4. Place the whisked milk and egg yolks into a shallow bowl and the panko crumbs in yet another one. And set up the bowls with the spiced flour, milk and egg yolks, and panko crumbs in a line. Working with a few sets of frog legs at a time, move them carefully from the flour to the milk mixture to the crumbs, taking great care to not drag along too much of the previous dredge. Place the breaded legs on a plate.

5. Fry the legs in batches, along with a few garlic scapes. Do not overload the fryer—it will cool your oil too much. When the legs look crisp and light brown, 2 to 3 minutes, transfer to a plate lined with paper towel. We recommend you cut the first set of legs open to check for doneness, so you can proceed in full confidence. Don't forget to let your oil return to 350°F (180°C) before plunging in the next batch of legs. We like to serve these with aioli, a few lemon wedges, or a red wine sauce.

How to hunt Wolverine

BY PETER KROTT

Photographs by the author

Dr. Krott, an Austrian by birth, is internationally famous for his work with wolverines carried on over many years in Finland, Sweden and Lapland. The translation from the German of Dr. Krott's manuscript by Dieter Schwanke was checked and revised by Clarence Tillenius.

...for her den a cave or a cleft in a snowdrift under a fallen tree, often where several trees have been felled across each other by wind or bowed down under a heavy burden of snow. The nest is usually located in marshland or at least close [...] or spring, one [...] at the garden [...] Europe, even as Without [...] hen except [...] the [...] en except [...] the [...] hope to [...] e to go look [...] mountain to it. It [...] rch, because at [...] and leaves early as [...] es continually [...] of March, when the mother stay [...] r close by. The situation the nest only t [...] ound looking for fo... changes consid [...] ritory, first to her r... mother wolverin [...] d early winter, and She goes on lon [...] noe rabbits, hiding [...] caches, put up by [...] prey [...] and moose. No... on hunts for fresh prey [...] caribou, and moose. No... snow dugouts, reindeer or caribou hunter to go into act... the time for the wolverine hunter to go into act...

At first you roam the area on skis or snow... stantly on the lookout for the tracks of a fema... The tracks of the female are distinguished... the male by the size, the female's being... To give measurements would be of no u...

Spruce Cough Drops

Makes 40 to 50 cough drops
(depending on mold size)

—~~—

You will need

Silicone chocolate/jelly/candy molds

Candy thermometer

Pyrex measuring cup

Because you'll have limited access to modern medicine, we've included a handy recipe for cough drops and a chart for other apocalyptic prescriptions kindly provided by Dr. Karl. This recipe is made using dried herbals, but if you want to use fresh herbs, triple the amounts indicated. These are all plants you can find in the woods, but they can also be purchased at most health food stores. Quantities of liquid, honey, and sugar in the recipe should be strictly adhered to, though amounts of herbals, et cetera, can be increased to suit your tastes.

1 tablespoon neutral oil for greasing the molds, with 1 or 2 drops of spruce essential oil mixed in

For dusting

2 tablespoons confectioners' sugar

1 tablespoon slippery elm bark, dried and ground to a fine powder

2 tablespoons cornstarch

For the flower infusion

1½ cups (375 ml) water

1½ tablespoons dried chamomile flowers

8 pieces young spruce tips

1 tablespoon dried common yarrow flowers

About 3 pieces wild ginger, finely chopped

2 tablespoons red clover flowers

For the syrup

½ cup (165 g) wildflower honey

1 cup (200 g) sugar

1 tablespoon apple cider vinegar

½ cup (120 ml) reserved flower infusion

1 teaspoon chaga powder

2 tablespoons slippery elm bark, dried, and ground to a fine powder

1 tablespoon Fernet Branca (optional)

1. Oil the candy molds or line sheet pans with parchment paper. Prepare the sugar to coat the drops: combine the confectioners' sugar, slippery elm bark, and cornstarch in a blender or food processor. Process until you have a fine powder.

2. For the flower infusion, bring the water to a boil in a small saucepan. Add the chamomile, spruce, yarrow, wild ginger, and clover flowers. Cover the pan and steep, off the heat, for 20 minutes.

3. Strain the flowers from the liquid, reserving ½ cup (120 ml) flower infusion for the syrup. (Stir some honey into whatever extra infusion you have, dilute it with a bit of hot water, and enjoy as a tea.) →

4. In a large heavy-bottomed pot, combine the honey, sugar, cider vinegar, and the ½ cup (120 ml) reserved flower infusion. Bring to a boil, put the candy thermometer into the pan, and cook over a medium-high heat, stirring occasionally. Keep a close eye on the proceedings: if the heat is too high, your syrup may boil over, and as you reach the candy stage, things can burn very quickly.

5. Cook the syrup to 300 °F (150 °C), lowering the heat as the syrup edges closer to the required temperature.

6. Remove the syrup from the heat and allow to cool slightly (wait until it stops bubbling). Stir in the chaga powder, slippery elm bark powder, and Fernet Branca, if using.

7. With the help of a silicone spatula, carefully transfer the mixture to a measuring cup, and fill the candy molds. Work quickly so that the syrup remains warm and easy to pour. If you find the syrup cools too much, warm it gently in the microwave, or return it to the pot and heat over very low heat.

8. Once the cough drops have cooled and set, about 60 minutes, unmold and toss them in the confectioners' sugar mix. Store in an airtight container. The cough drops can be wrapped individually in wax paper, if you so desire.

Note Silicone molds make nice shapes, but you can also make these drops freestyle directly onto parchment paper (see photograph page 30 for size reference).

List by: Dr. Karl Cernovitch.

Med list for the apocalypse.

Cuts — Tetanus Vaccine ASAP
  – Fucidin cream
  – dry dressings, Salt
Basic skin infections
  – Bacterial : Cephadroxil, Salt, Iodine
  – Fungal : Clotrimazole cream
Contact Dermatitis — cortisone cream.
  – Benadryl, Calamine
Burns – aloe vera, wet dressing
Trench foot – dry socks, Cephadroxil
Zombie bite/Fish hook injury/dirty wounds
  – Clindamycin for anaerobes.
Systemic/non-skin infections
  – respiratory – Moxifloxacin
  – Dental – Amoxi clavulin
  – Abdominal – Amoxi clavulin
  – Urinary tract – Septra & ciprofloxacin
  – Food-born illness – Ciprofloxacin
  – Viruses – Acyclovir/Valacyclovir
Animal bites – Fucidin cream, Clindamycin
Gun shot wound – Minor surgery kit, X-stat 30
MSK injuries – plaster rolls/Elastic bandages.
Rickettsia & Typhoid fevers – Doxycycline.
Pain – Hydromorphone, Cannabis, Tylenol/Advil.
Dental Abscess – pliers to extract tooth.
  – Surgical/surgical foam packing.
Systemic Fungal infections – clotrimazole cream.

Hilroy

Disclaimer: The list was provided by our friend Dr. Karl Cernovitch. While appropriate, this is not real-life medical advice.

5¢ CANADA POSTES · POSTAGE

ᛋ 1594   MARTIN FROBISHER

A commemorative postage stamp issued last year.

BY ALAN COOKE
now doing research in England on a Laval University fellowship, prepared with Dr Stefansson a short biography of Sir Martin Frobisher.

...ANADA'S ...RST GOLD RUSH

...ATTEMPT—and the first failure—to de- ...eral possibilities of Canada occurred nearly ...years ago when Martin Frobisher led a gold ... Island. The history of this premier mine ... pattern often followed in the generations

...spirit ran high in Elizabethan times, and ...ted in the general struggle for money, ...ver with a bold success that had made ...e ever he took up polar exploration. A ...e time, Frobisher still found time to ...hants and persons influential at court ... attempt to find a Northwest Passage. ... years of unsuccessful solicitation, he ... cause the influential director of the ...uscovy Company, Michael Lok. We know something about the financial arrangements of Frobisher's three voyages because they resulted in litigation. Had the voyages been profitable, no doubt these records would have been lost or destroyed with nearly all other business records of the time. For the first voyage, Frobisher and Lok had difficulty in raising £875 from eighteen of many persons asked to invest. The re-

maining cost, more than £700, Lok assumed personally. They built the *Gabriel*, a ship of about twenty tons, and bought the *Michael*, a ship of twenty-five tons, and a pinnace of about ten tons.

The little expedition sailed on 7 June 1576 and Queen Elizabeth herself waved them farewell. On July 1st they sighted Greenland, which Frobisher took to be Friesland, one of the non-existent islands that cluttered his inadequate charts. Near Greenland a great storm swamped the pinnace and its crew. The captain of the *Michael*, terrified by the ice, turned back and in London reported the rest of the expedition lost.

But Frobisher pushed on westward, "knowing," according to the account by George Best in 1578, "that the Sea at length must néedes haue an endyng, and that some lande shoulde haue a beginning that way." On 28 July they sighted new land, and on 11 August they entered "a greate gutte, bay, or passage" which Frobisher named for himself. It was not, as he supposed, a strait between Asia on the north and America on the south, but a huge bay, the one that continues to bear his name.

In late August some Eskimos came on board to trade. One of them agreed by signs to pilot them into the great sea to the west. But to Frobisher's astonishment and

disma... disapp... worrie... withou... surely... Near ... Charles ... bisher B... people . ... wintered ... that they ... put a ma... succeeded ... went, whi... The exa... own story, ... a stone, ".. dyd gyve r... land." Duri... stone to as ... and could f...

Map of Fro... map are the ... through then...

C·ROCLAND

WEST

...ho rowed the native ashore all ...ive return. Short-handed and ...e season, he had to turn back ...Vestern Sea, which he would ...Bay to be.

...rs later, in 1861-62, Captain ...from the Eskimos of Fro- ...en were captured by Innuit ...rs ago; that these men ...y lived among the Innuits; ...oomien (large boat), and ...ails; ... that finally they ...water, and away they ...or heard of them."

...egan, according to Lok's ...when Frobisher gave him ...nge to his promesse, he ...hat he found in the new- ...ok gave three bits of the ...of whom "made prooffe ..."In January, Lok gave

a fourth sample of the stone to John Baptista Agnello, an Italian assayer, who claimed to find gold in it, and found gold also in two more pieces. Lok marvelled greatly at this performance and asked him how he came to succeed where so many others had failed. The Italian begged the question gracefully, but his reply, "It is necessary to flatter nature," and the grains of gold, satisfied Lok.

Agnello continued to flatter nature as the winter wore on. He convinced Lok that here was a rich ore, although other assayers continued to declare the stone worthless. Lok submitted reports to the Queen and entered discussions with her representatives, who were at first convinced that Agnello "dyd but play the alchemist." At length a second assayer was found to agree with Agnello and, in spite of the burden of negative professional opinion, Lok's plans began to meet with a swell of enthusiasm. On 17 March 1577, Queen Elizabeth granted a charter and subscribed £1,000 to the Cathay Company, of which Lok was named Governor. The liabilities and assets of the first voyage were entered on the books of

...blished in 1578 by George Best who sailed with him, "Frobisshers Streights" on the ...ay and "The Mistaken Straightes" were later named for the man who first sailed

Dutch Babies

Makes one 10-inch (25-cm) pancake, serves 2 to 4

While we've all been deep in the Dutch baby game for a while now (perfect for kids! perfect for parents! perfect for lovers! perfect for families of four in a bunker!), we'll let David tell the backstory: "Many years ago, I worked at a seaside inn/restaurant on Vancouver Island called Sooke Harbour House. The deal was sweet: seaside, local day-boat fish, several gardeners on staff, foragers, all food was from a 5K surrounding area except the chocolate, orange juice, and coffee. 'You can't run an inn without chocolate, orange juice, or coffee, David,' Frédérique Philip, the innkeeper's wife, would say to me. The kitchen had windows, an ocean view, plants, hippie murals of children playing, and people seemed very happy.

"This was odd for me as I had come from the hell kitchens of other men's misery, competitive kill-or-be-killed environments, and was now getting big hugs from other cooks in the morning over seaside coffee. All that smiling was off-putting. Today, I credit Sooke Harbour House as the restaurant that most affected the cooking I did and still kind of do: loose menu, market-driven, an emphasis on the positive mental health of staff.

"Having been brought up in French kitchens, I had never seen a Dutch baby, but they were made daily at Sooke Harbour House: breakfast babies, herb and cheese babies, crab babies, clam babies, mushroom babies (to accompany roasted meats in lieu of a starch), dessert babies with foraged berries. Satisfying to cook and even better to eat."

⅔ cup (160 ml) whole milk

⅔ cup (90 g) all-purpose flour (or ½ cup/100 g gluten-free flour mix)

1 tablespoon sugar

Pinch of salt

Pinch of ground nutmeg

Pinch of ground cinnamon

3 large eggs

3 tablespoons unsalted butter

1. Preheat the oven to 450°F (230°C), including a cast-iron skillet, placed on the middle rack.

2. In a blender, combine the milk, flour, sugar, salt, nutmeg, cinnamon, and eggs, and blend until uniform, about 30 seconds.

3. When the oven reaches temperature, carefully remove the hot pan from the oven and coat it with 1 tablespoon of the butter, working promptly to avoid burning the butter and cooling the oven. Pour in the batter and return the pan immediately to the oven.

4. Bake undisturbed for 15 minutes, resisting the urge to poke, stroke, or inspect.

5. Remove from the oven, place on a trivet, and put the remaining 2 tablespoons butter to melt on top.

Note An 8-inch or 10-inch (20-cm or 25-cm) cast-iron pan is crucial to your success here: the heat it retains, its nonstick attributes, and the straight and tall walls. Don't attempt to make babies with anything less.

May we suggest a few Dutch baby variations? →

Comté, Girolles, Foie Gras, and Vin Jaune (Famille Ganevat)

2 tablespoons unsalted butter

2 cups (120 g) chanterelles, cleaned

¼ cup (60 ml) vin jaune or dry sherry

¼ cup (60 ml) heavy cream
(35 percent butterfat)

Salt and pepper

2 tablespoons chopped shallots

1 recipe Dutch Baby (page 35)

1 cup (80 g) grated Comté cheese

2 slices foie gras (2 oz or 60 g each)

I. Start by melting the butter until foaming in a large frying pan, over high heat, and sautéing the mushrooms until cooked—watch for burning, which would be tragic considering what you paid for them.

2. Add the vin jaune, then the cream, season with salt and pepper to taste, and, off the heat, add the shallots.

3. Make the basic Dutch baby.

4. Cover the baby with the grated Comté and the foie gras, and pour the mushroom sauce atop. Return to the oven and give it another 2 to 3 minutes so that the cheese can melt into the mushrooms.

Macerated Berries, Honey, and Quark

1 cup (140 g) mixed berries, sliced if you prefer

3 tablespoons sugar

1 teaspoon fresh lemon juice

¼ cup (60 ml) heavy cream
(35 percent butterfat)

¼ cup (60 g) fresh quark cheese

1 splash pure vanilla extract

1 recipe Dutch Baby (page 35)

A few drizzles of good honey

I. Combine the berries, 2 tablespoons of the sugar, and the lemon juice, toss, and let sit for 30 minutes at room temperature.

2. Whip the cream until soft peaks form. Fold in the cheese and mix in the vanilla and remaining 1 tablespoon sugar.

3. Make the Dutch baby.

4. Arrange the berries and cream on the baby and drizzle with honey.

Cultured Butter, Maple Syrup, and Cinnamon Sugar

3 tablespoons sugar

1 teaspoon ground cinnamon

½ pound (225 g) salted cultured butter, cold and cubed

1 recipe Dutch Baby (page 35)

Maple syrup

I. Combine the sugar and cinnamon. Set aside.

2. In the bowl of a stand mixer fitted with the paddle attachment, whip the butter until white and frothy, being careful not to melt it.

3. Make the Dutch baby.

4. Dress with the cinnamon sugar, then the whipped butter. Drizzle with maple syrup.

Igloo Mousse (or Winter Milk Jellies)

Makes four 6½ ounce
(200 ml) jellies

— ❧ —

You will need

4 whimsical molds

"There is something to be said about our impossible, nonsensical, and straight-up devotion to the absurd," says Meredith. "Like Marco driving seven hours to Abitibi to pick up two hundred and fifty pounds of caviar and driving back to Montreal on the same day. Like Fred's 2015 truck-stop beef tour of Texas. Or like my own attachment to these silicone igloo molds found in the basement of Dehillerin, a professional kitchen supplier in Paris, which I then trekked around for a month all over northern Italy during the 'Summer of Lucifer' so that we could make these here jellies." Truthfully, a dish, sometimes even an entire book, is a by-product of an obsession with a concept, usually in direct opposition to our time and wallet. Locally, France Décor has been an endless source of catalysts, through its enormous inventory of seemingly useless but actually invaluable kitchenwares and cake stuff.

2½ cups (625 ml) full-fat best-quality milk

¼ cup (40 g) milk powder

1 cinnamon stick

1 cardamom pod

10 black peppercorns

2 cloves

2 star anise

½ vanilla bean (not split open)

1 piece orange peel the size of a dollar bill folded into eighths

Pinch of sea salt

1 tablespoon powdered gelatin, bloomed according to the instructions on the packet

¼ cup (50 g) sugar

For the garnish

Crumbled macarons and birch syrup
or maple syrup

1. Combine the milk with the powdered milk (to create a super milk). Gently warm the milk over medium heat in a saucepan. Add the spices, vanilla, orange peel, and salt. Cover, set on low heat, and infuse for 15 minutes.

2. Stir in the gelatin and sugar, stir to dissolve, then strain into a measuring cup and pour into four whimsical molds such as the ones Meredith bought.

3. Refrigerate for 3 hours until set. Unmold onto tasteful dessert plates. Serve with white mulled wine. Garnish with crumbled macarons and a drizzle of birch syrup.

Note The vision here was to create a miniature northern Canadian scene of edible igloos, complete with confectioners' sugar snow, a bonfire atop jagged ice, and a thin electric blue (Jell-O) arctic river. You don't have to do that.

HEURES D'OUVERTURE
Lundi au Vendredi: 9h à 17 heures
Samedi: 9h à 12 heures

BUSINESS HOURS
Monday to Friday: 9:00 a.m. to 5:00 p.m.
Saturday: 9:00 a.m. to 12:00 p.m.

FRANCE DECOR CANADA

Two

Joe Beef, the Restaurant

People are often bewildered when they walk into our restaurant. A look of astonishment and disbelief washes over them as they realize they've just traveled a thousand miles to eat a piece of venison in what appears to be someone's woodshed.

But as the jackets are hung and the snow begins to melt off boots and the booze is poured, there is an ease that sets in: that the chalkboard is full of French classics, as is the wine list, that we're here to talk about our city, to show you the garden and the smoker, and that the evening will inescapably lead to having poire William in the workshop out back.

Someone told us that being at Joe Beef is like being with the uncle who takes you on a road trip, buys you hotdogs, introduces you to friends, and with whom you always catch a fish. We like that description.

Joe Beef is part French restaurant, part Northwest oyster bar, and part garden.

Since opening in 2005—when we waited anxiously for Hudson's Bay to have its "Bay Day" sales event where we could buy 40 percent off Jamie Oliver cookware that was already 50 percent off—our restaurants have grown in size, but a lot has remained the same: glabrous apprentices have departed, then returned bearded. An oyster shucker became a lawyer and then more shuckers followed. The garden grows and retracts with the four seasons, and our dishes are as generous as ever. We are still partial to eating leeks with ham and good cheese. We still serve soft-serve with cherries from our (much bigger)

cherry tree. The floor is still the red oxblood paint, our walls are cluttered (tastefully, we maintain) with maps, our friends' books, and trophies (Kevin: Best Eater).

There will never be tablecloths at Joe Beef. Nothing (still) makes us happier than Dover sole.

We still have a love-hate relationship with restaurants. Indeed: going to new restaurants at our age feels a bit like Tony Hawk jumping on a skateboard. The alley behind the three restaurants is still a geopolitical mystery: it's been used for car porn, and as a place to ditch stolen bikes . . . and, for a while, it didn't even appear on maps! For us, though, it's like the hallway in high school: a place to ferry stuff to and fro, a place for staff to catch up along the way.

Like a tree with its rings, Fred's closet tells the story of obsessions since Book One. If you peer inside you will see vapes, Alain Chapel cookbooks, shin pads and sparring gloves, a diving watch, a blacksmith's apron, a very large butcher knife, a circulator, hockey gear, a cyclo-cross bike, a ham radio, a fixed-lens camera, an alcohol stove from Sweden for hiking, wine-making supplies, eighteen paint cans, and chocolate molds.

It's been a long time that we have understood that we should let more talented people do their thing, and after all, all we (Fred and Dave) can do is cook with shallots, mustard, and white wine. We look with amazement at the younger generation, at what the younger cooks are coming up with. People can sling shit at the millennials, but these kids, unlike us at their age, have eaten in so many different restaurants growing up because that's what more and more families do now.

As always, writing a book is a therapeutic/beneficial experience for the restaurant. Digging up the archives in our mind of technical culinary information as well as the old plates in the basement that we forgot we had. Collectively reminiscing over the last decade, the hits and the failures. Like when Fred tried to make a *baumkuchen* in a rotisserie, or when *truite au bleu* seemed applicable, or just the idea of spaghetti ice cream. As you work on recipes, you realize there are so many better ways to make a dish. For us, inspiration has always come from the traditions of *L'Art culinaire Français,* from the Escoffier and the grand hotels, and from our hometown. There has always been a generosity of spirit. And of course, as we are still at heart Bocusian-Lyonnais market fare, it comes from the daily drop-ins of friends and purveyors of "what's good."

A restaurant is in a constant sway between changing itself to avoid a rut, between keeping creative and keeping classics, be it its food, its walls, or its playlist, to comfort returning guests.

We have to think solidly about traditions and whether they deserve to be maintained. It's something we think about a lot. If no one does Langue de Veau, Chicken Fricassée aux Écrevisses, or Lièvre à la Royale . . . if there is no museum to go to and eat it, then it's gone. We're very aware of this at Joe Beef, and it's indicative of our menus and also in the chapter that follows.

Joe Beef saved us, Fred and David, from our old jobs and our old selves. The base restaurant was David, Fred, Allison, Julie, John Bil, Vanya, Meredith, Kaunteya, and our dishwasher Rana. Our team is much bigger now and has created many paths along the way. We realize name-dropping within this book can feel a bit like watching *Game of Thrones* halfway through the series (Who is that? Is he good or bad? What is her magic power? Is he a zombie?). We know. But our little restaurant has been an apex for kindred culinary spirits (the idea of *atomes crochus* in French) and for that we're most proud. We've all suffered our own personal apocalypse, yet we all return at sunrise, to the Little Burgundy mothership that is Joe Beef, for a dozen oysters, lobster spaghetti, and a glass of Muscadet.

Joe Beef has changed the path of many, but it might not change yours.

—M.E., F.M., D.M.

Kidneys à la Monique

~~~

You will need

Meat thermometer with a probe, preferably ovenproof

Baking sheet

Montreal has potholes the size of resort hot tubs, obsolete futuristic highways, and crumbling overpasses. But we love this city with a love the size of Texas. Why? We can buy and eat rabbit, duck, horse, or offal within a two-mile radius of wherever we are on any given day. Indeed, the Montreal diner eats and loves kidneys for the meal that they are, not on a challenging dare, but because they are simply delicious!

A few years ago, Josée di Stasio, the grande dame of Quebec food media, introduced us to Monique Duveau and Olympe Versini, who were in town from France. Olympe is one of the first chefs to ditch the excruciating demands of the Michelin grind for a simpler bistro approach; Monique is a lady of the table, the best kind of food patron you could wish for. When we heard they were coming, we sent one of the cooks to the Atwater Market to fetch some *rognons* (veal kidneys). At the time, we were into putting a salt crust on everything: chicken, fish, potatoes, and each other . . . so we cleaned up the kidneys, wrapped them in a duxelles of chanterelles, wrapped that in caul fat, and then made the salt crust. We sculpted the crust to look like a young calf at rest on its flank, ruminating. Monique took that crust back to her house in Le Perche, where it sat displayed among many of her worldly finds, until time and moths got the best of it.

For the salt crust

4¾ cups (700 g) all-purpose flour

5 cups (1.5 kg) pickling salt

5 large egg whites

1½ cups (360 ml) water

For the kidneys

¼ cup (57 g) unsalted butter

¼ cup (35 g) minced shallots

½ pound (225 g) mushrooms (a mix of chanterelles, lobster, or firm white buttons), finely chopped

¼ cup (35 g) finely chopped white ham or Black Forest ham

¼ cup (60 ml) brandy

3 to 4 fresh flat-leaf parsley sprigs, minced

2 tablespoons Dijon mustard

Salt and pepper

½ teaspoon cayenne pepper

1 pair veal kidneys (1 pound/454 g each), cleaned and trimmed

3 tablespoons grapeseed oil or other neutral oil

1 pound (454 g) pork caul fat

For the egg wash

1 large egg, beaten

Suggested serving sauce

Sauce Madère Rapide (page 46)

I. Make the salt crust first. In a very large bowl, use a whisk to combine the flour and pickling salt. Using a wooden spoon, stir in the egg whites, then add the water slowly until a dough forms. Use your hands now to knead the dough until malleable but not sticky. Divide into 2 balls, wrap in plastic wrap, and refrigerate for at least 1 hour (overnight will work too).

2. Heat the butter in a sauté pan over medium heat. When it starts to foam, add the shallots and cook until translucent, about 2 minutes. Add the mushrooms and ham, cooking slowly over medium-low heat until the moisture is gone but before anything

starts to brown, about 10 minutes. Add the brandy and reduce until the pan contents are almost dry, about 3 minutes.

3. Add the parsley and mustard. Season with salt, pepper, and cayenne to taste, and set aside.

4. Season the kidneys and sear them briskly in a hot pan with the oil, using two spatulas to carefully turn them over, then set aside. You want to color them, not scorch them. Transfer them, trimmed underbelly side facing up, to a paper towel–lined plate.

5. Preheat the oven to 425°F (220°C).

6. Unroll the caul fat onto your work surface. Cut out four 12-inch- (30-cm-) wide circles. Place two layers of caul fat on your working surface, then transfer each kidney, underbelly side up, into the center of each caul "circle." Spoon half the mushroom mixture into each central cavity. Gather the edges of the caul up and overlap them to make a seal, maintaining the natural torpedo shape of the kidney. Repeat with the remaining kidney.

7. Roll out one ball of salt dough between two sheets of heavy-duty plastic wrap into a large circle about ½ inch thick. Discard the top sheet of plastic and cut out a 12-inch (300-mm) disk. Repeat with the second ball of dough.

8. Place a kidney bundle in the middle of each dough circle with the cavity/mushroom side up. Carefully close, gathering up the dough, using the plastic wrap as your support system, and overlap and press together to make a seal. Turn over the package and carefully transfer to a baking sheet. Feel free to add the calf legs and head or

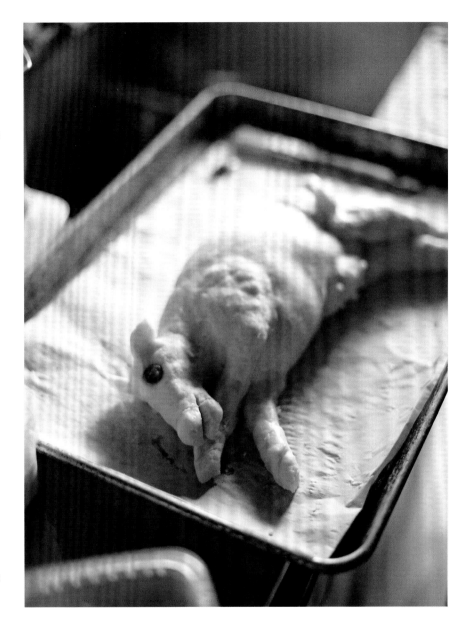

the crest of your alma mater with the remaining dough.

9. Brush both wrapped kidneys softly with the egg wash. Insert the probe of your meat thermometer through the salt crust into one of the lobes.

10. Bake for 25 to 30 minutes, until the internal temperature registers 135°F (57°C), then transfer to a large enough, pretty enough serving platter.

Pry the crust open with a blunt knife or with one of those very cool Fein saws, tableside, of course. Serve with Sauce Madère Rapide.

Note When it comes to kidneys, find out from your butcher what day of the week they come in; don't wait, they get funky after a while. Ask your butcher to trim away any fat and remove the bigger nerves.

Sauce Madère Rapide

Makes 1 ⅔ cups (400 ml) sauce

You will need

Fine-mesh strainer

3 tablespoons (45 g) plus ¼ pound (113 g) great unsalted butter

1 cup (150 g) roughly diced carrots

1 cup (175 g) roughly diced leeks

½ cup (10 g) dehydrated champignons de Paris or button mushrooms

2 garlic cloves, smashed

6 fresh thyme sprigs

1 tablespoon white peppercorns

1 tablespoon apple cider vinegar

1 cup (250 ml) dry Madeira wine

1 tablespoon Bragg liquid aminos

6 sheets leaf gelatin, soaked in 2 cups (500 ml) water

Salt and pepper

Squeeze of lemon

This sauce is a Joe Beef mainstay due to its fatty yet sweet proficiency with all things gamy or offal. We love it with kidneys, sweetbreads, quail, and, yes, even *cheval*.

1. In a medium, heavy-bottomed saucepan, over medium-high heat, melt 3 tablespoons of the butter.

2. Add the carrots, leeks, and mushrooms to the pan, and cook, stirring occasionally, until browned like steak and pleasantly fragrant, 5 to 7 minutes.

3. Reduce the heat to medium, add the garlic, thyme, and peppercorns, and cook for 2 to 3 minutes more.

4. Add the cider vinegar, Madeira, and liquid aminos. Reduce by half, about 5 minutes.

5. Stir in the gelatin and its blooming water, making sure it doesn't stick to the bottom of the pan. Reduce the heat and simmer slowly for about 20 minutes, until syrupy and a deep golden-brown hue.

6. Using a fine-mesh strainer, strain the sauce into a smaller saucepan, making sure you extract every last precious drop. Season to taste, then over medium-high heat, whisk in the remaining butter, one pat at a time, until melted and emulsified. Check the seasoning and adjust to taste with salt, pepper, and a squeeze or two of lemon.

Oeufs Mayonnaise

The French are smart. North Americans will feast on a three-egg bologna goat cheese fajita omelet with a stack of waffles, but the French will start a proper meal with one simple egg (which perhaps explains how they tend to fit into tight couture pants). And what better condiment for said egg than an emulsion of another egg with oil and mustard, aka mayonnaise.

A neat trick to determine if an egg is cooked or not is to drop it from a substantial height; the uncooked egg will be easily recognizable by the mess you just made.

For the eggs

4 large farm-fresh chicken eggs, at room temperature

2 quail eggs, at room temperature

For the mayonnaise

2 large egg yolks

2 tablespoons Dijon mustard

¼ teaspoon turmeric

Fresh lemon juice

1 cup (125 ml) grapeseed oil or other neutral oil

½ cup (125 ml) very lightly whipped unsweetened heavy cream (35 percent butterfat)

Salt and white pepper

To serve

¼ cup (42 g) hemp seeds

3 tablespoons fresh chives, minced

One 1.75-ounce (50 g) jar of your favorite fish eggs: mullet roe, whitefish roe, salmon roe, osetra (optional)

2 white hearts of celery, shaved, tossed in a drizzle of lemon, salt, and pepper

I. Place the chicken eggs and quail eggs in a medium saucepan and add enough water to cover by 1 inch (2.5 cm).

2. When the water comes to a boil, reduce the heat to low, cover, and simmer for 3 minutes. Using a slotted spoon, remove the quail eggs and transfer them to a bowl filled with cold water and ice.

3. Continue to simmer the chicken eggs for another 4 minutes. Drain the water and transfer the eggs to the ice water.

4. When the eggs are cool enough to handle, peel gently and set aside in a bowl on the counter.

5. **Now on to the mayonnaise:** In a medium bowl set over a damp cloth, whisk together the egg yolks, mustard, turmeric, and a small splash of lemon juice. Next, slowly drizzle the oil into the bowl, whisking continually until you have a smooth emulsion. Continue whisking and slowly adding the oil until you have a full bowl of mayonnaise. Whisk in the cream and adjust the seasoning with lemon juice, and salt and white pepper as desired.

6. Spoon 2 tablespoons of mayonnaise onto each plate. Cut the eggs into halves. Now's the time to channel your inner modernist when arranging the eggs (avian and piscine) on each plate. Add the hemp seeds and chives. Serve with the shaved celery tossed in lemon.

Notes   Peeling hard-boiled farm-fresh eggs can be an exercise in frustration. In order to get perfectly smooth eggs out of their shell, add 1 tablespoon baking soda to the cooking water.

If you just can't nail the Dijon-oil emulsion, it's okay to add a good splash of lemon juice and salt and pepper to 1 cup of Hellmann's and call it a day.

Onion Soup Toast, aka Soupe au Sandwich

Serves 6 to 8 or
two country lunches for 4

You will need

Loaf pan (8½ x 4½ x 2¾ inches/
21.5 x 11.5 x 7 cm)

Is there a Freudian root to the love of bread in broth? We love its motherly, soft, warm, nourishing, and tender embrace in the deep and darkest throes of February, when it has been three months of −20°C (−5°F), with still the hardest stretch ahead.

For the broth

2 tablespoons grapeseed oil or other neutral oil

8 bacon slices, cut into matchsticks

4 medium onions, thinly sliced

2 leek whites, thinly sliced

¼ cup (60 ml) sherry vinegar

½ cup (120 ml) dry sherry

2 tablespoons minced fresh lovage, celery, or flat-leaf parsley leaves

2 quarts (2 l) water

1¾ pounds (750 g) smoked ham or smoked ham shank

Salt and white pepper

For the cheese sauce

1 tablespoon all-purpose flour

1 cup (110 g) finely grated Gruyère or Comté cheese

1 cup (240 ml) whole milk

2 large egg yolks

For the sandwich

Unsalted butter, at room temperature, for the loaf pan

6 to 9 slices crustless white bread, toasted

1 shallot, minced

4 playing card–size slices (2¼ ounces/ 75 g each) foie gras terrine (see Microwaved Foie Gras, page 136)

1. To a wide, heavy-bottomed pan, add the grapeseed oil and bacon. Over medium heat, cook the bacon pieces until mildly crisped.

2. Stir in the onions and leeks, and continue to stir well while cooking. It takes a good 20 minutes of cooking and stirring to get to a nice golden retriever color on the alliums.

3. Add the sherry vinegar, dry sherry, and lovage. Stir to combine. Cook for a minute, then add the water and pork chunk, and bring to a boil. Reduce the heat, cover, and simmer gently for 1 hour.

4. Remove the pork from the soup and season the soup with salt and white pepper to taste.

5. Strain the broth, reserving the onions and leeks for your loaf. (The broth can be refrigerated now if you are making this ahead of time.) Set aside.

6. Thinly slice the pork chunk.

7. **For the sauce:** In a bowl, mix the flour and cheese with a fork. In a small pot, bring the milk to a boil. Pour the cheese mixture into the milk and stir until combined; cook briefly until →

Montreal restaurant icon Jacques Muller.

thickened. Whisk in the egg yolks, then set aside.

8. Preheat the oven to 325°F (160°C), and generously butter the loaf pan.

9. Build the "sandwich" in the loaf pan:
Place a layer of toast on the bottom of the pan to cover. It's okay to have some overlap, just make sure you're covering the whole surface of the pan. Next lay down the pork slices, followed by a sprinkling of shallots and the cheese sauce.

10. Lay down another layer of toast, then the foie gras terrine pieces. Squish them to make a nice flat layer, followed by the reserved onions and leeks. Top with a final layer of toast and press well, using a spatula.

11. Pour a few spoonfuls of the broth over the top layer of toast and bake for 30 minutes. Keep the rest of the broth hot until ready to serve.

12. Remove the loaf pan from the oven and, using the spatula again, press the top down lightly to ensure the sandwich comes together nicely. Bake for another 10 minutes, until the top is brown. (At this point, the baked sandwich can be refrigerated in its loaf pan until needed.)

13. To serve, cut the sandwich into 8 slices, approximately 1 inch (2.5 cm) thick. Transfer each slice to a shallow soup bowl and pour the steaming broth from a jug, table side, as they do in fancy restaurants.

Note The broth and "sandwich" can both be made ahead of time, assembled and refrigerated, and warmed up as needed.

Brains over Matar

The most important thing in the kitchen—other than being free of fecal coliforms—is a sense of humor. Long hours and rough work are unbearable in an environment of contemplative stiffness. Enter the pun: a way to break the seriousness rut in a kitchen, and a great way to make a dish—much better inspiration than fusion jazz or Arcimboldi, we think! For this one, we were riffing on the Hindi word for peas (*matar*) and a "*matar*cycle," but it wasn't really turning into a dish. We started thinking of calf brains, a classic of Montreal French dining: David would go through two pails of it every lunch service while cooking at Le Caveau (a classic Montreal institution, now closed).

For the brains

1 very fresh calf brain

1 cup (240 ml) whole milk

1 cup (160 g) gram flour (chickpea flour)

1 cup (140 g) all-purpose flour

2 tablespoons curry powder

1 teaspoon kosher salt

Canola oil for frying

For the peas

7 tablespoons (100 g) unsalted butter, cold

1 small onion, diced

1 tablespoon chopped fresh ginger

1 tablespoon chopped garlic

1 small tomato, seeded and chopped

1 small green apple, diced

1 tablespoon curry powder

2 tablespoons all-purpose flour

1 cup (240 ml) chicken stock

2 cups (480 ml) heavy cream (35 percent butterfat)

Salt and pepper

Hot sauce (optional)

1 cup (125 g) frozen peas

Squeeze of lemon juice

1. Cut the brain into ¾-inch-thick (2-cm-thick) slices and soak in a bowl of milk with a pinch of salt. Refrigerate.

2. In a separate bowl, combine the gram flour, all-purpose flour, curry, and salt, and mix well. Set aside.

3. In a 2-quart saucepan over medium heat, melt 6 tablespoons (85 g) of the butter and sweat the onion until translucent. Add the ginger, garlic, tomato, apple, and curry powder, reduce the heat to low, and sweat again for 3 to 4 minutes. Add the flour and mix well with a wooden spoon for about 2 minutes. Let the liaison (thickening) occur. Add the chicken stock and mix. Finally, add the cream and cook for 20 minutes more. Remove from the heat.

4. Carefully pass the mixture through a strainer and keep warm. Correct the seasoning with salt, pepper, and hot sauce, if warranted.

5. Barely cook the frozen peas in the sauce over low heat. Finish with the remaining tablespoon of butter, swirling the pan to blend in the butter, one teaspoon at a time, and a squeeze of lemon. Keep warm.

6. In a deep pot or, better yet, a deep fryer gifted to you by your insensitive significant other, heat the oil to 350°F (180°C), that is, perfect frying temp. Remove the brain slices from the milk and toss them in the gram flour mixture, getting a nice coating. Shake off any excess and fry the brains for 3 to 4 minutes, until firm-ish and crispy. Pat dry, lightly salt, and serve the brains over the *matar*.

Note Find out from your butcher when slaughter day is and make sure you don't purchase brains more than 3 to 5 days after that. Definitely not a weekend dish.

Duck Stroganoff

Serves 4

⟨⟨⟨—

You will need

Food processor to "grind" the meats, if your butcher can't help you.

Back when boeuf stroganoff was trending all over the Western world, and boys had posters of Samantha Fox on their walls, Fred was listening to Weird Al and enjoying a little Monsieur de Paris scalp tonic on his bowl cut. The McDonald's pizza was still around, but he preferred a steaming plate of Hamburger Helper, his "gold standard of good taste." That was then, and this is that dish now (nailing it without any yellow 5 dye in sight). Serve with store-bought pasta or dehydrated potatoes, cooked in at the end.

---

1 small onion, finely chopped

2 tablespoons grapeseed oil or other neutral oil

1 pound (450 g) duck hearts, ground

½ pound (225 g) lean bacon, cut into chunks, frozen for 30 minutes, then pulsed 5 times in a food processor

2 garlic cloves, minced

1 teaspoon chopped fresh thyme

1 tablespoon chopped fresh flat-leaf parsley

¼ cup (60 ml) vodka

Salt and white pepper

1 cup (240 ml) stock (brown is best)

1 cup (20 g) dried button mushrooms

½ cup (120 ml) heavy cream (35 percent butterfat)

Juice of ½ lemon

10 ounces (300 g) dried pasta (preferably egg noodles) cooked three-quarters of the recommended cooking time and chilled

For the garnish

Minced fresh chives

½ tablespoon toasted caraway seeds

Lemon cream—lightly whipped heavy cream (35 percent butterfat), with a squeeze of lemon and black pepper

Caviar (optional)

1. In a wide, heavy-bottomed pan over medium-high heat, sweat the onion in the oil until translucent, 5 to 7 minutes. Stir in the ground meats to make your stroganoff, and continue to sauté until browned, about 5 minutes.

2. Add the garlic, thyme, parsley, and vodka, reduce for a minute or two, and season with salt and white pepper to taste.

3. Add the stock and dried mushrooms. Bring to a boil over high heat, then cover, reduce the heat to low, and simmer for about 15 minutes. Strain the stroganoff and return the cooking juices (about 1¼ cups/300 ml) to the pan. Set aside the stroganoff.

4. Add 3 tablespoons of the cream to the cooking juices, and simmer for another 3 to 5 minutes, until the sauce has started to thicken and has reduced to ¾ cup (200 ml).

5. Whisk in the remaining 5 tablespoons (75 ml) cream and the lemon juice.

6. Stir the partially cooked pasta into the sauce and bring to a boil. Cover and cook until the pasta is done, about 5 minutes. Add water as needed to loosen up the sauce. Stir the stroganoff back into the pan.

7. Garnish with minced chives and caraway seeds. Serve with generous dollops of lemon cream and caviar, if you like.

Notes Talk to your butcher about ordering duck hearts. If not, check www .dartagnan.com. If your butcher won't grind the duck, coarsely chop it, then pulse it for 7 to 10 brief bursts in a food processor to medium-coarse.

Ground duck leg can be substituted.

Watercress Soup with Trout Quenelles

Serves 4

———

You will need

Food processor

Ice bath

We all love a good companionship story, like the couple who's been married for sixty-five years and die days apart from each other, or that movie with Schwarzenegger and Danny DeVito. There are very few such faithful pairings in the culinary world, except for shallots and thyme, and in this case, trout and watercress. In the limpid streams where one tackles trout, you'll often find watercress growing on the banks.

At Joe Beef, when we went looking for a clever way to legitimize our trout pond, we had no choice but to turn it into a watercress fertilizing device in order to have it make sense in our eyes, but mostly in the city inspector's eyes! We have no doubt that, by the time this book is published, watercress will have become the new kale; we apologize.

For the soup

Trout quenelles (page 121)

4 bunches watercress

3 tablespoons grapeseed oil

4 shallots, finely chopped

2 cups (300 g) Yukon gold potatoes, peeled and diced

4 cups (1 l) chicken stock

Salt and white pepper

½ cup (113 g) unsalted butter, cubed

Lemon

1. Prepare a pot of boiling, heavily salted water, as well as an ice bath. Wash the watercress carefully and chop the stems where they reach the leaves. Set aside the chopped stems.

2. Blanch the leaves for 30 seconds in the boiling water, drain, and transfer to the ice bath. When cold, drain and pat dry, then chop finely.

3. In a medium saucepan over medium heat, sweat the shallots in the oil until fragrant. Add the watercress stems, potatoes, chicken stock, and a pinch of salt. Cook for 30 minutes, or until the potatoes are crumbling.

4. Preheat the oven to 250°F (120°C).

5. Transfer the potatoes, watercress, and shallot mixture to a food processor and purée cautiously. Avoid long pulses that would turn the spuds and the soup gluey. Return to the pot.

6. In the oven, reheat 2 quenelles in each ovenproof soup bowl for 5 to 7 minutes.

7. Bring the soup to a boil and add the butter in chunks, whisking until fully incorporated. Adjust the seasoning—add a drop or two of lemon. Keep warm.

8. Pour piping-hot soup over the quenelles. Garnish as you like.

Note   This soup is delicious even without the trout quenelles. If you want to take the easy route, warm buttered trout with fish roe and even a poached egg as garnish. Otherwise, start by making the quenelles.

Buttered Turnip Soup,
aka Potage Télépathique

**Makes 5 cups (1¼ l) soup,
serves 3 to 4**

———— ∿ ————

You will need

Handheld immersion blender
or a blender

½ pound (225 g) unsalted butter

4 cups (550 g) peeled white turnips
(not rutabaga!), cut into ½-inch (1-cm)
cubes (4 to 6 turnips)

2½ to 3 cups (600 to 700 ml) chicken
stock or whole milk

1 teaspoon sea salt

¼ teaspoon white pepper

2 tablespoons maple syrup (optional)

The sad truth is that David and Fred can read each other's minds. Mostly, it's been helpful when picking out an outfit or shopping for an oversize roof rack. But there was this one time, back in the Globe restaurant days (our previous employer), when a call came in for Fred. It was Dave. As Fred tells it: "He was on a pay phone (the kind that, in a movie, a secret agent abandoned by his CIA handler will use to reach a hopefully friendly and tech-savvy journalist), after eating at a restaurant, telling me he was obsessing over a simple turnip and butter soup, which oddly enough I was precisely in the process of making, exactly in that moment."

I. In a Dutch oven or copper pot over low-medium heat, melt the butter. Add the turnips and stir, then cover. Sweat the turnips very slowly while stirring occasionally, keeping the pan covered the rest of the time. Give the vegetables a stir every 5 minutes until they are really soft, as only a European mother could appreciate, 35 to 40 minutes. Remove from the heat.

2. Add the chicken stock while blending with an immersion blender until the desired consistency. Season with the salt and pepper. Note that a touch of maple syrup is a delicious addition. Return to the heat to warm, if needed.

3. Serve with a mind-bent spoon.

Note This simple method of soup making can be applied to any number of root vegetables, but big white turnips are the most delicious and proper adult decision.

Thin T-Bone of Beef Bacon

Serves 4 (makes 8 small,
thin steaks)

━━━━━━━━━

You will need

Meat saw
(or ask your butcher to do the cutting)

Cold smoker

Bag of applewood or sugar maple chips

Large sheet pan

"We want to sit at a nice table, order a bottle of wine, have a dozen oysters each, and then eat a great plate of chops. Unpretentious thin chops, nicely browned, hot and salty, a heaping plate of them, in the middle of the table."

—Us, in our first book's "A Plea for Thin Chops"

This sentiment still holds true and was reinforced when Fred and Marco were in Miami and visited Playa Cafe just off the very busy South Beach strip. "It's delicious, cheap, and oddly enough felt way more Miami than any of the expensive restaurants on the strip. This recipe is inspired by their Palomilla Steak breakfast," says Marco. Still and always an ode to thin chops.

Eight ½-inch- (1- to 1.5-cm-) thick T-bone steaks, frozen, sliced thinly on the meat saw

2 tablespoons plus 1 teaspoon kosher salt

1 teaspoon brown sugar, packed

1 teaspoon granulated sugar

1 crushed bay leaf or ½ teaspoon ground bay leaf

1 teaspoon ground black pepper

I. In an appropriately sized nonreactive baking pan, mix the meat, salt, sugars, bay leaf, and pepper. Let sit overnight.

2. The following day, quickly rinse the meat under cold water and pat dry. Cold smoke for 1 hour.

3. To finish the steaks, cook them to your liking. We suggest a very hot cast-iron pan to imitate that griddle flavor from Playa Cafe. Florida serving suggestion: serve with eggs, hot sauce, and griddled onions.

Note In conjunction with the theme of the interlude, look for the standard meat, ungraded, the type that you usually shun.

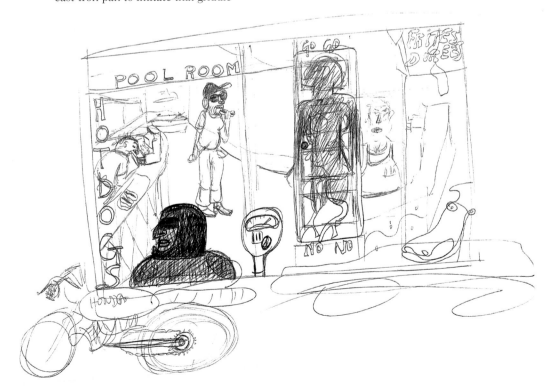

Tomato Marjolaine Butter

Makes 2½ cups (650 ml) sauce,
enough for a few meals

———— ✺ ————

You will need

Fine-mesh sieve

We've never quite believed in epic lists of ingredients and multiday processes, aside from Lièvre à la Royale, of course. This sauce, which combines only a few ingredients, is a perfect example of David's "save a sinking ship with a piece of gum" talent as a saucier. It's so easy; it emulsifies itself as it simmers, and seasoned appropriately, it's at home with scallops just as much as veal.

We like this as well with tongue, a thick slab of halibut, zucchini, or raviolis.

---

1 pound (454 g) butter, salted or not (you can adjust the seasoning at the end)

1 pound (454 g) pasty, not juicy, tomatoes (for example, plum tomatoes), coarsely chopped

1 generous handful fresh marjoram

3 garlic cloves

1 cup (240 ml) chicken stock

Salt, white pepper, cayenne, and water as needed

Juice of 1 lemon

I. In a heavy-bottomed pot as tall as it is wide, place the butter, tomatoes, marjoram, garlic, and chicken stock.

2. Over medium-low heat, bring to a slow but consistent simmer, and cook, uncovered, for about 1 hour. Keep an eye on the proceedings: as the stock and tomato juices start to cook off, the melted butter might start to look clear; if that happens, add ½ cup stock (120 ml) or water and give the sauce a vigorous stir—this will help get the emulsification back on track. The mother-of-pearl–like iridescence of the sauce is what gives it its mouthfeel and digestibility.

3. Strain the sauce through a fine-mesh sieve, pressing down on the tomatoes with a spoon to extract every last drop. Season with salt, white pepper, and cayenne as a sauce not a soup—assertively—then return the sauce to the saucepan. Add the lemon juice and briefly boil the sauce while maintaining that opacity, 1 to 2 minutes, adding a splash of water as needed to loosen the sauce.

Notes This sauce will keep refrigerated for 7 days, and 1 to 2 months in the freezer (frozen in an ice-cube tray, then unmolded and stored in a Ziploc bag).

Although we fancied a picture where the butters are molded (see image), the best option for storage is actually a widemouthed mason jar.

→ *We have included three butter recipes in all: the tomato marjoram butter; the one with All Dressed (BBQ to our friends south of the border, caliente BBQ to our friends south of that border) chips, because chips provide a minimum caloric requirement, and therefore are absolutely within the context of the apocalypse. And one version with healing chaga to maintain your lonely souls alive.*

Chips "All-Dressed" Butter

Makes a 1-pound
(454-g) slab

—∿—

You will need

Food processor

"All Dressed" chip flavor (which combines barbecue, sour cream and onion, ketchup, and salt and vinegar flavors) is a Quebec thing, kind of like *parfum de paprika* is a French thing. The use of bits of potato chips as a seasoning has been a tradition at Joe Beef; a delicious white potato soup with a handful of broken All Dressed chips is a marvel of culinary engineering, as is a few salted Ruffles blended into a potato pancake mix.

1 gas station bag all-dressed or BBQ potato chips

1 pound (907 kg) unsalted butter, at room temperature

2 tablespoons Frank's RedHot sauce

1. Blitz the chips to a fine crumb in the bowl of a food processor. Add the butter and mix until well combined.

2. Stir in the hot sauce. Refrigerate overnight.

Note This will keep refrigerated for 7 days, and 1 to 2 months in the freezer.

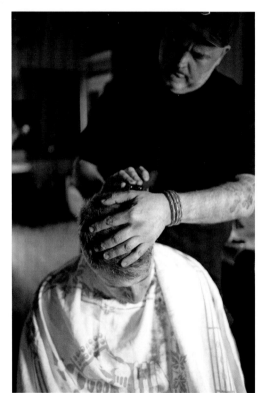

Chaga Ghee

Makes a 2-pound
(900-g) slab

Whether you want to live eternally in the occurrence of an apocalyptic event depends entirely on you. If the potential role of centenarian suits you, know that the chaga mushroom is your friend. Growing like a witch wart on the trunks of birches, it diverts the food supply of the host to fuel its own growth, hence it's full of betulinic acid and numerous beneficial compounds that "study for hire" universities research regularly.

From a culinary standpoint, it is pretty bland, so we add a few desiccated fungi of the Laurentian forest to the mix—such as lobster mushrooms and boletus.

Chaga ghee can be used for a seared steak, or in excess to poach a piece of salmon or trout.

2 pounds (900 g) unsalted butter

2 cups (80 g) clean and dried chaga mushroom chunks

1 cup (40 g) dried boletus, broken up

1 cup (40 g) dried maitake or lobster mushrooms, broken up

2 tablespoons apple cider vinegar

2 cups (480 ml) water

1 tablespoon sea salt

1. In a medium saucepan over medium-low heat, melt the butter. Add all the mushrooms, the cider vinegar, and ½ cup (120 ml) of the water.

2. Maintain a constant simmer, adding water regularly to keep the level to about ½ cup (120 ml) of liquid under the butter. Cook like that for 2 hours, then strain and place the water/butter mix in a flat container, preferably glass. Refrigerate overnight.

3. The next day, collect the hardened fat on top of the liquid and pat it dry with a paper towel; you may add the fat to sauces. Transfer to a bowl and leave at "hot yoga" room temperature until soft. Whisk in the salt and transfer to a sterile glass jar. Refrigerate.

Notes This will need to set overnight, so plan ahead.

It will keep refrigerated for 7 days, and 1 to 2 months in the freezer.

MONTREAL

LA DÉCOUPE
DE LA *Volaille*

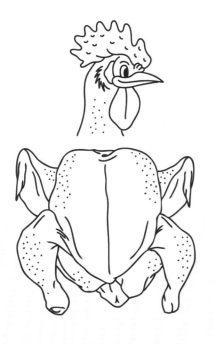

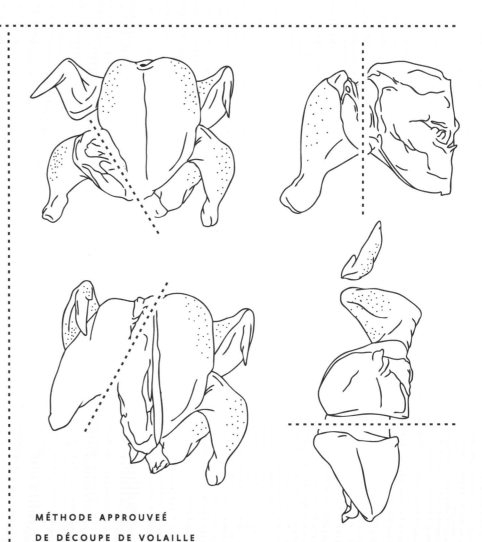

MÉTHODE APPROUVEÉ
DE DÉCOUPE DE VOLAILLE

ILLUSTRATION BY

DAN CLIMAN

Joe BEEF

B.S.T.

BAIT AND SCHLANG TATTOO
4929 NOTRE DAME WEST
ST. HENRI , MONTREAL , QC
H4C 1S9

Nose-to-Tail (or Beak-to-Butt) Volaille

Serves 4, gloriously

——————

You will need

Boning knife

Vitamix or good blender for the soup

Butcher's twine for the thighs

Cleaver or poultry shears

You've admired the Bresse capon, the plump avian emissary of French cuisine, since you were a young foodie with an Internet connection; you dream about the layer of fat that grows under its skin after its gonads are removed (it probably doesn't care, because it's just been castrated). Those blue feet, the comb that crowns its regal head, the way it gets wrapped in fine muslin, then dressed up with a sash and a medal, after the slaughter. You've read old menus the way kids used to pore over the Sears catalog before there was TV: Chapon de Bresse aux Morilles, pour deux, Sauce Aurore: wow! If you can get your hands on such a capon, follow our advice and bend the knee: nose-to-tail respect is due this bird.

This chicken three ways could be used like your grandma would stretch out a chicken for a whole family for the week. But we intended this as a *Big Night* feast. Before you can make the three main recipes, you'll need to prep: butcher the chicken, make a stock, and make a quick bisque. Nobody said full bird didn't involve commitment.

Step 1
Butchering the Chicken

One 6½-pound (3-kg) chapon de Bresse or any thoughtfully farmed chicken with an equally noble pedigree, raised slowly, 120 days and older

I. Working on a large cutting board, place the chicken with the cavity facing you. Remove each leg at the hip joint while cautiously also carving around the nugget of meat where the thighs meet in the lower back: Anglos call this nugget of dark meat the "oyster"; French people named it "le sot-l'y-laisse," literally "only an idiot would leave this behind."

2. With one confident cut of your knife, divide the drumstick from the thigh (hint: look for the visible line of fat where the drumstick meets the thigh and cut along it with your knife). If you encounter resistance, your knife is on the joint—move it around gently to find the space between the two joints and then cut through.

3. Now lift the breast off the chest plate: Starting with the cavity facing away from you, gently and superficially cut along one side of the central cartilage (starting at the cavity end) and, working with careful knife strokes, slowly cut deeper along the chest plate to slowly pry away the breast. Once you get to the wing end, keep sliding your knife to also cut away the wing, keeping it attached to the breast, along the wishbone. Rotate the chicken 180 degrees. Then repeat the same procedure for the other breast. Set the carcass aside for your stock.

4. Slide a finger under the skin of the breast to lift it from the flesh and pull it back toward the wing.

5. Cut the naked breast off from the wing, about 1 inch (2.5 cm) away from where the wing and breast meet, keeping the long piece of skin intact and attached to the wing—this will form a pocket for the stuffing. Repeat steps 4 and 5 with the remaining breast. Set the wings and breasts aside.

6. Place the chicken thighs back on the board, flesh side up. Using your nondominant hand to hold down the thigh, use your knife to cut through the meat following along the central bone; repeat this cut along the other side of the central bone, excavating the bone gradually by using short strokes of the tip of your knife. Cut around one end of the bone, then grab the end of →

the bone with your nondominant hand and use the knife to scrape the chicken flesh off the rest of the bone. Then, finally, cut around the other end of the bone to separate it from the meat. Trim away any excess fat and cartilage still stuck to the meat. Repeat with the remaining thigh and set aside those bones for your stock.

7. Roll each thigh onto itself, flesh side in, skin on the outside, and truss each with some butcher's twine to secure the rolled shape.

8. Refrigerate all your chicken pieces. Using a cleaver or poultry shears, break down the leftover carcass, bones, and neck (if you found one in the cavity) into chunks the size of a matchbook. Refrigerate until you're ready to make your stock.

Note Unless your fridge is packed like the Tokyo subway, you should refrigerate your naked chicken on a tray for a day or two: the cold draft of the fan will firm up the skin, and the skin will crisp up nicely later. It's what Nicolas Jongleux would have done, and it's what Marc-Olivier Frappier (Marco), our chef de cuisine, does.

Step 2
Making the Double Chicken Stock

Makes 6 cups (1½ l) stock

You will need

Fine-mesh sieve

Sauté pan, medium size

Instant-read thermometer or a meat thermometer with remote probe

Reserved bones of your nose-to-tail chicken, plus 1 pound (454 g) bones from one other chicken, necks, if any

1 decent-size celery root, peeled, trimmed, and cut into medium-size pieces

1 decent-size parsnip, peeled

1 small onion, studded with 1 clove

1 leek, white part only

2 garlic cloves

1 bay leaf

2 fresh flat-leaf parsley sprigs

1 tablespoon white peppercorns

1 tablespoon coriander seeds

6 cups (1.5 l) water

Salt and white pepper

1 cup (250 ml) dry sherry

3 tablespoons grapeseed oil

2 skinless chicken breasts, 2 drumsticks, and 2 rolled-up thighs (previously boned from your chicken)l

l. In a small stockpot, combine all the ingredients, except the sherry, oil, and boned chicken. Bring slowly to an elegant and consistent simmer and maintain it for 2 hours.

2. After 2 hours, carefully remove the celery root pieces and the parsnip, and set aside for use in the Velouté de Volaille aux Morilles (page 67).

3. Using a fine-mesh sieve, strain the stock into another large saucepan, discarding the aromatics, then add the sherry. Bring to a simmer over medium heat, then reduce the heat to low and cook for about 20 minutes to blend the sherry's incomparable aromas. Season with salt and white pepper to taste and keep warm.

4. Place the chicken breasts in the stock, and poach gently for 15 minutes, or until the internal temperature reads 165°F (74°C).

5. While the breasts are poaching, thoroughly season the chicken thighs and drumsticks with salt and white pepper. Heat the oil in a medium sauté pan over medium-high heat. When the oil is hot, put in the thighs and drumsticks, and sear them to a nice brown crisp on all sides, about 10 minutes. Transfer to a paper towel–lined plate.

6. Remove the breasts from the stock and set aside. Place the thighs and drumsticks in the seasoned stock, cover, and simmer over medium-low heat for 15 to 20 minutes.

7. Remove the thighs and drumsticks from what is now "double" stock. Strain the stock again, and measure out 3 cups (720 ml) to pour into a saucepan. Reserve 1 cup (240 ml) for the stuffed chicken wings (see page 71). Refrigerate or freeze the rest of the stock for another use.

Note Count on a good 3 hours to complete this stock and poaching of chicken pieces.

Step 3
Whipping Up a Bisque Rapide

Makes 2 cups (500 ml) bisque

You will need

Blender

Fine-mesh sieve

All our bisques sucked until we realized that French food can actually do with a little heat and some spices. Perhaps old-world French chefs had fatter fingers before they became filiform marathoners, and the size of the pinch got lost in translation? Anyway, this bisque is only a few notches away from a good butter chicken profile—no joke. The ginger is for warmth, not for poetry.

¼ cup (60 ml) ketchup

1 small onion, roughly chopped

4 garlic cloves, roughly chopped

1 tablespoon minced fresh ginger

¼ cup (7 g) roughly chopped fresh tarragon

2 teaspoons sweet paprika

2 tablespoons grapeseed oil

1 pound (454 g) crayfish, cut in half, tails reserved for garnish, or 4 lobster bodies

2 tablespoons all-purpose flour

¼ cup (60 ml) brandy

4 cups (1 l) water

¼ cup (57 g) cold unsalted butter, cut into 4 pieces

Squeeze of lemon

Salt and pepper

1. In a blender, blend the ketchup, onion, garlic, ginger, tarragon, and paprika until you get a nice, smooth paste.

2. Heat a large saucepan until shockingly hot, then add the grapeseed oil and the crayfish or lobster bodies. Stir vigorously, and when the shells are nice and red, about 5 minutes, stir in the ketchup paste.

3. Reduce the heat to medium-low, and cook until the contents of your pan look almost dry, 7 to 10 minutes.

4. Stir in the flour, then the brandy. Cook until almost dry, 1 to 2 minutes.

5. Add the water, scraping well around the bottom and edges of the pot, and bring to a boil. Reduce the heat to low, and simmer for 1 hour. Adjust the water level if need be.

6. Strain through a fine-mesh sieve, then return to the saucepan. Add the butter and whisk well, adjusting the seasoning with a squeeze of lemon juice and salt and pepper.

Note If you can't get crayfish, use lobster bodies instead. If you can find whole crayfish, save the tails as the garnish for the Fricassée de Volaille aux Écrevisses (page 68).

→ *Now that all the prep work has been taken care of, you'll find that bringing together the three recipes will happen fairly quickly—about 15 minutes for the soup, 45 or so minutes for the stuffed wings, and under 1 hour for the baked chicken legs.*

Recipe I: Velouté de Volaille aux Morilles

Makes 6 cups (1.5 L) soup

3 cups (700 ml) reserved Double Chicken Stock (page 64)

Reserved cooked celery root and parsnip from the Double Chicken Stock recipe (page 64)

¼ cup (50 g) crème fraîche, mixed with 1 tablespoon all-purpose flour

¼ pound (113 g) cold unsalted butter

Salt and white pepper

Squeeze of lemon

1 handful washed fresh morels, cut into thin round slices (cross section slices that look like O-ring washers)

2 reserved poached chicken breasts, cut into medium dice

1 bunch fresh chervil, plumes picked, or 1 bunch fresh chives, roughly chopped

1. Combine the seasoned stock, celery root, and parsnip with the crème fraîche mixture in the bowl of your high-speed blender. Blend until super smooth. Transfer to a medium saucepan.

2. Add ¼ cup (57 g) of the butter to the soup. Bring to a slow simmer over medium-low heat while stirring regularly, adjusting the seasoning with salt and pepper. Adding a squeeze of lemon now will make all the difference to this soup, revealing its depths and the butter as a most coherent accomplice. Reduce the heat to low and cover to keep warm.

3. In a medium frying pan, sauté the morels in 2 tablespoons of the butter. Set aside, season to taste, and keep warm.

4. In the same frying pan or saucepan over low heat, warm the diced chicken breast in the remaining 2 tablespoons butter, about 2 to 3 minutes.

5. To serve, divide the soup among four shallow soup bowls. Then portion out the chicken cubes and morels. Sprinkle with plumes of chervil or roughly chopped chives.

Note If you can't find fresh morels, rehydrate dry morels, pat dry, and proceed.

This recipe is dedicated in loving memory of "La Mère Michel," Micheline Delbuguet

Recipe 2: Fricassée de Volaille aux Écrevisses

2 cups (475 ml) fast crayfish bisque (see Bisque Rapide, page 65)

2 chicken drumsticks and 2 thighs, reserved from the Double Chicken Stock recipe (page 64)

1 tablespoon minced shallot, sautéed over low heat in 1 tablespoon butter

1 teaspoon finely chopped fresh tarragon

Splash of brandy

Squeeze of lemon

Salt and pepper

1. Preheat the oven to 350°F (180°C).

2. In a small saucepan, reheat the bisque. Nestle the drumsticks and thighs in a baking dish or a small Dutch oven or whatever ovenware you have that fits the vibe.

3. Pour the warm bisque over the chicken. Cover with the matching lid or a tightly wrapped piece of aluminum foil and bake for 30 minutes. Remove the cover, then bake for another 10 minutes.

4. Remove from the oven and use tongs to roll the chicken pieces in the sauce to coat them evenly. Add the shallot, tarragon, and a splash of brandy, and stir to incorporate. Add a squeeze of lemon and season with salt and pepper to taste.

5. Serve with hot buttered peas and Marrow Pilaf (page 196). Garnish with a nice, big, fat turned Champignon de Paris, "as learned from la technique Pépin."

LE BISTROT

PAUL BERT

Recipe 3: Ailerons de Volaille Farcis

Makes 2 wings, to be shared

You will need

Paring knife or boning knife

Butcher's twine

Small sheet pan lined with
parchment paper

Instant-read digital thermometer

2 reserved chicken wings with skin flap

5 ounces (150 g) seasoned classic sweet
pork sausage meat (make sure it's nice
and peppery, adding black pepper as
needed)

Salt and black pepper

2 shallots, minced

3 tablespoons unsalted butter

6 prunes, soaked in 1 cup (240 ml) red
wine overnight at room temperature

¼ cup (60 ml) prune juice

1 cup (240 ml) reserved Double Chicken
Stock (page 64)

1 tablespoon red wine vinegar

1. Preheat the oven to 450°F (230°C).

2. Using a sharp paring knife or boning
knife, cut a small slit to form a pocket
in the breast meat part of each wing.

3. Using your hands, stuff half the
amount of sausage meat into the
pocket, filling it as much as possible.
Carefully drape the skin flap back over
the chicken flesh and stuffing, and
using butcher's twine, tie it to make
a little parcel. Repeat with the other
chicken wing.

4. Place on a small sheet pan lined with
parchment paper and season well with
salt and pepper.

5. Bake for 10 minutes, then reduce
the oven temperature to 300°F
(150°C) and continue cooking until
the core of the stuffing registers
145°F (63°C) on an instant-read
thermometer, 10 to 12 minutes. Set the
pan of wings aside, but do not turn off
the oven.

6. In a small sauté pan over
medium-low heat, sweat the shallots in
2 tablespoons of the butter until
translucent and fragrant, about
3 minutes.

7. Set aside the prunes that have been
soaking overnight, and add the red wine
the prunes had been soaking in to the
pan. Add the prune juice, and proceed
to reduce the volume over medium-
high heat for 7 minutes, or until
almost dry.

8. Add the stock, bring up to a boil,
then bring the heat back to medium
and reduce the stock to ⅓ cup (80 ml)
total volume, 10 to 12 minutes.

9. Stir in the vinegar and adjust the
seasoning. Whisk in the remaining
1 tablespoon butter and add the prunes
to the sauce to warm them gently.

10. Return the wings to the oven,
and at regular intervals, spoon a bit of
the prune/wine sauce over the wings
to caramelize them. After about 10
minutes of this (say 3 or 4 times), when
sticky and mouthwatering, remove and
transfer to a serving dish. Transfer any
remaining sauce to a saucier. Add the
prunes to the dish. Serve with lightly
dressed watercress.

Note   The prunes need to be soaked
overnight at room temperature in 1 cup
(240 ml) red wine. Plan ahead.

The John Bil Fruit du Jour Cocktail

Serves 4

You will need

Juicer

One thing that hasn't changed since Book One is the assumption that Fred and David are lovers, which Fred only emboldens when he walks into the restaurant clutching tickets for "tonight's show" and two ferns from Planterra. Those early days remind us of our friend and brother John Bil, whom we dearly miss, who started the daily tradition of concocting a fruity cocktail for those less inclined to grapes and fine spirits. Without the booze, it's just a fruit cup for kids. With the booze, it's someone's little helper.

1968–2018

For the fruit juice

1 pineapple, peeled, cored, and quartered

1 orange, peeled

1 small cantaloupe, peeled and seeded

1 honeydew melon, peeled and seeded

1 nectarine, pitted

1 small papaya, peeled and seeded

1 mandarin orange, peeled

For the cocktail

Juice of 1 lime

1 ounce (30 ml) maraschino liqueur

10 ounces (300 ml) Jamaican rum

4 ounces (120 ml) Dry Curaçao

4 ounces (120 ml) simple syrup

Juice of 1 lemon

For the garnish

2 or 3 nice passion fruits, cut in half and scooped on top of the drinks

I. Dice a third of the nicest parts of each of the fruits into frozen vegetable–size pieces. Toss in the juice of a lime and the maraschino liqueur.

2. Pass the remaning fruits through the juicer.

3. Combine the juice with the rum, Dry Curaçao, simple syrup, and lemon juice.

4. Fill large tumblers, alternating between ice and fruit dices. Pour in the juice and garnish with the flesh of the passion fruit.

Smoked Meat Croquettes

Makes 30 croquettes

—————

You will need

Food processor

Digital scale (optional)

Deep fryer or heavy pot

Deep-frying thermometer

For the filling

¼ pound (113 g) cheese curds

¼ pound (113 g) smoked Cheddar, cubed

½ pound (225 g) Montreal smoked meat (lean), shredded

½ cup (30 g) sauerkraut, drained and finely chopped

1 tablespoon Montreal steak spice

2 tablespoons yellow mustard

½ cup (120 ml) Béchamel Rapide (recipe follows)

2 quarts (2 l) canola oil for deep-frying

For the breading

1 cup (75 g) flour

4 large eggs, beaten

1 cup (130 g) rye bread crumbs or plain bread crumbs mixed with 1 teaspoon ground caraway seeds

Salt

Water

Yellow mustard (optional)

Thousand Island dressing (optional)

1 kosher pickle, thinly sliced

When you're doing two hundred covers per night, it's imperative to have a winner in your arsenal, one that is all prep and little cook time during service. At home, well, this is the least healthy but the most rewarding of all "night-after" cures.

For our American readers, Montreal smoked meat is dry-cured beef brisket. It resembles pastrami the way that a Montreal bagel "resembles" a New York bagel.

___

I. Add the cheese curds and smoked Cheddar to the bowl of a food processor and pulse until evenly crumbled. Transfer to a large bowl.

2. Now pulse the smoked meat in the food processor until it looks like hamburger meat. Transfer to the cheese bowl.

3. Add the sauerkraut, steak spice, mustard, and béchamel, and using a spatula or gloved hands, mix well.

4. Use your hands to shape 30 cylinders into the size and shape of a wine cork. Transfer to a parchment-lined sheet pan as you work. Refrigerate the croquettes for 30 minutes to help them retain their shape.

5. To bread the croquettes: Set up three bowls, one with the flour, one with the eggs, and one with the rye bread crumbs. Dip each croquette into the flour, then the egg, then the bread crumbs. Set aside on a small tray.

6. Pour the canola oil into a deep fryer or heavy pot. The oil should be 350°F (180°C).

7. Fry the croquettes in batches of 5 or 6 for 2½ minutes, until golden brown. Keep an eye on the thermometer and adjust your heat up or down accordingly so that the croquettes don't brown too quickly: you want them to be hot in the center. Using a skimmer or slotted spoon, transfer to a paper towel–lined plate.

8. Serve with your choice of yellow mustard or Thousand Island dressing and slices of kosher pickle.

Note To make your own rye bread crumbs, process several slices of very dry rye bread in your food processor. Spread the fresh crumbs out on a sheet pan to stale completely. Process again until fine, pass through a sieve, and keep in an airtight container until ready to use.

BÉCHAMEL RAPIDE

Makes 2 cups (500 ml) sauce

———~~———

You will need

Handheld immersion blender

2 cups (500 ml) whole milk, cold

1 teaspoon ground nutmeg

½ cup (65 g) all-purpose flour

¼ cup (60 g) cold unsalted butter, diced

1. In a tall jar or container, combine the cold milk, nutmeg, and flour with an immersion blender.

2. Transfer to a small saucepan, and bring to a slow boil over medium heat.

3. Whisk in the butter: Whisk, whisk, whisk until well incorporated and the sauce visibly thickens—about 4 minutes. Cool to lukewarm, then stir into the croquettes filling (opposite).

Filet de Veau P.E.T.
(Pierre Elliott Trudeau)

Serves 4

~~~

You will need

Handheld immersion blender

In 1985, David was selling weed at a pool hall to people who were generally older than he. Dave says, "There was a chef who used to come around, a guy from Brittany who looked like he was straight out of *Asterix*. He worked in Sainte-Anne-de-Bellevue [on the western tip of the island of Montreal, where David was from] at an upscale place called Le Péché Mignon." They were friendly, and because David was good at dealing, he liked going to—and could afford—the nicer food places. One day, the Péché Mignon dishwasher quit before service, and this chef asked David to come and help out. He said sure. The second night he came in, the appetizer guy hadn't shown up, so the chef told him to work on the line, saying, "It's okay, I'll tell you what to do, you just have to listen." On the third or fourth night of working there, the *table d'hôte* was mussel soup and veal tenderloin. David was to make the mussel soup in the afternoon, and simply warm it to order during service, adding the nice plump mussels in at the end. The veal tenderloin was (oddly) roasted in an oven in a pan containing veal neck bones and served simply sliced with a brown butter reduction whipped lightly and topped with little mousseron mushrooms.

That night, one of the waiters popped his head in to say, "Don't fuck up," because Pierre Elliott Trudeau, Quebec nobility and the former prime minister, was in the dining room. Perhaps egged on by the chef, at the end of the night, P.E.T. came into the kitchen and loudly declared the soup was one of the best he'd ever tasted.

"True or not, this was a weird validation for me. He was the first person of note who told me I did something well. At the age of sixteen or seventeen, life wasn't working out as I hoped. I was not headed for college and didn't have the options I wanted. I realized that cooking was the only way I would get to meet a prime minister, and that this was the path for me. I worked at that restaurant for only a few months; eventually the chef got fired and a new guy came in and threatened to stab me, but that's another story." →

For the veal

One 2.2-pound (1-kg) veal tenderloin, preferably milk-fed

Salt and white pepper

2 tablespoons grapeseed oil or other neutral oil for searing

For the brown butter sauce

½ cup (approximately) brown butter made from ½ pound (113 g) unsalted butter, cubed

4 shallots, finely diced

Salt and white pepper

2 tablespoons walnut or hazelnut oil

¼ cup (60 ml) Champagne vinegar

1 cup (240 ml) reduced veal stock

2 tablespoons heavy cream (35 percent butterfat)

2 large egg whites, whipped until frothy to a soft peak

For the mushrooms

2 cups (120 g) mousseron mushrooms or small shiitake mushrooms stems removed

2 tablespoons olive oil

2 tablespoons unsalted butter

Salt and black pepper

Chive

1. Preheat the oven to 350°F (180°C).

2. Trim off the translucent silver skin from the tenderloin—a fish fillet knife is perfectly suited for the task. Alternatively, ask your butcher to do this for you. Season generously with salt and white pepper. Set aside.

3. **To make the brown butter:** Place the cubed butter into a small saucepan over medium heat, preferably a lighter-colored pan (easier to see the butter browning). Stir frequently so the butter melts and cooks evenly. The butter will foam as it melts, then subside. You'll notice the butter makes a snapping noise as it cooks, solids browning at the bottom of the pan, and a distinctive nutty aroma. The whole process should take 3 to 6 minutes. Take the butter off the heat, and get all the brown butter out of the pan and into a metal or glass container.

4. In a medium saucepan over medium heat, add the shallots, a pinch of white pepper, the walnut oil, and vinegar. Bring to a steady simmer and reduce to almost dry, about 15 minutes. Add the veal stock, and maintain an ebullition to amalgamate the flavors, not reduce.

5. Add the cream and whisk in the brown butter, a spoonful at a time. Keep warm.

6. Heat the 2 tablespoons grapeseed oil in a large ovenproof sauté pan over high heat. Sear the veal on all sides in the hot pan, 5 to 7 minutes. Transfer the pan to the oven and roast for 10 to 12 minutes. Remove from the oven and let the meat rest for 10 minutes before slicing.

7. In a separate pan, sauté the mushrooms in the olive oil and butter over medium-high heat, stirring frequently, for a few minutes, until nicely browned. Season to taste with salt and black pepper.

8. Slice the tenderloin and divide the slices among four plates or place on a distinguished serving dish.

9. Bring the brown butter sauce to a final boil. Season and add the egg whites away from the heat while whisking. Keep a supply of cold water and an immersion blender handy to rescue the splitting sauce.

10. Pour half the sauce over the tenderloin slices, and the other half into a porcelain gravy boat. Finish with the mushrooms, garnish with chive, and serve immediately.

Note We like to serve this dish with classic mashed potatoes, or see Munster Mash (page 251).

Turned Potatoes: A Meditation

A lot of kids who end up in kitchens in Montreal have been failed by the school system. David was one of those kids: "I hated turning vegetables with a passion. Hated it. One day, after sitting and watching other commis cooks before me do it, I fell into it. Like a daydream. Then the next thing I knew I was a complete machine at it, like faster than anyone. It's a rite of passage. I met some Italian cooks who speak of turning artichokes in the same tone. For me this was my transcendental meditation. I was so angry after high school, not getting into college, that this was a forced meditation and it calmed me and provided a focus."

It's done much less these days, really not in vogue. But we still do it.

6 to 8 yellow-fleshed potatoes, cut into fourths lengthwise

1 tablespoon kosher salt

Drop of white wine vinegar for the cooking water, not more

Obviously, the point here is not to use *primeurs* (baby veg/new potatoes) but rather the hearty straight-from-the earth-cellar large tubers. A handy result of turned potatoes is the stable cooking time the symmetry provides.

Although chefs would have you believe you must cut six to eight sides, there is no right or wrong way, just channel a country *maman:* always use a paring knife, never a peeler.

Grab the potato and a paring knife, whittle the 6 sides while moving the potato left at every cut. You're just cleaning up the edges really. We like our turned potatoes uneven and to have a slight curve like a banana. Transfer the potatoes to a large pot of cold water. Add the salt and vinegar. Turn the heat up to medium and bring to a gentle rolling simmer, ever so low. Cook with the lid on for 15 minutes. Check doneness by sliding the same paring knife in; the potato should be tender but not soft. Remove the potatoes from the water with a slotted spoon, and set aside to serve.

Lapin à la Moutarde

Until the age of twenty or so, we just assumed everyone ate rabbit. In Quebec and France, it's sometimes easier to find rabbit than chicken. Outside of Quebec, though, eating rabbit is what sets you apart as a Francophone. That and knowing every word of Céline Dion's *Incognito* album, before it was ironically acceptable.

This recipe is really tough to mess up: two pots, one rabbit, one cup of wine, one heaping tablespoon of salt, some herbs, and a simple mustard sauce. Even if you assembled all of the ingredients cold in a Le Creuset and banged it in the oven, it would still be good. In a restaurant, if you're frenching rabbit racks, you have too many *stagiaires* and you may have lost your way. At home, we don't see any point in deboning a rabbit unless it's Christmas or we're bent on making a *ballotine*.

For the rabbit

1 whole rabbit 2 to 2½ pounds (about 1 kg), fresh and local (ask your butcher to cut off the "shoulders"—the two small front legs—and to remove the liver and kidneys, if any)

1 cup (350 g) Confit Salt (The Cellar, page 9)

3 tablespoons grapeseed oil or other neutral oil

For the mustard sauce

1 small carrot, chopped to the size of a cork

1 small onion, chopped the same as the carrot

1 celery stalk, peeled and chopped, same as the onion, which is the same as the carrot

1 garlic clove

3 tablespoons grapeseed oil or other neutral oil

1 teaspoon chopped fresh thyme leaves

4 fresh tarragon sprigs, tied together

1 bay leaf

2 cups (480 ml) light stock (chicken or vegetable)

1 cup (240 ml) dry white wine

2 tablespoons apple cider vinegar

Salt and white pepper

¼ cup (60 g) Dijon mustard

1 cup (240 ml) heavy cream (35 percent butterfat)

2 to 3 tablespoons water, if needed

1 tablespoon chopped fresh flat-leaf parsley for garnish

For the hemp crust

2 tablespoons Dijon mustard

2 tablespoons grated Parmesan cheese

2 tablespoons fresh chervil, finely chopped

6 tablespoons hemp seeds

3 tablespoons hemp oil

Salt and black pepper

To serve

Turned Potatoes (page 79)

The first step in making and eating rabbit is not to give the creature a name.

1. Place the rabbit in a large container with the confit salt. Cover with plastic wrap. Refrigerate for 5 hours—so around lunchtime for the civilized dinner hour.

2. Remove the rabbit from the salt, using your hands to brush off any excess under cold running water, and pat dry. Preheat the oven to 325°F (160°C).

3. In a medium saucepan over medium-high heat, cook the carrot, onion, celery, and garlic in 3 tablespoons oil. Once the aroma is one of cooked vegetables, not raw, add the thyme, tarragon, bay leaf, stock, white wine, and cider vinegar. Simmer for a few seconds, then season with salt and white pepper and continue simmering while you sear the rabbit. $\rightarrow$

4. Place the rabbit in an oblong Creuset where the rabbit could lie unbent on its flank. Add 3 tablespoons oil. Over medium heat, carefully sear the beast until golden on each side. Remove from the heat. Tip the pan to remove the excess fat.

5. Add the mustard and cream to the sauce, and mix well.

6. Pour the sauce atop the rabbit, cover with a piece of buttered aluminum foil, and place in the oven for 1 hour.

7. To make the hemp crust, combine all the ingredients in a bowl and mix well. Set aside at room temperature.

8. After 1 hour of cooking, carefully remove the foil and, with the help of two spatulas, flip the rabbit onto its other flank, baste it, cover, and return to the oven for 30 minutes. Carefully monitor the amount of liquid, adding water as needed.

9. After 30 minutes, verify the doneness by poking the meat. A firm push from a finger should not return. Resilience is not what we seek, at least not in our dinner today. When the rabbit is ready, transfer it with your spatulas and ninja skills to an ovenproof oval dish. Cover with the foil while you finish the sauce and turn your oven to 425°F (220°C), on the broil setting.

10. Set the Creuset with sauce and veg on a burner at high heat. Reduce until it coats a spoon lusciously, about 6 minutes. Remove from the heat, taste, and season. Do not hesitate to add a bit of water, stock, or drops of vinegar if the taste is not quite there yet. Keep warm.

11. Remove the cover from the rabbit, cover with the hemp crust, and give it a brief tour under the broiler, barely a minute, just enough to color and lightly toast the crust. Remove and pour the sauce through a fine-mesh sieve over the rabbit. With elevated flavors and as opulent a sauce as this, the Turned Potatoes (page 79) is the perfect accoutrement, other than the culinary school classic of chopped fresh parsley.

Notes With a mustard sauce, we like to include the vegetables a rabbit eats: carrot, parsnip, and celery, for example. This rule applies to all animals, really: lamb with turnips, horse with apples, striped bass with clams, and so on and so on. You can play pretty fast and loose with a mustard sauce. You can stick with the recipe here and add only salt and pepper. In the past we've even added chervil or poached and diced apples. Up to you.

The hemp crust is inspired by our old friend and mentor Nicolas Jongleux: upon returning from the fish market an hour into service, with a trunk full of sea creatures bought in part for their deliciousness but more often because other chefs wouldn't get any if he took them all, Nicolas often whipped up this simple mix to crust fish and other proteins, sometimes including truffles. It's singularly great with halibut.

QC Spring Seafood Pie

Serves 6-ish
(feeds a family with leftovers
for the following day)

———

You will need

Ricer

Piping bag with the largest pastry tip

Large Pyrex or Le Creuset baking dish,
similar to what you use for
shepherd's pie

"We are geographically well off in Montreal, sitting on the shores of the seafood superhighway that is the St. Lawrence Seaway. From the Gaspé Peninsula to Kamouraska, Montreal to Portland, Maine, the seaway has a tremendous influence on what we eat." —Book One

April is a wild time in Montreal; the epitome of "twitterpated," as explained by the annoying yet wise owl to Bambi and Thumper and Flower. Our obsessive excitement is not for the opposite sex but rather for all that cold and fresh seafood on the banks of our icy maritime shores. And so, come early spring when we begin receiving our first snow crab, we throw reason out the window and set up tables in shoveled-out snowbanks in our garden terrace. Not warm enough for seafood platters on ice, we devised a warm seafood fish pie: lobster from Grande-Rivière, snow crab from Sainte-Anne-des-Monts, whelks from Sept-Îles, Matane shrimp, scallops from Jean-Paul Riopelle's Isle-aux-Grues, and Reine-like turbot from Rimouski. All cooked in a warm potato velouté. Enjoy feverishly in boots and parka.

For the pommes duchesse

4 Yukon gold potatoes, peeled

3 large egg yolks

2 tablespoons unsalted butter

2 tablespoons heavy cream
(35 percent butterfat)

Salt and white pepper

For the velouté

¼ cup (57 g) unsalted butter

1 tablespoon Dijon mustard

½ cup (60 g) all-purpose flour

3 cups (720 ml) whole milk

1 cup (240 ml) fish stock or clam juice

¼ cup (60 ml) heavy cream
(35 percent butterfat)

Pinch of cayenne pepper

1 tablespoon fresh lemon juice

Salt and white pepper

For the filling

4 ounces (120 g) cooked lobster meat
(from one 1-pound lobster)

4 ounces (120 g) whelk meat,
finely sliced (typically comes in a jar)

4 ounces (120 g) fresh or frozen Nordic
shrimp (aka Maine shrimp)

4 ounces (120 g) bay scallops

4 ounces (120 g) steamed and shelled
mussels (from one pound of mussels)

½ pound (225 g) turbot fillet

1 Yukon Gold potato, cut into cubes
the size of playing dice

7 ounces (200 g) lardons (bacon slices
cut into ½-inch-/1-cm-thick bâtons)

1 tablespoon minced fresh chives

1 tablespoon minced fresh chervil

1 tablespoon minced fresh flat-leaf parsley

For the garnish

Egg wash (1 large egg beaten with
3 tablespoons whole milk)

2 sets snow crab legs, thawed, and
cracked lengthwise (using kitchen shears)

1 tablespoon Old Bay seasoning

1. Preheat the oven to 375°F (190°C).

2. For the pommes duchesse: Place the potatoes in a large saucepan with enough cold water to cover them. Bring to a boil and cook until tender, about 20 minutes. Pass the potatoes through a ricer.

3. In a bowl, stir the potatoes with the egg yolks, butter, cream, and salt and white pepper. Reserve in a piping bag with the biggest piping tip, such as the classic plain #24 (¹¹⁄₁₆"').

4. For the velouté: Melt the butter in a large pot over medium heat. Add →

the mustard and flour and cook for 1 minute, stirring constantly. Add the milk, fish stock, cream, cayenne, and lemon juice, and slowly bring to a boil over medium heat, stirring occasionally. Season with salt and white pepper to taste.

5. Add all the filling ingredients to your velouté.

6. Butter the inside of a Pyrex/Le Creuset/copper pot. Transfer the filling mixture to your vessel. Inside the dish, pipe the pommes duchesse in a way to make it look like fish scales. If that's OTT (over the top), simply pipe in a spiral to follow the shape of the dish.

7. Brush with the egg wash. Just before putting the dish in the oven, place the crab legs sticking out of the dish as if it were crawling (see opposite).

8. Cook for 25 to 30 minutes, or until the pie is hot inside and golden brown outside. Finish with a dusting of Old Bay to garnish.

Joe Beef of Montreal, the Son of the People.

He cares not for Pope, Priest, Parson or King William of the Boyne; all Joe wants is the Coin. He trusts in God in summer time to keep him from all harm; when he sees the frost and snow poor old Joetrusts. in the Almighty Dollar and good old maple wood to keep his belly warm, for Churches, Chapels, Ranters, Preachers, Beechers and such stuff Montreal has already got enough.

From the "Evening Star," April 15th, 1876:

Mr. John Dougall, in the New York *Witness*, makes an appeal for "additional capital to the extent of fifty thousand dollars." He proposes to issue bonds of $10, $50, $100 and $500, payable in five years, and bearing 7 per cent. interest.   JOE BEEF.

Any Citizens, this day, having any of their Bonds on Hand, will please call at my Office from 10 a.m. to 12 a.m. daily, or at next door, the Rag Store, and they will get their full value, as far as old paper goes!

The Village Magistrate.

The City Councillor.

The Sunday School Bouncer.

The Blooming Rose, with the Temperance Nose.

All you Clergymen, Captains, Sailors, Bums, and Scurvy-Tailors, if you can walk or crawl, when you go on the spree, go and see JOE BEEF of Montreal.

JOE BEEF'S PROCLAMATION
TO THE PEOPLE.

TAVERNE
JOE BEEF inc.
TAVERN
"The Oldest Tavern in Old Montreal"
"Good Canadian Cuisine"

TAVERNE
JOE BEEF inc.
TAVERN
"The Oldest Tavern in Old Montreal"
"Good Canadian Cuisine"

Jambon Maquereau Persillé

You will need

Scale, precision in charcuterie is crucial

Butcher's twine

Fine-mesh sieve

Terrine mold, 8 inches (20 cm) long
x 3 inches (7.5 cm) wide x 4 inches
(10 cm) deep, lined with multiple layers
of plastic wrap

The charcuterie shop of our dreams: delicately smoked fish and impeccably sliced hams lie artfully nestled behind crystal-clean windows; pâtés and meat pies, ornate with noble crests and drenched in shimmering jellies, stand in tidy rows on the richest of opalescent marbles. Lovely condiments erupt from seemingly bottomless earthenware jars. Streams of friends from fellow kitchens drop in and deliver the finest fruits of their skilled labor. There are buttery brioches, crates of chilled cider, crops of turnips, and heaps of wild mushrooms freshly picked from the floor of the majestic boreal forests. In the corner would be this lovely jellied mackerel, treated the way a *jambon persillé* should be. The *persillé:* a Burgundian specialty of ham, cooked and set in a heavily parslied jellied broth.

For the ham

2.2 pounds (1 kg) ham hocks
(cooked according to the ham hock recipe
in The Cellar, page 10)

2 quarts (2 l) ham hock cooking liquid,
(from above)

For the mackerel

Two 1½-pound (675-g) Atlantic mackerels,
filleted, yielding 4 fillets, pin-boned

2 quarts (1 l) reserved ham cooking liquid

For the terrine

9 sheets (22 g) leaf gelatin, soaked in
cold water for 10 minutes

2 teaspoons kosher salt

1 cup (80 g) minced fresh flat-leaf parsley

Zest of 1 lemon

1 shallot, diced finely, cooked with ¼ cup
(60 ml) white wine and reduced

Buttered toast (optional)

Caviar (optional)

I. To poach the mackerel: Bring 1 quart (1 l) of the reserved ham hock cooking liquid to a boil over medium heat in a sauté pan. Add the mackerel, cover with foil, and turn off the heat. Let the fish sit in the poaching liquid for 5 minutes. Remove the fish using a slotted spoon or fish spatula and transfer to a plate. Discard the liquid and let the fish cool.

2. For the terrine: Bloom the gelatin sheets in a bowl of cold water for 10 minutes, or until ready for step 4.

3. Fill a medium saucepan with 1 quart (1 l) of the ham hock cooking liquid. Bring to a boil over medium heat, and reduce the liquid by half (2 cups/ 500 ml), skimming as foam and →

8. When you're ready to serve, using a hot sharp knife, slice ¾-inch- (2-cm-) wide pieces, plate, and serve with hot buttered toast and caviar (optional, of course). The terrine will keep for 7 days in the refrigerator.

Notes The brine for the ham will need 6 hours to be made and cooled. The ham hocks then need to be brined for 72 hours in advance.

The ham hock cooking liquid will yield an additional liter of deliciousness—freeze this as you would stock and keep it for a future blast of porky flavor or when you're ready to tackle Tripes à la Mode de Caen (page 95).

impurities rise to the top. Season with the salt.

4. Squeeze any excess water out of the soaked gelatin sheets and stir them into the hot reduced ham hock broth to dissolve. Keep at room temperature.

5. To assemble the terrine: Shred the ham meat into large chunks, discarding the skin, fat, and bones, keeping only the nice pink flesh. Place in a large bowl. Do the same with the mackerel in a separate bowl.

6. Add the parsley, lemon zest, and the reduced cooking liquid with gelatin to the ham. Then add the mackerel and the shallot. Mix well.

7. Start filling the terrine, one handful of filling at a time. There is no absolute way of building this; you just want all the ingredients evenly spread throughout the dish. Cover with an overlay of plastic wrap, press firmly, and put a weight on it. Place in the refrigerator for a minimum of 4 hours, or ideally overnight.

Base Sausage

Makes about twelve
4½-inch (12-cm) links,
about 3 pounds (1.4 kg)

You will need

Ice bath

Plastic or stainless-steel
sausage-stuffing funnel

Instant-read thermometer

Fine-mesh sieve

One 4- to 5-foot (1.2-m to 1.5-m) length
natural hog casing

4 garlic cloves, finely chopped

1 cup (250 ml) cold dry white wine
or brut cider

1 tablespoon kosher salt

¾ teaspoon finely ground white pepper

¾ teaspoon finely ground black pepper

½ teaspoon Prague Powder #1

1 tablespoon sugar

2.2 pounds (1 kg) coarsely ground fat
pork shoulder

8 ounces (250 g) of cured salami—
soft, like a soppressata—peeled,
cut into ¼-inch (6-mm) dice, and coarsely
ground in a food processor, 6 to 10 pulses

Sausage is the best food. That is, if you use great meat, sound seasonings, and extremely sanitary technique. Once you've found your groove, draw from history and your travels to customize this basic recipe: duck, pasture-raised beef, wild turkey. In the fall, a hunter might add game with a pinch of black pepper and some port. If your leanings are more vegetal, include the purée left over from your green juicing and a few hemp seeds. Just keep in mind that you need fat; it's not just a lubricant that stops you from choking on your food. Fat has finally been granted a nutritional pardon as decades of countrywide lipid abstinence has proved a majestic failure. Most sausage recipes call for fatback mixed with pork shoulder; we're using salami as well.

---

1. Wash your hands well. Rinse the casing by placing one end under the water tap and letting cold water run through until the water comes out the other end of the casing—this removes the preserving salt from inside of the casing. Repeat 2 to 3 times. Place the rinsed casing in a bowl of clean warm water to soak.

2. Combine the minced garlic and white wine in a small bowl. Let steep at room temperature for 20 minutes. Strain and discard the garlic, but keep the wine.

3. Stir the salt, peppers, Prague Powder, and sugar into the garlic-infused wine.

4. In a cold, large bowl, or in the bowl of a stand mixer fitted with the paddle attachment, combine the ground pork and salami, then mix in the seasoned wine. Place the bowl of meat over an ice bath, if possible.

5. In a small skillet over low heat, fry a small patty of the meat in a little oil until cooked through, 3 to 5 minutes. Taste it for seasoning. Season the bowl of meat as needed, adding salt or any spices and mixing the sausage mixture well (and always keeping it cold).

6. Remove the casing from the warm water and slide one end onto the horn of the stuffer. Keep gathering up the casing around the base of the funnel, until you have worked through all 4 to 5 feet. Tie a knot on the loose end. Set yourself up with a sheet pan moistened with ¼ cup (60 ml) water, next to your ice bath bowl holding the meat mixture.

7. In a large pot over high heat, bring 1 gallon (4 l) water to a simmer.

8. In the meantime, stuff the sausage, working gradually but with confidence. Hold the base of the funnel stuffer with your nondominant hand and, using your other hand, grab golf ball–size portions of meat and stuff them deep into the funnel using your →

thumb. Repeat. The sausage will slowly emerge as you work, sliding onto the pan, and you'll get a feel for pace and distribution. Every few moments, pause and manually squeeze the sausage to redistribute any uneven sections.

9. To form the links, start at the tied end of the casing. With your dominant hand, measure a good hand's length from the end of the casing and, using your index finger and your thumb, pinch the casing and twist the sausage two full rotations. The initial sausage should feel nice and tight. Measure another hand's length from the spot you just pinched and pinch again. This time, rotate the sausage two full rotations in the *opposite* direction from the last twist. As you twist the sausage in the opposite direction, you will feel the last sausage you twisted getting

tighter. Repeat this process for the entire length of the casing: pinch and twist one way, then pinch and twist the other way. This technique ensures that you do not untwist the link that you just made. Check for air gaps, and where there are gaps, pierce the casing lightly with the back of a sausage knife or the tip of a sharp knife.

10. Add the sausages to the simmering water, and reduce the heat to low. Poach—don't boil, the water shouldn't even appear to simmer— for 20 minutes, or until the internal temperature reaches 155°F (68°C) when tested with a digital meat thermometer.

11. If you're saving the poached sausages to eat later, transfer them for 2 minutes to ice water to let them cool,

then store in the refrigerator wrapped in plastic for up to 1 week, or in the freezer for 2 months. If you are going to eat the sausages right away, pat them dry, then warm a bit of oil in a frying pan over medium heat. Snip apart the sausages and cook for about 3 minutes on each side, until golden brown. (If cooking from cold, cook the sausages over medium-low heat for 7 to 10 minutes.)

Note Sausage can be done by hand, quickly, once you get the hang of it and, most important, with the proper stuffer. You just have to make sure to keep everything nice and cold. Pour about ¼ cup (60 ml) of water onto the surface of the sheet pan so that the casing will slide with ease and not tear as you stuff the sausage.

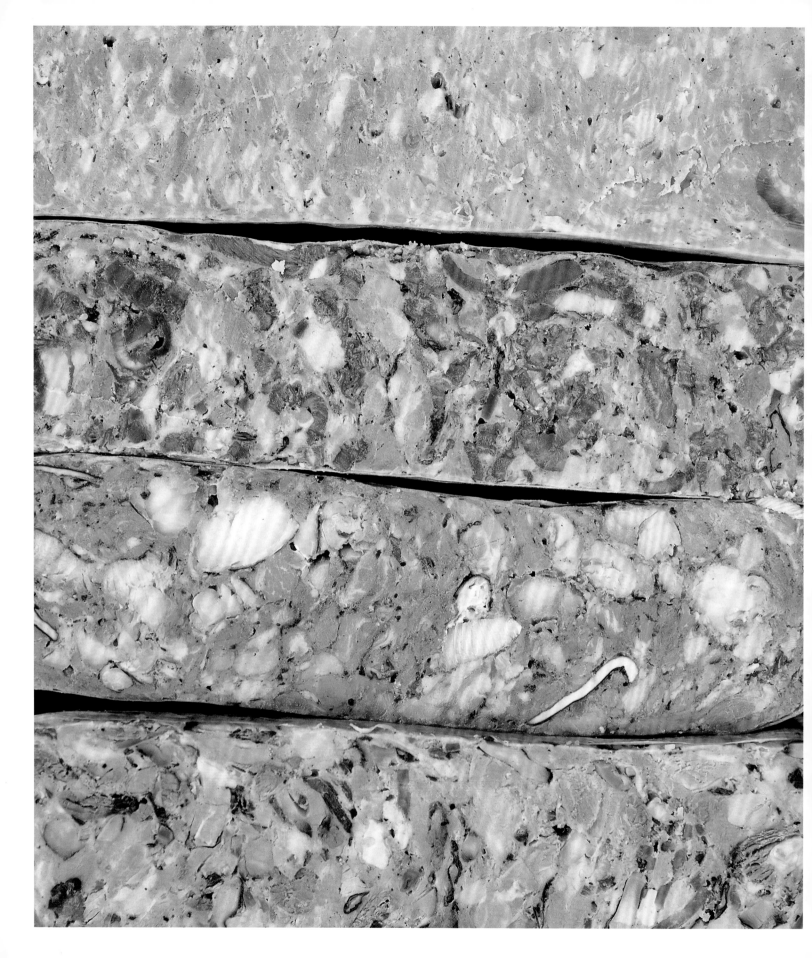

Lobster Sausage Variation

Makes fifteen 4½-inch (12-cm) links, about 4½ pounds (2 kg)

1. Combine the lobster stock with ½ cup (125 ml) infused wine. Add the shallots, parsley, tarragon, brandy, paprika, and cayenne to the infused wine and lobster stock.

2. Add the lobster meat to the base sausage mixture at step 4, then mix in ½ cup (125 ml) seasoned wine only and the ½ cup (125 ml) lobster stock.

1 recipe Base Sausage (page 89)

½ cup (125 ml) lobster stock
(to replace ½ cup [125 ml] of the 1 cup [250ml] infused wine from above)

½ cup (70 g) roughly chopped shallots

½ cup (40 g) chopped fresh flat-leaf parsley

⅓ cup (20 g) chopped fresh tarragon

2 tablespoons brandy

1 tablespoon paprika

Pinch of cayenne pepper

1 pound (454 g) cooked lobster meat, cut into small pieces (a few pulses in your food processor) that will fit through the stuffer

Egg Roll Salad Sausage Variation

Serves 4 as a salad;
makes fifteen 4½-inch (12-cm)
links, about 4 pounds (2 kg)

━━━◆◆◆━━━

You will need

Grill, deep fryer, or heavy-bottomed pot

Charcoal for the grill, or oil for frying

1 Savoy cabbage, cut into 8 to 12 wedges, core still on

8 large shiitake mushrooms, stems removed, thinly sliced and sautéed briefly

2 tablespoons sesame oil

2 tablespoons olive oil, plus more as needed

1 large carrot, cut into matchsticks

¼ cup (10 g) wood ear mushrooms, rehydrated and thinly sliced

2 tablespoons minced fresh ginger

1 garlic clove, minced

2 tablespoons toasted sesame seeds

¼ cup (60 g) water chestnuts, sliced

6 tablespoons apple cider vinegar

2 tablespoons maple syrup

¼ cup (25 g) each chopped fresh cilantro, garlic chives, and mint (20 g)

Salt and pepper

Hot sauce

1 pound (454 g) smoked brisket or pork belly

This is not a gastro-anthropological treatise about the mighty egg roll. What this recipe consists of is the insides of a Montreal-style egg roll turned into a salad. There's something about that smell of deep-fried stray cabbage—jettisoned from the inside of the mother roll; it's the smell of Sunday dinners at La Maison Egg Roll, the smell of growing up next to the back door of a buffet Chinois, which were everywhere in nineties' western Montreal.

I. Heat the oil to 340°F (170°C) in a tall, heavy-bottomed pot or a deep fryer. Alternatively, light your coals, if using a grill.

2. Fry the cabbage wedges until golden, but still crunchy on the inside, 3 to 4 minutes. Transfer to paper towels to drain. If using a grill, char the cabbage on both sides. Transfer to a bowl, cover, and set aside.

3. Sauté the shiitake in the sesame oil and 2 tablespoons of the olive oil in a large frying pan; remove from the pan and set aside. Sauté the carrots, adding oil to the same pan if needed but keeping the carrots crunchy. Finish by sautéing the wood ears briefly. Combine the mushrooms and carrots in a bowl, adding the ginger, garlic, sesame seeds, water chestnuts, cider vinegar, maple syrup, and the chopped herbs. Mix well and season with salt and pepper and hot sauce.

4. Cut away the cabbage cores from the wedges, then add the wedges to the vegetable mix, tossing vigorously to coat.

5. If the salad is your final destination, serve it with the brisket or belly, pulled or cubed, tossed in or on top. If you're making an egg roll sausage, blitz the salad in the food processor until coarsely ground, 5 or 6 pulses.

Note To turn this into a sausage, use one whole recipe of this salad (minus the brisket or pork belly), chopped small, and add to the Base Sausage (page 89) mix.

Tripes à la Mode de Caen (White Tripe with Cider)

Serves 4 to 6

You will need

Butcher's twine

Cheesecloth

Fred loves tripe. Not in that lyrical, erotic memory à la *Chef's Table*. Once in a while he gets the urge to eat it. If it's not on the Joe Beef menu that day, he heads for the Italian grocer like a lemming for the cliffs, buys too much tripe, pig's trotters, or a calf's foot, and some mirepoix vegetables. Fred says, "I can't say that the mood at my house on those days is blissful, for many don't partake in my primal drive to ingest trainloads of tripe. In cooking school, tripe was my self-administered hazing, the required initiation before I could be allowed farther down the path of *la bonne cuisine française*. The smell that first time wasn't so great; now, it opens the floodgates of my appetites." Try it once, then many more times, and you will see.

For the pâte à luter or "dead dough" to seal your pot

4 cups (about 500 g) all-purpose flour

1 teaspoon kosher salt

2 large egg whites

¾ cup (200 ml) water

For the tripe stew

2 bay leaves

1 clove

1 tablespoon black peppercorns

1 tablespoon white peppercorns

2 fresh pig's trotters or 1 calf's foot

2 pounds (900 g) honeycomb tripe, cut into 1-inch (2.5-cm) pieces

1 pound (454 g) leaf tripe, cut into 1-inch (2.5-cm) pieces

2 cups (500 ml) ham hock stock (see the ham hock recipe in The Cellar, page 10), optional

1 large onion, thinly sliced

1 large whole carrot

6 garlic cloves, crushed

2 teaspoons kosher salt

1½ cups (350 ml) brut cider

To garnish

1 tablespoon minced fresh chervil

1 tablespoon minced fresh flat-leaf parsley

I. Make the dough to seal your pot: In a bowl, use a wooden spoon to mix the flour, salt, egg whites, and water together until you have a homogenous paste. Let the mixture sit, covered with plastic wrap, for 30 minutes.

2. Preheat the oven to 300°F (150°C).

3. For the stew: Wrap the bay leaves, clove, and black and white peppercorns in a cheesecloth bundle, and tie it off with some butcher's twine. Also tie a length of twine tightly around the joint in one of the pig's feet, leaving a 12-inch (30-cm) twine tail.

4. Combine all the remaining stew ingredients except the cider in a large Dutch oven. Nestle in the aromatics' cheesecloth bundle and then pour the cider over everything. Use your hands to press down and submerge any stray ingredient. Make sure the twine attached to the pig's foot is hanging over the edge of the pot. Cover with the pot's lid.

5. Roll out the dough as you would a Play-Doh snake, long enough to wrap around the circumference of your Dutch oven. Wrap the dough all around the edges of the lid, pressing firmly as you go, to make a seal, leaving a small gap around where the twine is sticking out. This "caulking" keeps all the flavor and aroma of the tripe inside the pot during its long cooking period.

6. Braise in the oven for 8 hours.

7. The pig's feet bring a lot of collagen to this dish, but they also act as your doneness check: the tripe is ready when you give the twine around the pig's foot a little yank, sectioning the now-tender foot at the joint. Crack into the pot, discarding the cheesecloth bundle.

8. Serve the contents of the pot steaming hot with a generous sprinkle of chervil and parsley. This would be delicious with some steamed →

pommes de terre vapeur, "turned" potatoes (see page 79). The richness of the tripe calls for an unbuttered accompaniment.

9. If you're planning on making tripe sausages (you should be), manually remove all the bones and joints that were released into the pot during cooking. You'll be left with about

2 cups (500 ml) cooking juices and 2.2 pounds (1 kg) tripe stew (now that the bones and cheesecloth bundle have been discarded). Blitz half of the tripe stew in a food processor until it looks coarsely ground. Drain and cool the tripe prior (to avoid a gummy mess). And proceed with the Base Sausage recipe (page 89). Makes about 4½ pounds (2 kg) finished sausage.

Notes We like to use two types of beef tripe, honeycomb and leaf, so called based on their appearance. If you have any pork trimmings left from making charcuterie, add them to your pot.

To make a tripe sausage, use one-half of this recipe's yield, drained, chopped (small enough to fit through your sausage-stuffing funnel), and perfectly cooled to add to the Base Sausage mix (page 89).

Interlude

What a Long, Free-Range Trip It's Been

We were perhaps a little naïve, believing that if our first book had good reach, we would have a line of small cattle farmers just dying to show us their cherished goods for us to source. Not so much— though of course there are always the unannounced drop-ins and the cold calls from reps, eager and proud to show us their house brand of beef, tastefully vintaged. But, vacuum-packed beef strip loin is still vacuum-packed beef strip loin, no matter how dynamic an in-house graphics department you have.

The sheer size of a cattle, upward of two thousand pounds, kills the idea of nose-to-tail, farm-to-table before it even starts. It is a lengthier and costlier process to produce great beef, much more than say, turnips, and the market is ruled by a price that is not "officially" set, while pretending it is.

What do we mean?

The whole of the steak industry (we're covering only Canada here) is controlled by two or three main meat packers that can alter the market at whim, therefore setting the rules for the smallish farms to play by. Restaurateurs and customers alike are often in the dark about the real needs of rural communities, and fall for the myth and image of a family farm where they make their own soap and sew their overalls to feed the most distinguished city-dweller eaters in the cores of our metropolises a handcrafted, artisanal, pasture-raised, *and* not-too-expensive meat.

If we want beef from smaller farms, then, to thrive beyond subsistence, a farm *needs* to grow. To grow it needs space, but also margins and fair prices. Transportation costs in a country as big as Canada are a massive obstacle.

For example: we did try to get in touch with cattle farms that claimed they had their herds in outdoor pastures in the north of Quebec, feeding on northern plants and roaming peacefully in the long days of boreal summers. But even if there was a website, a branding program, and a few official retailers, there was no meat. On the few occasions when there was meat, there was limited transport or it was prohibitively onerous. This highlights one of the major risks of pushing rural areas farther and farther away from urban centers: transportation logistics.

While in the cities ride-sharing apps abound, to get a case of sturgeon or a half lamb from the St. Lawrence Valley, someone still needs to bring it to the local Greyhound bus depot and someone needs to pick it up in town, most often in traffic. After a few well-intentioned orders, placed to interesting producers, doing so was rapidly deemed a bad idea. Moving big pieces of meat is expensive at every point of the business. And so, lots of bovines of the Angus type peacefully roam the pastures—you can see them, pet them if you dare—but try to find the beef they become. They are sent

most often to feedlots in Ontario and sold as carcasses to be graded and sold as Canada A, AA, AAA, or prime, or, in some cases, USDA graded meat.

We dealt for a while with a local company that offered high-quality Quebec beef, with an intelligent method of traceability, but they couldn't withstand the state of the market and quickly went under. A year later, we got involved with a company that took over the program. And that's the closest local beef we've been able to find, ever.

The beef business is still dominated by steaks and burgers; people want giant cuts of cheap beef, burgers at a buck a pop, and such mathematics is only possible with huge shortcuts at every step of the "field-to-grill" process. Just like the public, we (Joe Beef and all the individuals that that entails) often forget that we are part of the solution. We want decent working conditions for slaughterhouse workers, humane farming methods, and animals raised at a less infernal pace, and yet we still eat a half pound of meat, and we want it cheap. Choosing the right farmer, grocer, or restaurant and paying a fair price matter, even if that means eating a quarter pound of steak instead of a half pound.

What's more: the difference between prime and tertiary cuts does not always materialize on the fork. We live in a world where *tender* and *juicy* are the utmost compliments a bite of steak can receive; the real *carne* will sometimes fail to impress.

Which brings us to an option we can all exercise now: to support tertiary/odd cuts.

 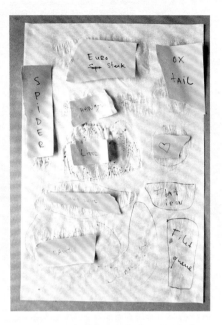

The secondary and tertiary cuts often have what the French call *mâche,* a certain chew, and in that light, require different cooking methods, condiments, and instrumentation. A well-aged, marbled Angus tenderloin will be tasty with barely a shaving of horseradish, yet a shoulder piece of some more poetic French steak will require a little lubrication with a generous pat of butter.

Our expectations have to change for us to appreciate texture instead of lack of texture. And sometimes you have to take the gristle. Although this is not a legitimate Darwinian statement, we need to use our teeth for something other than selfies or they will fall out. Indeed, we often say that if people chose their partners like they do their meat, most of us oppressed by the figures of beauty would have remained untouched!

We try to adopt little changes, like to dry age the "lesser" cuts the way one would loins. We do that with top sirloin (which differs from the primal sirloin cut most know, striploin) to great effect. The dining room staff's skills and language are crucial in the process of serving other parts; for customers to enjoy this difference, you need amazing and smart individuals who comprehend meat beyond simply mastering "the house" discourse on steaks. Heart tartare, beef neck stew, oxtail ragù, cured and smoked brisket, sweetbreads are all delicious with different qualities, and if servers are able to steer (get it!?) diners into a choice that they will appreciate, then it could (gradually) alter consumer behavior and trigger durable and impactful changes that will help rural communities and smart farms.

As George Orwell said, it's the sharp knives that make a good French restaurant.

Ambassador Steak

Serves 4

You will need

Slow cooker (If you don't have one, buy one. The best stores in the world have them on permanent sale rotation.)

Grill and charcoal

We have complained about today's restaurants' egos and lack of fun. Though Fred found a good one: The Big Texan in Amarillo. He says, "I had the good fortune to visit there with our great friend John Bil, though you too have probably been there, as this type of establishment has been featured in countless movies. It's the place with the "free" steak: the only caveat is you must eat all seventy-two ounces of it, bun, and breaded shrimps. Honestly, I am prone to regrets, and to this day I consider myself a lesser person for opting for the quarter feast, eighteen ounces (hold the bun, for I am celiac). Against all expectations, the meat was top notch, the vibe was amazing, and the lovely waitress made our day when she came back with a napkin drawing of a cow to show us where the steak came from."

½ cup (113 g) unsalted butter

2 garlic cloves, sliced

6 fresh thyme sprigs

5 ounces (150 ml) Worcestershire sauce (or make your own, page 106)

72 ounces (4½ pounds/2 kg) sliced top sirloin 1½ inches (4 cm) thick, cleaned of big sinew and fat by your butcher

Coarse salt and cracked black pepper

Small bunch of fresh chives, chopped

1. Preset your slow cooker to warm, or the oven to the lowest setting. Place the butter, garlic, thyme, and Worcestershire in the bowl of your slow cooker (or the sad oven alternative: a sheet pan).

2. Place the big steak in the butter mix to coat. Keep the butter mix for later.

3. Cook the steak for 20 minutes in the slow cooker or oven. In the meantime, prepare the coals in your grill.

4. Turn off the cooker and leave the steak there. When the BBQ is hot, season the steak generously with salt and pepper, and place on the grill. Make magazine-perfect grill marks, always 45 degrees to the steak, and flip. We say 3 minutes on one side, then 2 on the other. Slice the steak open to check— better safe than sorry!

5. Warm the butter mix in a small saucepan, and combine with chives for the most delicious drizzle.

6. Drizzle the butter over the steak. Slice thinly. Texas serving suggestion: baked potato, shrimps, a side of salad, a bun, and a good friend.

→ Cheat Sauces

Stock is a beautiful thing. It adds a unique depth and flavor to a sauce, a necessity in a food tradition such as *la cuisine française* that relies very little on strong spices and powerful herbs. Like most traditions, making stock became normal in French kitchens for a multitude of reasons, some (if not most) of them now irrelevant. Most establishments had a butcher on-site and would purchase only whole animals. Refrigeration was not at its peak, so it was crucial to break down and transform carcasses quickly. Any respectable establishment had

a plethora of apprentices learning the trade in exchange for room and board, so labor-intensive processes didn't pose the cost issue that they do nowadays.

Even with "modern" refrigeration, having dozens of gallons of tepid meat infusion around is not the best idea. Moving steaming stock in five-gallon pots in an already-way-too-hot kitchen is dumb. We admit it is a hard transition to go to a no-stock kitchen. The commercial offerings are weak, and the tradition seems to be built deeply into every cook's DNA.

Like the pager and Blockbuster Video, cooking stocks will fade away, not because they aren't good but because we will find alternatives that will be both delicious and smart. Like the cubes we included on page 104. Similar to bouillon cubes, these cheat stocks are easier on the back. And save time. Like cheating without the guilt. These are meant to be fast and loose, as much concept encouragement as recipes. Hence no yields. Here are three variations:

Sauce Volaille

We used to brown our full amount of chicken carcasses, simmer the stocks, and reduce them for an hour for this classic sauce made of reduced brown chicken stock, reduced white wine, and butter. Things have changed; it is no longer cute and nerdy to turn our kitchens into a tannery every weekend. We still reduce a bit of white wine, cheat with some white wine vinegar to require less wine, and add a dash of mushroom soy and lots of cold chunks of butter.

---

2 cups (480 ml) of not too sweet white wine

3 tablespoons white wine vinegar

3 to 4 tablespoons soy sauce

¼ to ⅓ pound (113 to 150 g) unsalted butter, cut into chunks

Salt and white pepper

Canned pimiento

Tabasco sauce

I. Reduce the wine and vinegar in a nonreactive saucepan on medium heat until you have about ¼ cup (60 ml) left (figure out the level it represents on the side of your saucepan by measuring the amount with water first).

2. Add the soy and butter by swirling the pan. If the sauce doesn't hit the high note, add more vinegar or soy, and adjust with salt or white pepper. It's also a good idea to add chopped canned pimiento to this sauce and a dash of Tabasco.

Crème de Soya

This easy two-component sauce was Nicolas Jongleux's recipe. He served it on snails with a royale of rabbit liver, which we still do once in a while at the restaurant. This sauce is also very delicious on sweetbreads.

We measure 1 tablespoon good soy sauce and 3 tablespoons soft whipped cream (no sugar, of course) per person. A small saucepan is crucial; also, make the sauce à la last minute. When you are ready to plate, heat your soy. When it bubbles, whisk in the cream, warm through, and serve immediately.

Strong Tea Jus

Let's say you are roasting duck breast. And you're using a steel pan to get it sticking a bit. You also have strong tea brewed, probably left over. When your meat is done, of course you kept it on the underdone side to allow for time to deglaze the pan. Get rid of the cooking fat and add a good cup (240 ml) strong tea, reduce and season, and don't forget a squeeze of lemon or a dash of vinegar.

Or if you're making beef or venison or bison, adding red wine vinegar is perfect—a tablespoon will do. Reduce and correct the seasoning; we use white pepper. Swirl in some butter, add tea, taste, repeat.

Faux Vin Rouge

½ small beet, diced

1 large shallot, peeled and sliced

1 tablespoon unsalted butter, plus ¼ cup (57 g) for finishing the sauce

1 tablespoon white pepper, plus more for seasoning

3 tablespoons water

3 tablespoons cheap-ass balsamic vinegar

1 tablespoon soy sauce

Salt

1. In a small saucepan over medium heat, sweat the beet and shallot in the tablespoon of butter until they smell cooked, 4 to 5 minutes. Add the white pepper. Lower the heat, add the water and vinegar, reduce a bit, add the soy sauce, and reduce again by half.

2. Cube and add the ¼ cup (57 g) butter and swirl the pan to emulsify. Strain and season with salt and white pepper.

Bouillon Cubes

An old-school chef may throw you to the wolves at the mere mention of instant bouillon, and your philanthropic heritage won't matter anymore. Unless the bouillon cubes are made *à la main* (by hand), with honorable ingredients and care. These three variations will definitely help elevate your shelter fare.

We have yet to find a better source than hoosierhillfarm.com for all things dried and powdered.

For the meat jus pucks

2 tablespoons mushroom powder

¼ teaspoon red wine vinegar powder

1 teaspoon black pepper

1 teaspoon garlic powder

1 teaspoon powdered thyme

2 tablespoons nutritional yeast

1 teaspoon dried soy sauce

1 teaspoon ground lovage

2 tablespoons sea salt

1 teaspoon smoke powder

Pinch of cayenne pepper

1 tablespoon maple sugar

1 tablespoon coconut oil

¼ cup (60 ml) tightly reduced veal stock

For the lobster pucks

2 tablespoons tomato powder

¼ teaspoon red vinegar powder

½ teaspoon white pepper

¼ teaspoon garlic powder

2 teaspoons ground tarragon

2 tablespoons nutritional yeast

2 tablespoons powdered kelp or dulse seaweed

1 tablespoon sea salt

Pinch of cayenne pepper

Pinch of ground fennel

1 tablespoon sugar

1 tablespoon coconut oil

¼ cup (60 ml) shellfish syrup

For the vegetable pucks

2 tablespoons tomato powder

2 tablespoons mushroom powder

2 tablespoons nutritional yeast

2 tablespoons dried soy powder

2 tablespoons kale powder

2 tablespoons sea salt

1 teaspoon black pepper

1 teaspoon garlic powder

1 tablespoon lovage powder

Pinch of cayenne pepper

1 tablespoon coconut oil

1 tablespoon honey

Directions for all three variations:
Combine the dry ingredients, including the salt, in a bowl and mix them well. Then add the the coconut oil and mix well again. Add the syrupy stuff. Mix well again. Using the hashish press, compress into amazing flavor pucks that will brighten the most boring of bunker broths.

Note   The recipe is amazingly simple; most of the work is done online! Companies like Amazon will be of great help with the less-conventional ingredients, such as the powdered soy and smoke powder. OliveNation has a list that's the dream of every gastronome survivalist! As far as the most awkward part of this recipe, the hashish press, any head shop or Amazon carries it under the name of pollen or herb press. It's a little metal cylinder with a threaded piston that can exert great pressure and compact matter into a solid puck.

Worcestershire Sauce

Makes 2 quarts (2 l)
once filtered

———— ~⁓~ ————

You will need

1-gallon glass jug with air lock

Fred was born in Montreal and went to French schools, but he married Allison Cunningham (English), and David McMillan (Scottish) is his best friend, and he writes books with Meredith (English) and is a big fan of *The Howard Stern Show* (definitely not French). In spite of this near-total English immersion, he's still quite unable to pronounce the name of this deep, delicious, and historically relevant condiment.

We fill glass demijohns and let them sit in the Joe Beef cellar for six months. We suggest you do the same at home. The sauces will keep for up to a year (approximately, let your nose decide!), stored in a cool place. For us, Worcestershire sauce is a staple with grilled beef.

---

2 cups (480 ml) water

4 cups (1 l) apple cider vinegar

2 cups (480 ml) dark maple syrup (we use the dark stuff from our friends in Saint-Armand)

¼ cup (60 g) salt

1 cup (240 ml) naturally fermented fish sauce

1¼ cups (300 ml) tamarind paste

¼ cup (60 ml) onion juice

2 tablespoons whole black peppercorns

1 cinnamon stick, 3 to 4 inches (7.5 to 10 cm)

1 teaspoon whole cloves

5 green onions, chopped

5 garlic cloves

1 teaspoon dried ginger

¼ cup (45 g) whole salted anchovies

1 teaspoon whole mace

5 small dried chiles

1. Combine everything in the glass jug with the help of a funnel.

2. Affix the air lock on the jug and shake well. Leave in a sunny window for 1 month, then store in your cellar or a cool, dry place for at least 4 more months. Or (attention New Yorkers) in your parking garage or your friend's parking garage—you can repay them with this sauce; there's enough.

3. When ready to use, filter through a cheesecloth and bottle.

Note The photo we included is of a 10-liter (2½-gallon) demijohn with a bubble cap. It does not represent the intended yield of your 2 liters. This recipe takes 5 months.

Onglet Sous-Marin "Spécial A.A."

Serves 2

One backbone of our after-hours routine that keeps our staff going is A.A. Sous-Marin, a submarine/poutine/hotdog staple of our Saint-Henri neighborhood since the eighties. Here, André is boss; he takes orders, cooks, serves, and throws out drunks.

A.A. is open late. So late, in fact, that if it's closed, you know it's time for home. The bread is replaced by steak here, so the recipe is as gluten-free as your pepperoni!

One 1-pound (454-g) *onglet* (hanger) steak

½ small white onion, sliced

8 white button mushrooms

3 tablespoons canola oil

5 large slices capicola

1 small garlic clove, chopped

Pinch of dried oregano

Pinch of red pepper flakes

Dash of Worcestershire sauce

Salt and pepper

2 tablespoons grapeseed oil

5 large pepperoni slices

4 provolone cheese slices

Handful of shredded iceberg lettuce

Zesty Italian dressing, your choice

2 beefsteak tomato slices

Handful of chopped fresh chives

1. An hour before you're ready to cook your steak, remove the meat from the refrigerator.

2. In a small pan, sauté the onions and mushrooms in the canola oil over medium-high heat for 5 to 6 minutes. You want that smell and feel of a diner where heaps of onions and mushrooms are piled high and you can feel the heat off the griddle.

3. Place the capicola on top of the onions and mushroom mix. Turn the heat to low. Add the garlic, oregano, red pepper flakes, and Worcestershire sauce. Cook for another 4 minutes.

4. To cook the steak: Heat a thick cast-iron frying pan over medium-high heat. It should get very hot. Season your steak liberally with salt and some pepper. Add the oil to the hot pan, carefully add the steak, and lower the heat to medium. Cook for 4 minutes on one side and then 2 minutes on the other for rare. We're undercooking it slightly here because we're going to finish it under the broiler. Remove from the heat and let the hanger rest for 5 minutes.

5. Preheat the broil setting on your oven to high.

6. To build the sandwich: Place the steak on a plate. Pile the onion mix atop. Cover with the pepperoni. Same with the provolone. Broil for 3 to 4 minutes.

7. Remove from the oven. Mix the lettuce with Italian dressing and gingerly place on top. Finish with the tomatoes and chives.

Sweetbreads "Prince of Darkness"

Serves 2

━━━ ∼∼∼ ━━━

You will need

Grill and charcoal

It is a little-known fact that Ozzy Osbourne did not chew the heads off any real bats; instead, educated gastronome that he is, he enjoyed feasting on sweetbreads cooked with charcoal honey and licorice, a dish he discovered in some form, probably at Chez Thibert in Dijon when David was working there. We'd sworn to never do Instagram-perfect shock-value black food . . . until we learned that charcoal has a very appeasing effect on gas and bloating, making road trips more enjoyable. As we write this, though, we're discovering that black licorice consumed in high doses could decrease your sex drive. But . . . if you are planning on living through the long aftermath of some *Mad Max* disaster in a crowded bunker, you might want to forgo the call of mating for a while, at least until the eternal night comes to a dawn, and you are both deemed fit to repopulate the gene pool.

This is also a nice date dish.

Two 8-ounce (230-g, approximately) pieces veal sweetbreads, trimmed of excess fat, and very fresh

2 tablespoons olive oil

2 teaspoons fresh lemon juice

1 tablespoon chopped fresh thyme

1 garlic clove, smashed

1 teaspoon salt, plus more for seasoning

1 teaspoon black pepper, plus more for seasoning

6 tablespoons (90 ml) very fragrant honey, such as Manuka

½ teaspoon activated charcoal powder (see Note)

1 cup (240 ml) heavy cream (35 percent butterfat)

1 tablespoon chopped soft black licorice candy, such as Panda brand

3 licorice root sticks, washed

Charred onion

I. Place the sweetbreads in a glass bowl. Add the oil, 1 teaspoon of the lemon juice, the thyme, garlic, salt, and pepper. Refrigerate for 1 hour.

2. Meanwhile, build a coal fire and brush off your grill. In a small bowl, stir the honey and charcoal powder until combined.

3. In a small saucepan over medium-high heat, bring the cream to a simmer and slowly dissolve the licorice candies in it. Add 1 of the 3 licorice sticks. When the cream has reduced by half and the candy is dissolved, 10 to 15 minutes, add the remaining 1 teaspoon lemon juice, season with salt and pepper to taste, and set aside.

4. Sharpen the ends of the remaining 2 licorice sticks. Stab each sweetbread across with a stick as if it were a vampire and the licorice a vampire-slaying stake. Place on the medium-hot grill and cook for 20 minutes or so, flipping often and brushing with some of the black honey mixture. You want the insides of the sweetbreads to be firm and not gluey.

5. Serve on a hot plate with a dollop of licorice cream under the sweetbreads and a drizzle of honey on top, alongside a charred onion as a garnish.

Note Look for activated charcoal powder in the toothpaste section of health food stores (yes, counterintuitive!) or online.

Hamburger "Catalina"

There is a little *casse-croûte* east of us in Kamouraska where they used to, maybe still do, make a hamburger covered in Catalina dressing. The beef was fresh, there were Styrofoam plates, and the dressing was a "food service deliverable"; deliciously unique nonetheless. This recipe is a throwback to before our day, a time when ice cream wouldn't melt and burgers didn't come with disclaimers.

1½ pounds (680 g) ground meat (chuck and brisket, lean, fat, loin and bacon, whatever you like), shaped loosely into 4 patties

1 teaspoon kosher salt

1 teaspoon black pepper

2 tablespoons grapeseed oil or other neutral oil

¼ cup (57 g) unsalted butter

¼ cup (60 ml) steak sauce, something like HP

4 hamburger buns, unseeded

1 cup tomato marjoram butter sauce (see page 58), warmed and blitzed with your immersion blender or simply go for Catalina dressing!

1. Bring a skillet to high heat.

2. Season the patties with the salt and pepper. Cook the patties in the oil over moderate heat until well browned on the outside and pink on the inside, about 4 minutes.

3. Remove the patties and place on a plate. Drain the pan and add the butter and steak sauce, then return the patties to the skillet and finish cooking in the butter sauce mix, about 2 minutes, just enough to incorporate the flavors.

4. Place a patty on a bottom bun, spoon on some sauce mix, place the top bun over, and sauce with the tomato marjoram butter. Serve *tout de suite, mon chéri.*

Chips

Makes enough for 2 snacks
or 4 sides

You will need

A deep fryer with a sober fryer operator

Mandoline

Clean dish towels

2 big russet potatoes that avoided
the fridge, peeled

4 quarts (4 l) water

1 tablespoon white vinegar

A good amount of frying oil—canola
works—enough for your fryer

Fine salt (pulse in a coffee grinder to get
a perfect Golden Arches salt texture)

1. Four hours before frying, slice the potatoes as thick as a Popsicle stick on a mandoline. Plunge them in the water and vinegar and let them soak for 4 hours in the fridge.

2. Heat the oil to 335°F (170°C).

3. Remove the potatoes from the water and pat dry on a clean cloth.

4. Fry in small batches until crispy, turning one by one. Dry on a paper towel placed on a sheet pan. Season as you wish.

Note

At home, we wash all kitchen linens with unscented soap. I screwed great wines by washing decanters with guava-linden dish soaps and failed at foie gras torchon because the rag involved was washed with Platinum Rush gym soap.

—Fred

Potato Chips Road Map

❧❧

The road trip has lost its soul, its most fascinating philosophical quest: the gas station foods. The same breakfast burritos, the same cream-filled cakes granted eternal life by inert gas packaging—one hundred miles used to guarantee a change in snack scenery, but no more. Except for one thing, perhaps by sheer virtue of shipping difficulties: the humble yet delicious potato chip has survived this extinction of flavor. With the potato chip,

you can taste where you are. In the Northwest, the flavor tastes hippie; Napa has a yuppie flair packed in a health-conscious format; in the Southwest it's a bag of salsita within the bag of chips. Meredith's favorites are Tim's Cascade from Oregon or Better Made, when in the Motor City. On and on, chips are the last bastion of road food, and we shall stand for it!

They are also a great side dish.

Three

Sunday Dinners at Home

One day it just happens: you pull up to a red light, glance sideways at the car next to you, and everything you see in that sensible, safe station wagon makes you cringe. You have pulled up next to yourself: dark tinted windows and a bike rack on your powerful yet really practical station wagon; taking the kids somewhere your folks never took you, out of love, but mostly spite; the windows are down, pumping some enormously popular dub version of Max Romeo's "Chase the Devil" from a subscription music service meant to distill your creative self to a simple algorithm.

Of course, you're happy and proud to be a dad/mom, a husband/wife, and a chef (or whatever people claim boldly on their Twitter bylines), but these days, evening shifts are tougher. Your culinary drive is set to toddler gear.

So you do what most chefs do before they buy the sports car: you write a book on Sunday dinners at home, and you start giving interviews on the state of school lunches and composting. Unsurprisingly, *this* chapter is called "Sunday Dinners at Home." And in typical Joe Beef fashion, this is where you will find the most complex recipes because beautiful Limoges and exquisite table manners *matter*.

→ The Choice of a Menu

Let an old *Larousse Gastronomique* dictate the path your dinner should follow; whatever you set out to prepare that night should stay true to the theme of your choosing.

If any of your guests, even if they live in your basement (hello, John Bil),

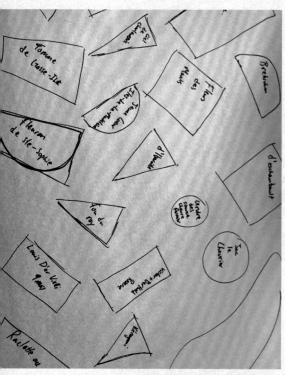

are dressed inappropriately for the occasion, lend them a cardigan.

As for the children: they shall wear bow ties. Allison Cunningham, Fred's partner and the third owner of Joe Beef, opts for outfitting the kids in pressed trousers, button-down shirts, and smart dinner jackets, with a penchant for seersucker, or a flowery dress and again a cardigan. This is the time for "children [to] be seen but not heard." They will have plenty of occasions to voice their opinion. Now is not that time.

Flowers will be present at the table. They will respect the season and theme of the meal—peonies, pear blossoms, or tulips. You would never see blue carnations in Mionnay (the home of Alain Chapel)! Always remember, as Meredith's mom, Mary, does, that flowers are arranged in odd numbers. Plan abundantly for that "carefree abandon" look. Don't buy your flowers at the grocery store: it can barely sell you good food. It would be miraculous if it lived up to your floral expectations.

Conversation: Our David is an expert, based on years of observation and gathering information. We have never seen anything like it. Like him, call obsolete knowledge from your mind to recite entertaining tales,

be it Roman history or muscle cars, even if you don't share the passion exhibited by your diners on said topic; they will appreciate knowing there is someone out there who knew a ham radio operator once. In other words, don't just research your menu and flowers, research your guests as well.

Now is not a time for restraint: as a host, you should be the provider of laughs, cool dancing tunes, and, later, hangovers. Keep the drinks stiff and the wine flowing. Refuse, categorically, the help offered by your smashed, guilt-ridden guests: hide the dishes in a few large Rubbermaid boxes until tomorrow.

✢ Why French Cuisine Rocks at a Dinner Party

Contrary to what one might think based on the complex offerings of modern tasting menus, the progression of a great French meal is actually a grandiose display of simplicity. It's a carefree offering: one or two bang-in-season vegetables, prepared simply, followed by one or two of the freshest shellfish the closest coasts have to offer; then, perhaps a slice of some skilled *ouvrier*'s pâté en croûte, before hitting up a shoulder of lamb with wire-thin green beans. Then cheese—always after—spirits, and a tight little café.

Of course, this is the kind of menu we would recommend to a culinary neophyte. What our at-home guests are served can range from Lièvre à la Royale to the most beautiful suckling pig you have ever seen, simply followed by an irrational amount of French cheeses (now mostly from Quebec), all served at perfect levels of ripeness. Serving such a meal family style, in pretty platters, is the way to go: the bird and the ogre can get their fill without being put in the spotlight.

One tradition that has fallen out of grace that we practice occasionally is the sorbet midway through the meal, or *trou normand*. It's also a wonderful opportunity to purchase an otherwise totally useless ice cream maker and another pitch-perfect way to highlight any regional or very seasonal ingredient: yellow plum sorbet at the end of August with a few drops of potent mirabelle eau-de-vie is definitely chat-worthy food.

We know most of you will be discouraged by our deranged enthusiasm for this kind of Sunday dinner, but it's an amazingly simple menu to cook. The challenge lies in the sourcing and shopping.

—F.M.

Camembert

There is actually solid science behind the tradition of enjoying some raw-milk cheese at the end of a meal. Fat is the most potent trigger to signal satiety, and probiotics, which the cheese is loaded with, won't be facing an empty stomach with hostile pH. After a nice dinner, the good bacteria and yeasts have a chance to make their way down your digestive tract, where they can establish helpful colonies.

Quenelles de Truite
(can be done as Gâteaux)

Serves 4

Serves 4

You will need

Food processor

Four ¾-cup ramekins (10 cm diameter)

9 x 13-inch (23 x 33-cm) roasting/
Pyrex dish

Purists will argue that a quenelle is made of pike, puréed by hand in a mortar with a pestle, painstakingly forced through a muslin sieve to rid it of pike's infamously tiny bones. Quenelles are then shaped by the emaciated hands of an apprentice who left home too early and who cries himself to sleep at night in the overpacked dormitory above the coal-furnaced kitchen.

As much as we are lovers of *la bonne cuisine française,* the fact remains that "French restaurant" cuisine flourished in large part on the backs of very young and very affordable labor (we're talking about the establishments stuck in the cogs of the Michelin machine, not farmhouse cuisine). Then came the food processor, a machine that these purists would shun. We like it. Although a Robot Coupe is the price of a small dirt bike (Dave and Fred both still profoundly resent their own parents for never getting them dirt bikes), it's well worth the money and will save you from repetitive strain injury.

Although we call it a quenelle, and shape it as such, this recipe is also the base for the gâteaux de truite, in which case you would cook the mixture in buttered ramekins placed in a water bath as opposed to shaping it with spoons and poaching it directly in water. →

7 ounces (200 g) bay scallops

7 ounces (200 g) trout (speckled, rainbow, char, etc.), pin bones out, skin off, cut into chunks the size of the scallops

2 tablespoons dry white vermouth

1 teaspoon salt

Generous pinch of white pepper

2 whole large eggs, plus 1 large egg white

1 cup (250 ml) heavy cream
(35 percent butterfat)

½ cup (113 g) softened butter,
plus extra for greasing the ramekins

To serve

1 cup (240 ml) lobster or crayfish bisque,
with added chunks of cooked lobster
(see page 65)

Minced fresh chives

1. Preheat the oven to 325 ° F (160 ° C).

2. In a small bowl, combine the scallops, trout, vermouth, salt, and white pepper. Freeze for 30 minutes, along with your food processor bowl and blade.

3. Bring 6 to 8 cups (1.5 to 2 l) water to a boil in a kettle or saucepan.

4. Transfer the seafood mixture to a food processor bowl. Pulse until coarsely chopped, then add the eggs and egg white, one at a time, and pulse until mixed well. Clean the sides of the bowl with a spatula. Next, add the cream, pulsing briefly—do not overtax because the cream might split. Pulse in the butter.

5. Butter the ramekins very well, and, using a spoon, divide the seafood mousse equally among them.

6. Place a sheet of paper towel or a thin tea towel in the base of a roasting dish large enough to contain the 4 ramekins. Add the ramekins, and carefully pour in the boiling water until it reaches halfway up the ramekins. Bake until set, about 20 minutes.

7. While the seafood gâteaux are baking, slowly heat the lobster bisque in a small saucepan. Season to taste.

8. Gently unmold each ramekin onto a plate embossed with your family crest, spooning ¼ cup (60 ml) seasoned bisque over each, and topping with too many chives.

QUENELLES

Although not true pike quenelles in the eyes of the purist, these gâteaux cooked like quenelles in simmering water followed by a pass under the broiler, then drenched in bisque d'ecrevisse, is above and beyond an acceptable substitute to the Lyonnais classic.

1. Bring a wide shallow pan of water to a simmer, salt, and taste (it should taste like mild sea water).

2. With the help of two oval large serving spoons of identical shape, form a little football while scooping the fish mix from one spoon to the other, holding the spoons in opposing fashion.

3. Drop each quenelle carefully into the water, rinse the spoon, and start again until no more mixture remains.

4. Cover and maintain a gentle simmer for about 12 minutes.

5. Remove with a slotted spoon and transfer to a clean tray lined with absorbent paper. The quenelles can now be refrigerated.

6. When ready to serve, preheat the oven to 425° F (200° C), place the quenelles in a beautiful copper au gratin dish, and cover with sauce—some might sprinkle on some grated Gruyère—and bake for 15 to 17 minutes, until the quenelles are slightly browned and the sauce is bubbly. Serve the remaining sauce, piping hot, on the side.

Armagnac à la truffe du Périgord

Looser regulations and much less stringent distilling
procedures make Armagnac a more diverse and pleasant
reflection of the land and the people who make it.

The Armagnac trade never quite reached the elite-platinum-
gold level of Cognac, which gives you a much better product for
your coins. Forgotten barrels are discovered frequently and you
won't have to sell your smart car to taste a spirit that predates
your parents' first date.

You can sip it alongside a nice demitasse, or as we
prefer, when you get some, sink in a few clippings of *Tuber
melanosporum* (Périgord truffle), swirl a bit, and enjoy.

Truffes du Vaucluse au Sésame

Serves 4

~~~

You will need

Very sharp mandoline or
truffle slicer

As much as we think of ourselves as excessive and obsessive (positive traits of character!), Martin Picard, of Au Pied de Cochon and Cabane à Sucre fame, takes the blue ribbon: when he wants fresh truffles, he doesn't just place a call, he books airfare and hotel and travels right to the source, coming home bearing the tastiest, smelliest specimens of *Tuber melanosporum* straight from Avignon, in the Vaucluse. Being the great brother that he is, we get to benefit from his dealings. This recipe is a simple match between sesame and truffles, odd but it works.

¼ cup (60 ml) organic tahini

¼ cup (57 g) unsalted butter

A few drops of fresh lemon juice

Salt and black pepper

4 slices great bread (seeded, sourdough, or whatever will make solid toast)

1 nice *Tuber melanosporum* truffle, brushed and scrubbed

1. Combine the tahini with the butter, add the lemon juice, and mix well. Season with salt and pepper to taste.

2. Toast the bread over an open fire or under a hot broiler to get some char.

3. Spread the sesame butter on the toast.

4. Slice the truffle thinly, distributing it among the 4 slices of bread. Add a twist from ye olde pepper mill.

Note Although truffles are best when ripe and fresh, the tradition of high-quality preserved truffles is very interesting. We prefer Pébeyre above all others.

Dulse Bagged Potatoes

Serves 4

———— ᕦᕤ ————

You will need

Two 6 x 10-inch (15 x 25-cm) paper bags, one carefully stuffed into the other

Butcher's twine

Spray bottle filled with water

Grand Manan is a maritime island in the Bay of Fundy, part of New Brunswick. It is by far the best place to find dulse, specifically at a place called Roland's Sea Vegetables. Here, they harvest dulse by hand and collect it on dories. Then they lay this edible seaweed (that looks like a leafy, red lettuce) out on the rocks to air-dry in the salty breeze under the sun. Grand Manan gets so much fog in the summer, hence its iconic lighthouses, that the dulse can take ages to dry. A sign of good dulse is that it is crisp with a bit of salinity.

This has the feeling of Jiffy Pop yet is nothing at all like Jiffy Pop. The absolute best campfire meal.

16 fingerling potatoes
(approximately 1¼ pounds or 600 g),
scrubbed and scored with a cross
along the length of each

4 garlic cloves, smashed

2 tablespoons dulse or kelp,
soaked in water, then minced

2 tablespoons kosher salt

2 tablespoons neutral oil

To serve

Minced fresh chives

¼ cup (60 g) whipped butter

1. Preheat the oven to 350°F (180°C).

2. Toss the potatoes, garlic, dulse, salt, and oil in a bowl to combine.

3. Transfer to the double paper bag, tying the top shut with some butcher's twine. Place in an ovenproof dish or on a small sheet pan.

4. Working in the sink or close to it, spray the bag with water until it is completely soaked. Transfer to the oven and bake until the potatoes are tender, about 1 hour. After 30 minutes, check the bag, spritzing it with more water if it has started to look dry.

5. Rip the bag open and transfer the contents to a bowl. Shower with chives and serve with whipped butter alongside.

Civet de Homard au Calvados

Bernard Pacaud, the chef of L'Ambroisie in Paris, is like the genius introverted sound engineer who has quietly mixed the greatest albums of our generation. Pacaud brought the potato to prominence, stayed humble, and preached deliciousness through decades of nouvelle cuisine . . . an Adam Yauch lookalike, sporting a Lacoste polo while shaving half a black truffle over some banker's food in the opulent salons of the Marais.

If you were to find yourself, a young *stagiaire* abroad, standing outside his establishment, expecting a glimpse of the man himself or, at the very least, the loot from the market, poring over the menu—you'd sense that each dish was grammatically structured, rhythmic and delicious to read before you'd even catch a glimpse of it through the kitchen window. This is how, reading L'Ambroisie's menu back then, we imagined this *civet* to be.

⅓ cup (90 g) sea salt

Kelp (optional)

One 3-pound (approximately 1.3-kg) lobster

¼ cup (60 ml) neutral oil

1 cup diced mirepoix (½ small onion, 1 carrot, 1 celery stalk)

1 garlic clove, smashed

2 teaspoons apple cider vinegar

1 cup (250 ml) dry (sparkling) apple cider

1 cup (250 ml) chicken stock

1 tablespoon chopped fresh tarragon

¼ cup (57 g) cultured unsalted butter

2 shallots, finely chopped

¼ cup (60 g) bacon lardons, blanched for 3 minutes

1 Golden Delicious apple, peeled, cored, and cut into 8 wedges

½ cup (120 g) crème fraîche

2 tablespoons Calvados or apple cider vinegar, plus more as needed

Salt and white pepper

To serve

1 bunch fresh chervil, minced

Black truffle (optional)

1. Combine the salt with 6 quarts (6 l) water in a very large pot, and bring to a boil over high heat. If you have kelp, geek out and put some in there and simmer for a few minutes. Plunge the lobster in. When the water returns to boiling, cook for 4 minutes only. Transfer the lobster to a bowl filled with ice.

2. Working on a large sheet pan, with a bowl or two at the ready, break into the lobster with your hands and some lobster crackers: remove the meat from the tail, knuckles, and claws, reserving the shells in one bowl and the meat in the other. Refrigerate the lobster meat. Discard the contents of the head, but clean the head shell and set aside for garnishing purposes. →

3. In a heavy-bottomed pot that feels French enough for the dish, heat the oil until smoking hot. Add in the shells and cook, stirring over high heat, until all the liquid has evaporated, about 5 minutes. Stir in the mirepoix and garlic, reduce the heat to medium-low, and cook slowly until fragrant, about 5 minutes. Next, add the cider vinegar and the cider, bring to a boil, then simmer to reduce until sticky, about 15 minutes. Add the chicken stock and tarragon, return to a simmer, and cook for a further 20 minutes over low heat.

4. Strain the sauce, discarding the shells and aromatics. You should have about 1 cup (240 ml) of sauce. Set aside.

5. In the same French saucepan over medium-low heat, melt the butter and sweat the shallots until soft, about 3 minutes. Add the lardons and apple, cooking for a further 3 to 4 minutes. Set aside.

6. In a different saucepan, combine the lobster sauce with the crème fraîche, bring to a simmer over medium-high heat, and reduce until thick, about 5 minutes. Add the lobster meat to the sauce, reduce the heat to medium-low,

and poach gently for 2 to 3 minutes before stirring in the Calvados.

7. Return the reserved lardons and apple mixture to the sauce, stirring gently but well to coat the lobster. Adjust the seasoning with salt and pepper now, adding a splash of Calvados or vinegar as needed. Should the sauce look too thick, thin it out with a little water.

8. Serve in a beautiful dish, topped with chervil, shavings of truffle (if using), and the reserved shell of the head. Serve alongside Dulse Bagged Potatoes (page 126).

You may attempt to flambé!

Pithivier de Perdrix (Partridge Pie)

Serves 6

Here in Quebec, wild game can be hunted but not sold for commercial use. So any game we get tends to be farmed, but the partridges we source are actually delicious, in part because they've retained the texture of wild meat. In a nod to tradition, partridges are always sold as a pair, or brace, as it's called . . . and should, ahem, a country gentleman pop into the restaurant to treat us to some fresh game birds for our personal consumption, the partridges would be in a brace.

For the filling

¼ cup (80 g) pickling salt

1 tablespoon black peppercorns

1 tablespoon chopped fresh thyme

1 brace oven-ready partridges, about 10 ounces (300 g) each

8 cups (2 l) duck fat

1 pound (454 g) fresh pork belly, skin off, cut into ½-inch (1-cm) cubes

For the shallot compote

8 shallots, thinly sliced

3 tablespoons brunoised red beet (1 small beet diced in ⅛-inch [3-mm] cubes)

1 teaspoon sherry vinegar, plus more for finishing the shallot compote

⅔ cup (150 ml) port

Salt and black pepper

1 teaspoon red currant jelly

2 tablespoons cultured butter, plus more for finishing the compote

8 peeled chestnuts (look for the vacuum-packed kind), coarsely chopped

Chicken stock, as needed, for stretching the compote

For the dough

2.2 pounds (1 kg) puff pastry, rolled to ¼-inch (6-mm) thinness and cut into one 10-inch (25-cm) disk and a 12-inch (30-cm) disk, chilled

1 egg yolk whisked with 2 tablespoons cold water for the egg wash

To serve

1 small black truffle (optional)

1. Mix the pickling salt, peppercorns, and thyme together in a small bowl, then rub the spice mixture all over the partridges. Transfer to a container, cover, and refrigerate for 2 hours.

2. Preheat the oven to 300°F (180°C).

3. In a large Dutch oven, melt the duck fat over medium-high heat.

4. Place the partridge and pork belly in the pot and cover. Transfer to the oven and confit for about 2 hours: the bubbles in the fat shouldn't be more intense than the ones you see in a glass of ginger ale on your bedside table. If they are, reduce the thermostat of your ill-functioning oven.

5. While the meat is slow-cooking away, make the shallot compote. In a medium saucepan over medium heat, sweat the shallots and beets in a few spoons of duck fat stolen from the confit pot. Cook until fully translucent and on the verge of caramelization, about 10 minutes. Add the vinegar and port and, still over medium heat, reduce the amount of liquid by two-thirds, 13 to 15 minutes. Season with salt and pepper to taste, being generous with the pepper. Stir in the jelly, followed by the butter. Set aside.

6. After 2 hours, check the meat for doneness: when poked, it shouldn't bounce. Strain, reserving the fat for future use (when you're cooking paleo for your CrossFit friend if he hasn't dumped you for new CrossFit friends).

7. Working on a plate or small tray, shred the meats, feeling carefully for bones—just like that time you made Lièvre à la Royale. Discard the bones and reserve the pulled meat.

8. In a medium bowl, combine the meat, chopped chestnuts, and half of the shallot compote, mixing well. The filling should taste deep and supple: add salt, pepper, vinegar, and/or →

a bit of butter to attain pitch-perfect flavor. Let the mixture cool.

9. Line a sheet pan with parchment paper. Lay the larger dough disk down on the parchment, then spoon the filling in the center of the circle, leaving a 1-inch (2.5-cm) margin all around. Brush the border with egg wash (avoid brushing the sides of the dough as this will inhibit the even puffing of the dough during cooking), then lay the remaining dough disk over the top. Press down gently around the perimeter of the dough to encourage the seal.

10. Using a sharp knife, score the top of the pie in a circular, decorative motif. Next, score around the edges in straight lines. Brush the pie with egg wash (again, avoiding the sides of the pie),

and refrigerate for 1 hour until very well chilled.

11. Preheat the oven to 425°F (220°C).

12. Brush the pie once more with egg wash, and bake for 35 to 45 minutes until the filling is olfactorily arousing and the pastry is puffed and golden brown.

13. Serve with the remaining shallot compote (which can be stretched with stock) and under a generous shaving of truffles (if using).

Notes Find a butcher that specializes in game to order the partridge. Duck fat is more readily available.

Count on 2 hours for marinating the partridge and another 2 hours for cooking it.

Crêpes Vonnassiennes

Makes eight 4-inch
(10-cm) crêpes

You will need

Nonstick frying pan

1 pound (454 g) lukewarm mashed russet potatoes, salted but no butter or milk added

2 large eggs, separated, plus 1 large egg white

3 tablespoons heavy cream (35 percent butterfat)

3 tablespoons all-purpose flour

Salt and white pepper

Canola oil for frying

Like a bribe of a sticker book at the grocery store, this is the X factor that keeps your kids eating.

1. Once your mashed potatoes are lukewarm, transfer them to a large mixing bowl.

2. In a medium bowl, whip the 3 egg whites by hand until slightly stiff.

3. Mix the 2 yolks with the cream in a small bowl, then stir into the potatoes with a spatula. Sprinkle in the flour and mix gently.

4. Gently fold in the egg whites, then check the seasoning for salt and white pepper.

5. Pour 1 to 2 tablespoons oil into a nonstick frying pan, and warm over medium-high heat. Cook the crêpes in batches, dolloping a generous spoonful of batter per crêpe into the pan, leaving space around each crêpe. Cook until golden brown, flipping the crêpes after 2 minutes. They should puff up and have that nice hazelnut ring around the edge. This won't happen if your pan is not hot enough, so you may have to adjust the heat upward of medium-high. Cook for another minute or two, then remove the crêpes from the pan.

6. Enjoy immediately (or with Paupiettes de Saumon au Cerfeuil, page 135).

Paupiettes de Saumon au Cerfeuil

Serves 2

You will need

French-looking baking dish

Serve salmon these days and you can expect stares of disapproval like you would get driving a monster truck through Manhattan with the windows rolled down, three kids with no seat belts on the front bench, and a cigarette planted in the middle of your sunburned face—not cool. But those of us fortunate enough to have experienced salmon fishing in the rivers of Gaspé or off the coast of British Columbia will understand: wild-caught salmon, the good kind (not the sick, sea lice–stricken kind), is a wonderful fish. At Joe Beef, we serve Pacific line-caught salmon when it's available—sockeye, coho, king—prepared with white mushrooms, chervil, and white wine. We suggest Crêpes Vonnassiennes (page 133) as a garnish, a simple potato pancake from Vonnas, France, brought into the limelight by the now-often-underestimated Georges Blanc.

---

2 tablespoons chopped leeks

6 tablespoons (85 g) unsalted butter (includes 2 tablespoons, softened)

¼ cup (20 g) finely chopped mushrooms (chanterelles are great, but button mushrooms are just fine)

½ cup (120 ml) dry Riesling

¼ cup (40 g) blanched spinach leaves, squeezed dry, chopped finely (about 1½ cups/60 g raw)

2 tablespoons chopped fresh chervil

1 tablespoon chopped fresh flat-leaf parsley

Salt and white pepper

Two 5-ounce (150-g) tail-end wild salmon fillets, skin removed

Two 12-inch (30-cm) squares caul fat (about 2.5 ounces/75 g total)

¼ cup (60 ml) heavy cream (35 percent butterfat)

Squeeze of lemon

1 tablespoon dulse seaweed, rehydrated in warm water, then squeezed and coarsely chopped

1. Preheat the oven to 450°F (230°C).

2. In a small pan over medium heat, sweat the leeks in 2 tablespoons of the butter, until translucent but not colored, about 4 minutes. Add the mushrooms and cook until soft and not sizzling, another 4 minutes. Pour in ¼ cup (60 ml) of the wine and reduce cautiously, over medium heat, until almost dry, 5 to 6 minutes.

3. Away from the heat, add the spinach, chervil, and parsley to the pan, seasoning with salt and pepper to taste. Spread the mixture onto a plate and place in the freezer to cool quickly.

4. Lay the pieces of salmon flat on a work surface, with the "skin side" (now removed) facing down, and season them lightly. Divide the filling in two, and spread it out to cover each piece of salmon. Fold the tail of the salmon over the filling, as if closing a book, pressing down firmly with your hand to have it stay put.

5. Spread the 2 pieces of caul fat out on your work surface and rub about

1 tablespoon of the softened butter over the pieces. Wrap your salmon pockets neatly, pressing the butter evenly. Use scissors to trim any excess/unruly caul fat.

6. Nestle the paupiettes in a baking dish, pour in the remaining ¼ cup (60 ml) wine, and roast for 7 minutes, or until the paupiettes look pink and the caul fat is translucent.

7. Pour the cooking liquid from the dish into a small saucepan, and cover the paupiettes with foil.

8. Over medium heat, reduce the wine and salmon juices until almost dry, add the cream and the remaining 2 tablespoons butter, giving it a brief boil to bring the sauce together. Stir in the lemon and dulse, and adjust the seasoning to taste. You should have ½ cup (120 ml) sauce.

9. Serve the paupiettes with this seaweed sauce, accompanied by Crêpes Vonnassiennes (page 133).

Microwaved Foie Gras

Serves 8 to 10

~~~

You will need

Digital scale

Microwave oven
(set at 900 watts cooking power)

Dish to fit the foie, such as the
classic Pyrex

Legend has it that radar men, back in the day, would lay their stews on the radar's transmitter coils, and that by lunchtime the electromagnetic microwaves from the coil would have heated their daube just nicely. It's not clear to us why the microwave oven failed at carving its niche among the thermal circulators and the nitrous oxide canisters in the hallways of modernist cuisine. As a former bachelor and a gastronome, Fred can attest that the humble microwave cooking device lives up to a few gastronomical cooking challenges beyond the sorrow-filled theme of "cooking for one" manuals!

For the cure (good for 1 kg foie gras)

14 grams kosher salt

8 grams sugar

4 grams freshly ground white pepper

2 grams Prague Powder #1 or Prague Powder #2

1 whole duck foie gras (generally around 1½ pounds or 650 g)

2 tablespoons good-quality sweet white wine, like a Monbazillac or John Bil's favorite, Sauternes

1 black truffle, preferably from Maison Pébeyre, sliced thin

½ teaspoon fleur de sel

Freshly ground black pepper

I. Calculate how much cure you will need based on the size of foie you purchased (see Notes). Prepare the full amount of cure, then weigh out what you actually need.

2. In a large Ziploc bag, combine the foie, the cure, and sweet wine. Make sure you extract as much air from the bag as possible before sealing it. Refrigerate overnight.

3. Remove the foie from the fridge and let it come to room temperature for 1½ hours.

4. Remove from the bag and pat dry with paper towels, then place in a Pyrex-type glass cooking vessel: the foie should be nestled in snugly. Cover tightly with plastic wrap.

5. Microwave at 900 watts in 30-second bursts, with 30 seconds of rest between each burst, for a total of 5 cooking bursts. The foie will have rendered a good amount of fat. Drain it cautiously in a small bowl and save the fat for the next step.

6. Cover with sliced truffles, then spoon the reserved fat over the truffles, and sprinkle the fleur de sel and pepper generously all over. Wrap the bowl in a double layer of plastic wrap, pushing down gently and carefully to expel any air and flatten the foie lightly. Refrigerate for 5 days for maximum gastronomical goodness. Serve simply, on toasted bread, or on the Partridge Pie (page 131) or on the Moose Stew (page 279).

Notes While the foie gras does indeed get cooked in a microwave, it will taste its absolute best if you patiently let it cure overnight before cooking, then let it rest for at least 5 days after cooking. Your wait will be rewarded.

The amount of cure (28 g) is given for 1 kg (1,000 g) of foie gras. To calculate how much cure you'll need, this is the magic formula: $x = (y \times 28) \div 1,000$. X is the amount of cure needed, y is the weight in grams of your foie gras. So, for example, a 650-gram lobe of foie would call for 18 grams of cure.

MICROWAVED FOIE GRAS

FRED MORIN

Gâteau Renversé aux Truffes

Serves 8

You will need

One 8-inch (20-cm) nonstick springform pan, buttered and lined with an 8-inch (20-cm) parchment circle

¼ cup (60 ml) pear nectar

2 tablespoons butter, plus some for greasing the mold and ⅓ cup (80 ml), melted

2 tablespoons runny honey

2 tablespoons cocoa nibs

Six to eight 0.7-ounce (20-g) truffles, the cheapest you can find, brushed and cleaned and cut into ¼-inch- (6-mm-) thick rounds

3 large eggs

¾ cup (160 g) raw sugar

Pinch of salt

⅓ cup (85 g) cashew butter

¾ cup (75 g) almond flour plus ⅓ cup (55 g) buckwheat flour, combined and sifted

2 tablespoons XO Cognac

1 tablespoon flaxseeds

This is the cake Lil Yachty would wear if it were a piece of bling. Rest assured that (aside from when we were testing this recipe) we do not eat ostentatious victuals like this ever, but if the bomb were to be dropped, and the bunker was full of canned truffles, we wouldn't hesitate for a second. The cake itself is pretty good, even without the truffles. Also, serving it with small pieces of seared foie gras is not bad.

1. Preheat the oven to 325°F (160°C).

2. In a small pan, combine the pear nectar, 2 tablespoons of the butter, the honey, and cocoa nibs. Over medium-high heat, bring to a simmer, then reduce by half until syrupy, about 10 minutes.

3. Add the truffles to the syrup, reducing the heat to low, and cook gently for a minute or two. Pour into the prepared springform pan, arranging the truffle slices and cocoa nibs manually to cover the bottom of the pan evenly. Freeze the pan for 10 to 15 minutes to set the syrup.

4. In a mixing bowl, whisk the eggs and sugar until pale and frothy, about 2 minutes, then add the salt and stir in the cashew butter.

5. Using a spatula, stir in the almond-buckwheat flour mixture, followed by the melted butter and the Cognac.

6. Gently pour the cake batter into the chilled springform pan—the batter will be fairly runny so should cover the truffles easily and completely. Sprinkle with the flaxseeds. Place on a sheet pan and transfer to the oven.

7. Bake for 40 minutes, until golden brown and a knife or cake tester inserted into the center comes out clean. Transfer to a rack to cool for 10 minutes before releasing the mold.

8. Lay a plate onto the flaxseed side of the cake, then flip the springform base over. Lift the bottom of the springform pan off slowly, then peel the parchment off if it didn't come off with the base. Rearrange any errant, glistening truffles.

Omelette Soufflée au Kirsch, Compote de Griottes "Parc Vinet"

Serves 2

——～～——

You will need

Nonstick frying pan

Flambéing tools: 2 skewers and propane torch

Fred used to own a MINI Cooper and remembers driving back from the garden nursery with a little cherry tree sitting on top of him. Now there is a wall of jars in the basement cellar, filled with our own delicious preserved Montmorency cherries, or *griottes,* as the French call them.

We have always been proponents of Breakfast for Dinner, so much so we almost had an entire chapter about it in Book One. This is the perfect Sunday dinner: kids love a flambé, and parents love any excuse to use kirsch.

For the cherry compote

4 cups (600 g) pitted sour cherries, 12 pits crushed and wrapped in a cloth

1 cup (200 g) sugar

2 leaves from the cherry tree

For the omelet

4 large farm-fresh free-range eggs, separated

½ vanilla bean, seeds scraped into 2 tablespoons sugar

Pinch of salt

3 tablespoons unsalted butter

To serve

Confectioners' sugar for dusting

2 to 4 tablespoons (30 to 60 ml) kirsch for flambéing

I. Combine the cherries, pits, sugar, and leaves in a bowl. Refrigerate, covered, overnight.

2. Discard pits and leaves. Transfer the pitted cherries to a saucepan, bring to a boil, then simmer for 30 minutes. Transfer to a glass jar and refrigerate until needed.

3. Preheat the oven to 300°F (130°C). Place a nice serving plate in the oven to warm while you make the omelet.

4. In a large bowl, whisk the egg yolks and vanilla sugar until pale and frothy, about 2 minutes. In a separate bowl or using your stand mixer, proceed to whisk the egg whites and a pinch of salt to stiff peaks, 3 to 4 minutes at medium speed, if using the mixer. Gently fold the egg whites into the yolk mixture.

5. In a nonstick frying pan over medium heat, melt 1 to 2 tablespoons of the butter. Spoon the eggs into the pan carefully, spreading them evenly into a circle. Reduce the heat to low and cook slowly until set, about 3 minutes. Note the "filling" will be puffy, warm but still very airy. That's perfect.

6. Remove the warmed plate from the oven.

7. Dollop a spoonful or three of the cherry compote into the center of the omelet and fold the omelet over itself. Carefully transfer to the warm plate.

8. Dust with confectioners' sugar, then use the torch to heat the skewers to red-hot and make your faux grill marks.

9. At the table, pour kirsch around the omelet and light it on fire.

Notes If you have two metal skewers and a propane torch lying around, you can pull off these fictitious but nonetheless thrilling grill marks. Have someone work on heating the skewers until absolutely red-hot while you cook the omelet.

If it's not stealing-sour-cherries-from-your-neighbor's-tree season, replace fresh cherries with 4 cups (600 g) frozen cherries.

This recipe requires prep the night before.

Bavarian Cream à la Doris

Makes 2 quarts (2 l)
Bavarian cream

You will need

Ice bath

Instant-read thermometer

Handsome crystal bowl

My beloved grandmother, Margot Cloutier Hayfield, and my mother, Doris, both made this dessert every holiday dinner. They used pineapples from cans, and we had a big beautiful Christofle bowl that I felt as a child was kind of the nicest thing we owned. One day it broke, then there was no more *bavarois*. A few years later I mentioned how much I loved that dessert and what a shame it was that one of our family traditions had ended; the next year there was a new bowl, and it was back. Bliss.

Fred in his infinite kindness to me and his ability to remember even the tiniest details of anything I've told him over our twenty-five-year career, made this version for the book. That said, it's also highly annoying to have someone close remember every detail of everything you might have said at one time.

—D.M.

4 cups (1 l) whole milk

6 chamomile tea bags or ⅓ cup dried chamomile flowers

8 sheets (0.7 ounce/21 g) leaf gelatin

8 large egg yolks

⅔ cup (150 ml) clear, mild honey

2 cups (500 ml) heavy cream (35 percent butterfat)

To serve

Candied angelica stems and violets

Glacée cherries; 2 oranges, peeled and sliced

Oatmeal cookies (optional— never optional)

I. In a heavy-bottomed pot, bring the milk to a simmer, then add the tea bags or flowers. Cover and remove from the heat. Let sit for 10 to 15 minutes, or until the milk tastes of chamomile.

2. Place the gelatin sheets, one at a time (so that they don't all stick together), in a large bowl of cold water. Let them soften, about 10 minutes.

3. Strain the milk and return to the saucepan. Bring the milk to a simmer. Squeeze the gelatin to remove all excess water, then whisk the gelatin into the hot milk. Reduce the heat to the lowest setting.

4. In a large bowl, whisk the egg yolks and honey until pale. Ladle a small amount of hot milk into the egg mixture and whisk. Continue this process, one ladleful at a time, to temper the egg mixture so that it doesn't curdle, until all the infused milk has been incorporated.

5. Clean your milk saucepan (so that the custard doesn't scorch as it cooks) and return the chamomile custard to the saucepan. Set up a clean large bowl over an ice bath next to the stove.

6. Over medium-low heat, cook the custard, stirring constantly, until the temperature reaches 180°F (82°C) on an instant-read thermometer (there is a trick to knowing the custard is just

right involving the trail it leaves on the back of a spoon, but that never worked for us). *Any hotter and it will curdle.* As soon as it hits 180°F, pour the custard into the bowl set over the ice bath. Stir a few times to start the cooling process.

7. In a large bowl or using a standing mixer, whip the cream to medium peaks and refrigerate, until ready to use.

8. When the chamomile custard has reached room temperature (about 30 minutes) and before the gelatin starts to set, stir in the whipped cream in batches and pour into the mold of your choosing, in our case, Doris's very own crystal bowl. Refrigerate for 4 to 5 hours to set.

9. Garnish the top to make it pretty with candied fruits. Each portion of Bavarian cream can be served with an oatmeal cookie.

Mousse au Chocolat, Chantilly à la Praline Rose

Makes 1½ quarts (1.5 l)

You will need

Instant-read thermometer

Pretty bowl for the mousse

We have seen mousses swoop in, all guns a-blazing, to fill that airy void between foamy layers of tropical fruit gels and food-cost-friendly cakes. Then they retreat, leaving in their wake a trail of *crémeux* and *petits pots*. In a world where all expenses are accounted for and wine is too often poured to right under the line, putting a big soup tureen full of chocolate mousse down on the table is an awesome gesture of sharing and generosity.

Serve the mousse with some Chantilly with pink praline on the side. Pralines roses are a typically Lyonnais confection, almonds in a coating of pink sugar—simple enough, but when you bake them into something or, in this case, when you crush them and mix them into whipped cream, the cream will turn a nice pink, part confident-man-shirt pink, part Molly Ringwald–teenage room pink. Since this is a very simple recipe, spend the time and money to source the best chocolate, eggs, and dairy: you'll taste the difference.

For the chocolate mousse

2 ½ cups (350 g) 64% chocolate (pistoles or broken into large pieces)

1¾ cups (450 ml) heavy cream (35 percent butterfat)

1⅓ cups (300 ml) crème anglaise (see below)

For the crème anglaise

½ cup (120 ml) whole milk

½ cup (120 ml) heavy cream (35 percent butterfat)

4 large egg yolks

1 tablespoon plus 2 teaspoons (25 g) sugar

½ teaspoon instant coffee

To serve

2 cups (500 ml) heavy cream (35 percent butterfat)

2 tablespoons confectioners' sugar

½ cup (90 g) chopped pink praline

1. For the chocolate mousse: Manually whisk (or using a stand mixer, whip) the cream until soft peaks form. Set aside.

2. Make the crème anglaise: In a small saucepan over medium heat, combine the milk and cream and bring to a simmer.

3. In the meantime, in a medium bowl, whisk the egg yolks and sugar until pale. Whisk in the coffee powder.

4. Pour a small amount of the hot milk and cream into the egg yolk mixture and stir, to temper. Continue whisking in the hot milk and cream, working gradually until all the milk mixture has been incorporated.

5. Put the chocolate in a large bowl.

6. Return the custard base to the saucepan and cook over medium-low heat, stirring constantly, until the temperature reaches 180°F (82°C), 3 to 4 minutes. As soon as the custard reaches 180°F, pour it over the chocolate pieces. Using a spatula, stir until well combined and the chocolate is smooth.

7. Gently stir in the softly whipped cream from step 1. Pour into a mold of your choosing and refrigerate for 2 to 3 hours.

8. To serve: Combine the heavy cream with the confectioners' sugar in a bowl and whip until medium peaks form. Stir in the crushed pink praline. Transfer to a pretty bowl and refrigerate until ready to serve alongside the mousse. Let people help themselves.

Note You can source pink praline on Amazon.com.

Four

Liverpool House

Nestled in the middle, between Joe Beef and Vin Papillon, is Liverpool House. This geographic reality applies metaphorically, as it is indeed the middle child.

Liverpool is the good son. The quiet one. The smart one who always does his homework. The one on time and who does not cause any ripples. We don't stay up late worrying about him. We don't ask him to check in. If anything goes awry, we will hear it quickly and directly from our weekly locals, guys like Bobby Sontag and Lenny Lighter.

Vin Papillon is the third child and the baby. She is feminine and treated as a suck; shiny, newish, "She's so cute!" people will say. And they're right, she is. But that's not where LPH is at. LPH doesn't want to get noticed, and if you say something cute, he might roll his eyes.

Like a pub or an old friend, Liverpool House hasn't really changed. Not since the first book, not since ever. It has a bustling bar where there is always someone you know, and most nights four of the eight stools are taken by industry folk. A TV is tucked away in one corner for watching *Nos Glorieux* Canadiens play. It's a great place to be during a blizzard, which happens to be all of the time. In the summer, there is a shaded terrace with potted plants and overgrown trees and diners eat BBQ. If anyone is looking for me, LPH is the first stop. Joe Beef has, over the years, become popular with the traveling dining crowd, and many nights I don't know anyone there. So Liverpool House has become my chosen companion.

The building is a beautiful Victorian. It has a double entrance, and from the outside it looks like two side-by-side soda-pop shops. The floors are a Canadian

National Railway green. It is full of Peter Hoffer truck paintings, a couple of cedar canoes, an old fridge, maple benches, a framed picture of a Nike box stuffed with cash, and has always had the feel of a simple Laurentian cottage (albeit one of hoarders). It is perhaps the most Montreal of the restaurants, which is to say it is Waspy, Jewish, French, and Italian all at the same time.

Ari Schor is the LPH chef. In spring and summer, the menu is jammed with smoked fish and French BBQ, and then come October, you would think you're eating in Warsaw as the menu is full of stuffed cabbage, pierogis, pelmeni, and kielbasa. But

somehow it all works, and that's because of Ari.

Born in Buenos Aires, Ari was raised in Winnipeg. In 2012, after reading the first Joe Beef cookbook, he promptly left Manitoba and applied for a job with us. Thank god for that. "My idea for the place is that you could eat here on a weekly basis and still feel healthy. I grew up eating Argentine peasant food: grilled meats, cooked vegetables, lots of condiments, Spanish and Italian accents. Every Sunday my family would host a BBQ atop a very long table and you would eat with your hands, and as the hours went by, so did the bottles."

LPH has also been the test kitchen for many young chefs, managers, and owners. Our friends Emma Cardarelli and Ryan Gray opened Liverpool House and worked there for years before opening their own Italian restaurant, Nora Gray.

Omar Zabuair, who now owns Le Coq de l'Est, gave it his own spin for a good stretch (you can see his Dungeness Crab Curry on page 181). Currently James Simpkins and the very loved Chris Morgan, our two managers, run it as their own restaurant, and we're thrilled with that.

—D.M.

Ari's Lamb Ribs and Eggplant

Serves 4

—~~—

You will need

Outdoor grill or indoor grill pan

This is Ari's brainchild, so we'll let him tell it: "To satisfy my ego, I wanted to make a wicked press of lamb belly from the whole lamb. It's a very old-school French technique. I tried ordering the bellies from Boucherie de Tours (our butcher at Atwater Market), but they sent me the ribs by accident. I played with the method a bit and settled on the recipe below. Charred, they remind me of the lamb asados we ate in my hometown of Ushuaia."

For the lamb ribs

1 tablespoon tomato paste

1 tablespoon fresh lemon juice

¼ teaspoon ground cumin

½ teaspoon black pepper

5 fresh oregano sprigs, chopped

2 garlic cloves, minced

2 tablespoons Fermented Chile Butter (page 159), melted

2 racks lamb ribs, 1 pound (454 g) each

2 teaspoons salt

For the eggplant

2 tablespoons chicken fat

1 large eggplant

Salt and black pepper

For the sauce

2 shallots, thinly sliced

¼ cup (60 ml) dry white wine

¼ cup (60 ml) dry sherry

1 teaspoon black peppercorns

½ teaspoon mustard seeds

½ teaspoon coriander seeds

4 fresh thyme sprigs, chopped

1 cup (240 ml) lamb stock

1 cup (240 ml) veal stock

For the garnish

2 cups (490 g) full-fat plain yogurt

2 tablespoons chopped fresh mint

2 tablespoons chopped fresh cilantro

2 tablespoons chopped fresh flat-leaf parsley

1. For the ribs: Mix the tomato paste, lemon juice, cumin, black pepper, and oregano. Combine the minced garlic with the melted chile butter, then stir into the tomato paste mixture.

2. Season the lamb ribs with salt and rub thoroughly with the marinade. Wrap tightly in plastic wrap, followed by aluminum foil. Refrigerate overnight.

3. Next day, preheat the oven to 300°F (150°C). Bake the ribs on a sheet pan for 4 hours, or until very tender. Set aside.

4. Increase the oven temperature to 400°F (200°C).

5. For the eggplant: Melt the chicken fat. Peel the eggplant from top to bottom using a vegetable peeler. Brush the eggplant with the melted chicken fat, and season with salt and pepper. The chicken fat helps the seasoning stick. →

6. Place the eggplant on a sheet pan and roast for 18 to 20 minutes, or until it begins to break down. Allow to cool to room temperature.

7. For the sauce: Combine the shallots with the white wine, sherry, peppercorns, mustard seeds, coriander seeds, and thyme in a small pot. Reduce by three-quarters over medium-high heat, about 12 minutes. Add the meat stocks and reduce by half, another 15 minutes. Strain through a fine-mesh sieve and keep warm.

8. Unwrap the ribs and cut into individual bones with a sharp knife. Turn on the grill to medium-high heat. Char the ribs thoroughly, 4 to 5 minutes. (These could also be seared indoors on a grill pan.) Season with salt and pepper once they come off the grill.

9. While charring the ribs, cut the eggplant in half lengthwise, then into large semicircles about 1 inch (2.5 cm) thick. Once the ribs come off the grill, char the eggplant, a couple of minutes on each side.

10. Spoon the yogurt onto the bottom of a plate, pile the ribs onto the yogurt, drizzle the sauce on the ribs, and scatter the herbs all over the place. Eat with your hands.

Notes These ribs need to marinate overnight. They also grill up even better if they've been refrigerated and firmed up after their four-hour slow braise in the oven. Plan accordingly.

Don't worry about keeping the ribs wrapped in plastic and aluminum foil for their long, slow oven braise—they will steam in their own marinade and juices, and still stay moist. Think of it as a no-fuss/makeshift sous vide!

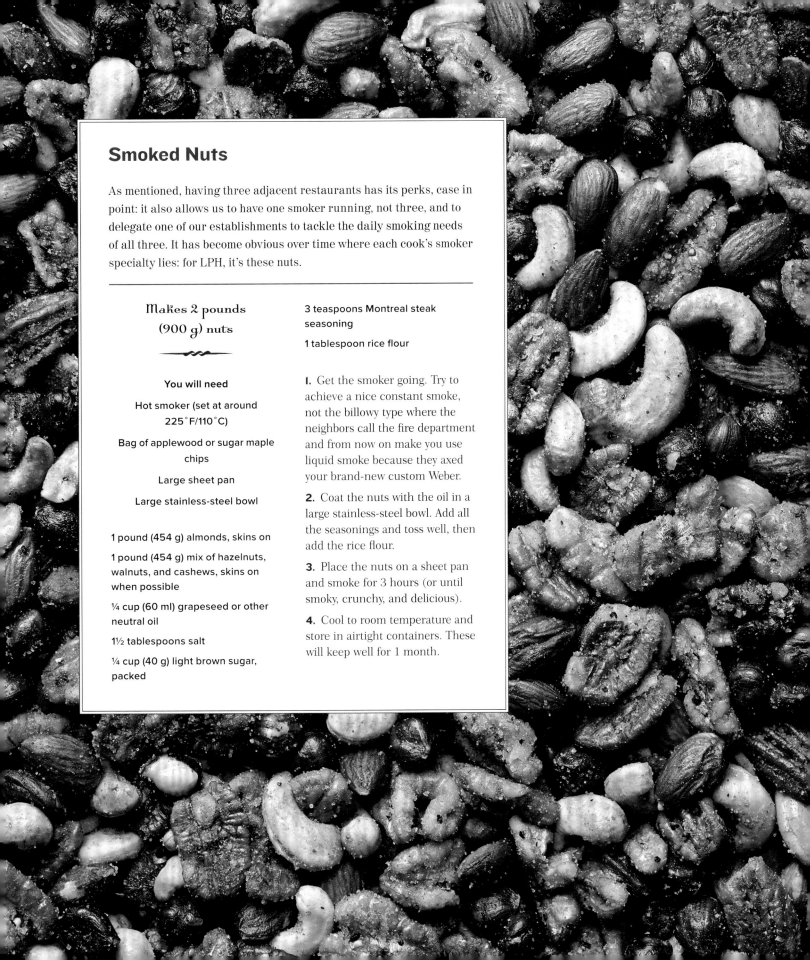

Smoked Nuts

As mentioned, having three adjacent restaurants has its perks, case in point: it also allows us to have one smoker running, not three, and to delegate one of our establishments to tackle the daily smoking needs of all three. It has become obvious over time where each cook's smoker specialty lies: for LPH, it's these nuts.

Makes 2 pounds (900 g) nuts

You will need

Hot smoker (set at around 225°F/110°C)

Bag of applewood or sugar maple chips

Large sheet pan

Large stainless-steel bowl

1 pound (454 g) almonds, skins on

1 pound (454 g) mix of hazelnuts, walnuts, and cashews, skins on when possible

¼ cup (60 ml) grapeseed or other neutral oil

1½ tablespoons salt

¼ cup (40 g) light brown sugar, packed

3 teaspoons Montreal steak seasoning

1 tablespoon rice flour

1. Get the smoker going. Try to achieve a nice constant smoke, not the billowy type where the neighbors call the fire department and from now on make you use liquid smoke because they axed your brand-new custom Weber.

2. Coat the nuts with the oil in a large stainless-steel bowl. Add all the seasonings and toss well, then add the rice flour.

3. Place the nuts on a sheet pan and smoke for 3 hours (or until smoky, crunchy, and delicious).

4. Cool to room temperature and store in airtight containers. These will keep well for 1 month.

Buffalo Bison Tartare

Serves 6

You will need

Very sharp knife for cutting the meat
or meat grinder that's been frozen
for 2 hours prior

2 stainless-steel bowls, one filled with ice,
the other resting atop the ice

1¼ pounds (570 g) fresh bison meat,
preferably rump or sirloin

½ pound (225 g) chicken skin
(ask your butcher ahead of time to
save you some or steal from bone-in
skin-on thighs)

Kosher salt and black pepper

1 small shallot, minced

1 teaspoon capers, drained and minced

1 whole kosher dill pickle, diced small

2 tablespoons minced celery heart

2 tablespoons olive oil

1 teaspoon Dijon mustard

2 teaspoons ketchup

4 teaspoons (20 ml) fresh lemon juice

¼ cup (57 g) Fermented Chile Butter
(recipe follows), softened

To serve

4 ounces (113 g) blue cheese
(we use Bleu d'Élizabeth from Quebec,
but Stilton is also great), crumbled

Celery heart leaves, minced

Toasted bread

Montreal doesn't do wings well. Never has. So whenever we land in an American city, we go straight to a sports bar for Buffalo wings.

After a dozen oysters, along with an ice-cold beer, Liverpool House serves this farmed bison tartare. It has the same flavor profile of your favorite basket of Buffalo wings. This dish is made for watching hockey.

---

1. Preheat the oven to 325°F (160°C). Set up the cold bowl/ice bowl combination next to your cutting board.

2. Work in small batches to dice the meat: cut thin layers, then cut sticks that you rotate 90 degrees to cut into small dices. Transfer the diced meat to the cold bowl.

3. Stretch the chicken skins out on a sheet pan lined with parchment paper—the skins can be close together, but not overlapping. Lay a sheet of parchment paper on top of the skins. Top the parchment with another sheet pan. Bake for 45 minutes, or until the skin is golden brown and crispy. Season immediately with ½ teaspoon salt and a dash of black pepper, and allow the skin to cool, uncovered, on the pan placed on a cooling rack for 30 minutes. Crumble the skins by hand or chop them to crumbs with a knife. Transfer to a paper towel on a sheet pan, uncovered, while assembling the rest of the dish.

4. Combine the shallots, capers, and diced pickle in a small bowl.

5. Season the minced meat with 1 tablespoon kosher salt and ¼ teaspoon black pepper. Stir in the shallots/capers/pickle mix, the minced celery heart, as well as the olive oil, mustard, ketchup, and lemon juice. Finish with the chile butter. Transfer to a serving bowl and garnish with crumbled chicken skin, blue cheese, and minced celery leaves. Serve with toasted bread.

Fermented Chile Butter

Makes 1 pound (454 g)

You will need

1-quart (1-l) widemouthed mason jar, sterilized

Cheesecloth and butcher's twine or elastic band

1 pound (454 g) fresh cherry bomb or red jalapeño peppers, washed

1 tablespoon kosher salt

1 quart (1 l) bottled water

1 pound (454 g) unsalted butter

This butter applies to almost anything where a bit of heat is needed. There's a shit ton of applications, really: mixed in with a tartare (see opposite), as a hot sauce on the lamb ribs (see page 155), mixed in with potatoes (roasted or not), or brushed on a good piece of fish.

I. Slice the peppers in half lengthwise and toss in a bowl with the salt. Very carefully place all the peppers and seeds inside the mason jar—once the peppers are salted, they typically start to release pepper "fumes" into the air, which can make people cough. Let the peppers sit in the jar at room temperature for 1 hour.

2. Cover the peppers with the bottled water (to ensure sterilization). Cover the top of the jar with cheesecloth, tying it around the mouth of the jar with twine or an elastic, and move to a cool, dark place. Allow the peppers to ferment for 2 weeks. They will become mushy, and the water will turn cloudy. If any white mold rises to the surface, skim it off. If the mold is not white, throw the contents out and restart the process. (Once fermented, the peppers will keep, covered, for up to 1 month refrigerated.)

3. To make the butter: Carefully extract the peppers from the liquid. Combine with the butter in a small saucepan, and cook over low heat until the butter clarifies (it will look clear but with a reddish hue and have a strong pepper aroma). Strain and use immediately, or store, covered, in the refrigerator for 1 week (or freezer for 1 month).

Note The peppers need 2 weeks to ferment before you can make the butter.

Horse Ceviche

Serves 4

———— ～ ————

You will need

Very sharp knife to slice the meat.
Alternatively, you can freeze the meat
for 30 minutes prior to slicing to help
cut very thin slices.

Mandoline for the onion and carrot

1 pound (454 g) horse fillet

½ teaspoon sea salt

3 tablespoons fresh lime juice

1½ tablespoons olive oil

½ red onion, sliced into very thin rings
(use a mandoline)

1 small carrot, sliced very thin

1 tablespoon Pickled Jalapeños
(page 165)

1 head Little Gem lettuce, leaves
separated

To serve

½ cup (30 g) fresh cilantro leaves
with (short) stems

1 lime wedge

What's the one thing that's never been ceviched?
Voilà.

---

1. Slice the horse fillet with a very sharp knife: you want it very, very thin.

2. Place the slices in a shallow bowl, and dress with the salt, lime juice, and olive oil. Refrigerate for 30 minutes.

3. Lift the slices of meat out of the marinade (but do not discard the marinade). Roll them into small cigarlike rolls and arrange on a small platter.

4. Toss the onion, carrot, pickled jalapeños, and lettuce leaves in the marinade. Adjust the seasoning with salt, olive oil, and more lime juice as required.

5. Garnish the horse rolls with the vegetables, finishing with the cilantro and a wedge of lime.

Note Depending on where you live, sourcing fresh horsemeat could prove tricky. Ask your butcher for recommendations.

Artichokes Bravas

Serves 6

You will need

Blender or immersion blender

Deep fryer or heavy-bottomed, tall-sided pot

Deep-frying thermometer

Custom *Steal Your Face* plate (kidding, but that's what we use)

In the last five years, our customers have definitely changed how they eat. It used to be: appetizer, main course, dessert. Or a pasta followed by a piece of meat and one bottle. Today, it's all about first courses shared among friends, "crushing" bottles or trying many offerings by the glass, and just ordering three or four appetizers total. Artichokes Bravas is one such appetizer.

For the Brava sauce

3 red bell peppers

2 pounds (900 g) very ripe tomatoes

Salt and pepper

1 small onion, cut into thin disks

4 garlic cloves, thinly sliced

3 tablespoons sherry vinegar

1 tablespoon Pickled Jalapeños (page 165)

1 tablespoon Spanish pimentón

¼ cup (60 ml) olive oil

For the artichokes

Juice of 4 lemons

12 medium artichokes

1 pound (454 g) sunchokes/ Jerusalem artichokes

4 quarts (4 l) canola oil for frying

Kosher salt and freshly ground black pepper

To serve

1 cup (220 g) your favorite aioli recipe

2 tablespoons finely chopped fresh flat-leaf parsley

Lemon wedges

1. Heat your grill to medium heat or turn on your oven broiler to high.

2. Grill or broil the red bell peppers on all sides until well charred. Transfer to a bowl and cover for 10 minutes. Peel roughly and remove the seeds. Set aside.

3. Cut the tomatoes in half, across their equator. Season their open faces with salt and pepper. Grill with the tomatoes face side up and the grill cover down, 15 to 20 minutes, or until the bottoms are charred and the faces are dry and wrinkly. Remove from the heat and allow to cool before chopping finely.

4. Grill the onion disks until charred and fragrant, about 4 minutes per side, flipping delicately.

5. Combine the red peppers, tomatoes, onion, garlic, sherry vinegar, jalapeños, and pimentón in a medium saucepan. Add the oil and simmer slowly over medium-low heat for 15 minutes. Transfer to a blender and purée. Season with salt and pepper to taste, then transfer to a small container and refrigerate.

6. For the artichokes: Combine the lemon juice with 2 quarts (2 l) cold water in a large bowl.

7. Peel off all the looser outer leaves of the artichokes until you find tender green leaves. Trim the tops and stems. With an espresso spoon, dig into the center of the artichokes and remove the hairy chokes. Place the artichokes in the acidulated water to avoid browning.

8. Heat the oil in your fryer or pot to 275°F (135°C).

9. Fry the artichokes in batches, maintaining the oil at 275°F, for 5 to 6 minutes, or until a toothpick goes through with ease and they are soft but still hold their shape. Transfer to paper towels to cool and drain. Once cool, press them down lightly until they resemble opened-up flowers.

10. Rinse the sunchokes well with water and pat them dry. Cut them in half lengthwise. Repeat the frying procedure above.

11. Increase the temperature of the oil to 365°F (185°C). →

12. Working in batches, fry the artichokes and sunchokes again until golden brown, 4 to 5 minutes. Transfer to fresh paper towels to drain. Season immediately with the salt and pepper.

13. Serve on a custom *Steal Your Face* plate with Brava sauce on the bottom and aioli and minced parsley on top, and, of course, plenty of lemon wedges.

Note Look for firm artichokes that feel heavy for their size. Avoid ones with open leaves. Bruised leaves aren't much of a problem since you trim them anyway.

Pickled Jalapeños

You will need

One 1-quart (1-l) mason jar

As Ari tells it: "Usually we have a new employee at the end of summer. The litmus test for them is to see if they can slice forty pounds of jalapeños by hand. I learned to make pickled jalapeños back home from my friend Jon Hochman, who runs a deli. Come September, we make enough to last us a whole year. They are perfect for adding heat to braises and soffritto because they retain their freshness. Perfect addition to staff sandwiches at the end of the night."

---

1 pound (454 g) jalapeño peppers (15 or so peppers), sliced into very thin rings

2 tablespoons kosher salt

½ cup (120 ml) apple cider vinegar

¼ cup (60 ml) tequila (nothing fancy)

6 garlic cloves, smashed

2 cups (475 ml) neutral oil

1. In a bowl, toss the jalapeño slices with the salt. Let them sit at room temperature for 2 hours, until the juices are expressed. Rinse and pat dry.

2. Bring the cider vinegar to a boil in a small saucepan, then pour it over the jalapeños. Add the tequila and garlic, and let sit overnight.

3. The next day, strain the jalapeños and transfer them to a clean mason jar. Leave the garlic in. Cover with the oil, and refrigerate for a few days before you start using the pickled peppers. Keep refrigerated.

Note These will need to sit overnight, so plan accordingly.

Deer Beer Belly

Serves 8

You will need

Large, inexpensive tea towel

Butcher's twine

Deep fryer

Deep-frying thermometer

We are fortunate in Quebec to have some of the best venison farms around, where the animals live in near-wilderness conditions, yet are still close enough to the city for HBO access, a juice bar, and a great brunch spot nearby.

This recipe is built on our love of puns, because what grows a beer belly better than beer, fries, pickles, and bar snacks? The size of a belly makes this the perfect dinner for a nice date with seven other people. Serve with Tater Tot Galette (page 178).

For the belly

One 6-pound (2.7-kg) deer belly

1 cup (240 ml) neutral oil for frying (if you're not using a deep fryer)

2 nice, big yellow-flesh potatoes, peeled and diced into ¼-inch (6-mm) cubes

Salt and pepper

2 tablespoons apple cider vinegar

2 pounds (900 g) basic sausage stuffing—ask your butcher for his favorite or use our Base Sausage (page 89) mixed well with 2 large whole kosher dill pickles and 3 karnatzel (Montreal smoked dried beef sausage), all cut into ¼-inch (6-mm) cubes

8 hard-boiled large eggs, peeled

For the braise

¼ cup (60 ml) grapeseed oil or other neutral oil

4 carrots, cut into 4 pieces

4 celery stalks, cut into 4 pieces

2 large yellow onions, chopped into 8 wedges

2 heads garlic

1½ tablespoons black pepper

1 tablespoon mustard powder

3 whole cloves

¼ teaspoon ground cinnamon

¼ nutmeg, grated

1 tablespoon picked fresh thyme leaves

12 bay leaves

½ cup (80 g) light brown sugar, packed

4 ounces (120 ml) bourbon

¼ cup (60 ml) apple cider vinegar

2 cans beer of your liking

8 cups (2 l) beef or veal stock or water

1. Clean out the deer belly of any excess hard fat, as it will not render in the cooking process. To remove said fat you may use CrossFit or the blade of a well-honed knife in the hands of a specialist. Place the deer belly, skin side down, on a clean counter or cutting board. The grain of the meat should be going from right to left, not top to bottom.

2. Heat the oil to optimal frying temperature, 350° F (180° C), and pat dry the potato dices. Fry them in batches until very crisp. Drain on paper towels and toss in salt and cider vinegar.

3. Cover the deer belly with the sausage mixture, leaving a clean, untouched, pure edge of meat on the "top" section of the belly of about 2 inches (5 cm). Press the fries into the sausage mix in an even fashion. Once the fries are into the sausage, make a furrow across →

the meat, from left to right, where the eggs will be nestled. Cut the apex of each egg ever so slightly so that they fit snugly in a row. Press them into their designated groove. Roll the belly from bottom to top, carefully leaving the eggs lined up. Tie 10 tight and evenly spaced knots with butcher's twine around the belly, making sure to secure the ends. Season as you would a steak, then wrap in a large, clean (unscented) tea towel, secured at both ends with twine. Let the belly set up in the fridge for at least 3 hours or overnight, if possible.

4. Preheat the oven to 425°F (220°C).

5. Place a large roasting pan, thick and heavy bottomed, in the oven. When the pan is nice and hot, pour the oil in the pan, followed by the carrots, celery, and onions. Close the door and let brown, while stirring occasionally, for about 10 minutes.

6. Add the garlic, spices, thyme leaves, bay leaves, and brown sugar. Give a good stir, then add the bourbon, cider vinegar, and beer—the browning liquid—and reduce by half, with the door closed, then add the stock. Very carefully add the wrapped belly to the roasting pan, spoon some juice over, and cover with aluminum foil. Lower the oven temperature to 325°F (160°C) and close the door.

7. Let the belly braise slowly, basting it every 30 minutes or so. After 4 hours, it should be ready—the probe of a thermometer inserted into its deepest part should indicate 165°F (75°C), and the deer meat should yield to a gentle touch. Let temper in the liquid before carefully removing the tea towel. Slice with a serrated knife, with the sauce that has been reduced a little and seasoned as to stand up properly to this majestic belly. Serve with Tater Tot Galette (page 178).

Notes Should you find yourself in the countryside, you'll have an easier time sourcing deer belly—a hunting friend can point you in the right direction, or you can talk to a venison purveyor. Otherwise, contact your butcher and pre-order a veal belly, which works just as well here.

To make your own basic sausage meat: for every pound of ground pork, add 1 teaspoon salt, 1 teaspoon black pepper, 1 smashed garlic clove.

Also, if you are looking for the gateway drug to venison and this seems overwhelming, we suggest the Carbonnade of Deer Necks (page 185).

"Beauty's Special" Saint Honoré

Serves 6

You will need

2 piping bags (embrace the disposable kind, much more hygienic)

½-inch (13-mm) star tip

¼-inch (6-mm) plain tip

Pastry brush

Patience (for the swans)

For the whitefish salad

1½ cups (200 g) smoked whitefish, picked and inspected for bones

½ cup (120 ml) sour cream

1 celery stalk, finely chopped

3 scallions, thinly sliced

3 tablespoons mayonnaise

1 tablespoon fresh lemon juice

Salt and pepper

For the herbed cream cheese

One 8-ounce (226-g) package cream cheese, softened

1 cup (240 ml) sour cream

¼ cup (15 g) chopped fresh chives

1 tablespoon chopped fresh dill sprigs

Salt and freshly ground black pepper

For the choux swans

1 cup (240 ml) water

½ teaspoon salt

½ teaspoon sugar

7 tablespoons (100 g) butter

1 cup (128 g) all-purpose flour

4 large eggs

1 tablespoon poppy seeds

For the egg wash

1 large egg, whisked with a fork

For the smoked fish

2 cups (300 g) cured char, thinly sliced

2 cups (300 g) smoked sturgeon or smoked fish of your choice, thinly sliced

For the puff pastry base

1½ pounds (about 700 g) thawed but still cold puff pastry, rolled out to a thinness of ¼ inch (6 mm), into a 12 x 12-inch- (30-cm-) square, approximately

For the garnish

8 fresh dill sprigs

1 small shallot, sliced thin

3½ ounces (100 g) caviar (whitefish or trout)

First there was the Smorgasbord (Book One, insert following page 132). Then we tried the Deli-Fish Plate. Then there was a Savory Fish Paris Brest. Now *this,* for when you want to mess with your Jewish relatives (or in our case, the Battat family) in the best way possible; or, if you're looking for a Jewish family's embrace, bring this on a High Holiday and it will be game over. Good for breakfast, lunch, or dinner.

Disclaimer: Sourcing the fish you need for this and making the choux swans are a bit of a process. David says, "Just don't do it."

---

1. In a bowl, combine all the ingredients for the whitefish salad with a fork, seasoning to taste. Cover and refrigerate.

2. In a medium bowl, using a wooden spoon or whisk, mix the cream cheese, sour cream, chives, and dill until well combined. Season with salt and pepper to taste, then transfer to a piping →

bag fitted with a ½-inch (13-mm) star tip, and refrigerate.

3. Preheat the oven to 375°F (190°C).

4. Make the choux dough: In a medium saucepan, combine the water, salt, sugar, and butter, and bring to a simmer. When the butter has melted completely and the liquids are boiling, stir in the flour, off the heat, with a wooden spoon. Then, return the saucepan to medium heat and stir vigorously for 30 seconds. Transfer to a mixing bowl.

5. Continue to give the choux dough a few stirs to let the steam escape, then add the eggs, one by one, mixing each until fully integrated before adding the next. Transfer into a piping bag fitted with a ¼-inch (6-mm) plain tip. Set aside.

6. Line a large sheet pan with parchment paper. With a pencil, trace 10 or so 1½-inch (3.8-cm) circles 3 inches (7.5 cm) apart. In the spaces between the circles, trace 2-inch- (5-cm-) tall S letters, drawing as many or more as you have rounds.

7. Turn the parchment over (so that the graphite doesn't come in contact with the dough) onto the pan. Pipe the choux dough into each circle, starting in the center of the circle and moving the dough until it reaches the edges of the traced circle. Next, pipe the S shapes—the trick is to do it with a quick movement of your wrist, akin to cursive writing. Let the dough rest for 10 minutes, then brush the rounds gently with the egg wash. Same with the swans. (Keep the remaining dough in the bag just in case you mess up a swan or two. This happens very easily.)

8. Bake for 20 minutes, or until puffed and golden. Turn off the oven, remove the choux, and brush lightly with the wash. Add the poppy seeds, return to the oven, and let cool and dry out gently, with the oven door ajar, about 20 minutes.

9. Time to make some swans: Cut the top third off each round choux. Slice each of these "caps" in two down the center—those will be your wings. The remaining shells will be stuffed with the whitefish salad.

10. Preheat the oven to 400°F (200°C).

11. Lightly dust your work surface with some flour, and lay the rolled-out puff pastry square on it. Using a lid or upside-down pie dish, trace then cut a 9- to 10-inch (23-cm to 25-cm) circle with the tip of a sharp knife. Prick the dough all over with a fork. Transfer to a parchment–lined sheet pan, then cover with another sheet of parchment and a sheet pan over the top. Bake for 15 minutes, then remove the top pan and parchment and bake a further 10 minutes, until light brown and crisp. Transfer to a rack to cool.

12. Fill the puff rounds with the whitefish salad—a little overflow is nothing to worry about—and set aside on your work surface or a sheet pan.

13. Dab a dot of herbed cream cheese on the bottom of the puff pastry circle and place it on a beautiful plate, pressing down slightly to help it stick. Next, dab a little cream cheese on the bottom of the whitefish-stuffed rounds as you work to place them, one by one, around the perimeter of the puff pastry circle.

14. Pipe the cream cheese in the center first. Arrange the smoked fish in concentric circles, with every rolled slice acting like the petal of a greater oceanic lily. Delicately place the poppy seed wings on each swan, and tuck their necks (the S) into the whitefish salad (see final image for visual direction).

15. Garnish your creation with fresh dill, thin slices of shallot, and the caviar of your liking.

Lobster Pelmeni

Makes 40 to 50 pelmeni,
serves 4

————⌇⌇⌇————

You will need

Large pot of very salty boiling water
to cook the lobsters

Stand mixer

4-inch (10-cm) cookie cutter or ring mold

Floured sheet pan

Tray oiled with 3 tablespoons neutral oil,
to prevent cooked pelmeni from
sticking to one another

David loves ravioli. David also loves pierogis. And soup dumplings.
And wontons. And anything resembling stuffed dough. Remember that old
Sesame Street pierogi skit? It had a vaguely operatic song in which ladies
handling dough were just chanting "pierogi" over and over again. That's
David's favorite song. Russian grocery stores have the best selection of
imported commercial pierogi. One day, while torso-deep in the freezer section,
David came across a bag of Siberian pelmeni. The label was handwritten.
Pelmeni are the sophisticated cousins of pierogi. The dough is thinner, the
filling is higher in protein. It's less heavy. I guess you could call this Lobster
Spaghetti 2.0.

Two 2-pound (900-g) lobsters, parboiled
for 4 minutes, meat extracted and shells
reserved (steps 1 and 2)

For the sauce

Lobster shells (reserved from above)

3 tablespoons neutral oil

3 garlic cloves, roughly chopped

2 fresh tarragon sprigs

1 teaspoon sweet paprika

¼ teaspoon freshly ground black pepper,
plus more for seasoning

2 cups (500 ml) heavy cream
(35 percent butterfat)

1 to 2 cups (240 to 500 ml) water

Salt

1 cup (240 ml) fresh-pressed carrot juice

Cayenne pepper

Juice of ½ lemon, or to taste

¼ cup (57 g) cold unsalted butter

For the dough

2 large eggs

4 cups (500 g) all-purpose flour,
plus extra for dusting

Pinch of salt

¾ cup to 1¼ cups (200 to 300 ml) cold
water

For the pelmeni filling

1 pound (454 g) ground pork

1 large egg plus 1 large egg yolk

2 garlic cloves, minced

2 tablespoons finely chopped fresh
tarragon

2 tablespoons finely chopped fresh chives

¼ cup (60 ml) Calvados

Salt and white pepper

To serve

1 cup (240 ml) sour cream

3 tablespoons chopped fresh chives

1. Cut the lobster meat into small pieces
the size of peas, transfer to a container,
and refrigerate.

2. Strain away any excess liquid from
the lobster shells.

3. For the lobster sauce: In a heavy-
bottomed pot, heat the oil until smoking
hot. Add in the shells and cook, stirring
vigorously, over high heat, until all the
liquid has evaporated, about 5 minutes.
Stir in the garlic, tarragon, paprika,
and black pepper. Cook for a few
seconds, then add the cream and water.
Reduce the heat and simmer gently
for 30 minutes. Strain into a small
container and season with salt and
black pepper to taste.

**4. While the lobster sauce is
simmering, make the pelmeni dough.**
In the bowl of a stand mixer, combine
the eggs, flour, salt, and ¾ cup
(200 ml) water. Mix on low speed to
form a smooth dough, 8 to 10 minutes,
adding a splash of water here and →

there as needed: keep in mind that the dough will become considerably looser and softer as it rests, so you will likely not have to use more than 1 cup (240 ml) water total. In humid weather, err on the firmer side. Manually knead the dough on the counter a few times, then toss with a little flour and transfer to a container or Ziploc bag. Let the dough rest for at least 30 minutes, preferably longer.

5. To make the filling: In a large bowl, combine the chopped lobster meat with the ground pork, the egg and the egg yolk, the minced garlic, tarragon, chives, Calvados, and salt and white pepper. Mix well with your hands. We encourage you to test-fry a small amount to assess the seasoning and adjust as needed.

6. On a floured work surface, roll out the dough into a large circle about ⅛ inch (3 mm) thick. Using a floured 4-inch (10-cm) ring mold, cut out as many circles as you can, and place them side by side on a floured sheet pan.

7. In the center of each dough circle, place a tablespoonful of pelmeni filling. Using your fingertip, brush a little water or egg wash around the edges, then fold in half, pressing down on the top edge to seal—like a boss. Grab the tips of the semicircle and press them together, as if it's going to hug itself. Transfer back to the floured sheet pan, make the rest of the pelmeni, then refrigerate.

8. Finish the lobster sauce: In a medium saucepan, reduce the carrot juice by half, add the cream mixture, and reduce at a tranquil simmer for 30 to 40 minutes, until still unctuous but not stiff. Season with salt, black pepper, and cayenne to taste, add the lemon juice, and whisk in the cold butter. Set aside but keep warm.

9. Bring a large pot of salted water to a boil. Cook the pelmeni in small batches to avoid overcrowding them like Smurfs in Gargamel's cauldron—maintaining a slow but even simmer, 2 to 3 minutes. As always, it's a lot easier to test one for doneness than to send your guests an apology letter later. Transfer pelmeni to a sheet pan that's been oiled, and continue cooking the next batch.

10. Transfer the pelmeni to a large pan, and cover them in the lobster sauce. Over medium-low heat, bring to a slow simmer, cover, and cook for 5 to 6 minutes. Some of the sauce will be absorbed, so add a splash of water to extend it, and adjust the seasoning accordingly. Serve with the sour cream and chives.

Hot and Sauer Soup

Makes 4½ quarts (4½ l)

As much as we love our smoker, we acknowledge that some people are just better at smoking meat than we are, and that's how we feel about the charcuterie at Slovenia, an old-world meat haven on St-Laurent Boulevard. Whenever we have the chance at domestic duties, we buy the lamb necks there and the Hungarian pork sausage for our personal stash. Any mention of Slovenia in conversation is also a great bonding technique for our chef Marc-Olivier Frappier with his father-in-law, Momir Filipovic (our partner Vanya's dad).

2.2 pounds (1 kg) lamb necks, cut into large chunks

Kosher salt and black pepper

¼ cup (60 ml) canola oil

One 9-ounce (250-g) Hungarian pork sausage, cut into pieces

1 white onion, thinly sliced

4 garlic cloves, thinly sliced

1 teaspoon Vegeta seasoning

1 teaspoon caraway seeds

2 fresh thyme sprigs, picked and chopped

1 tablespoon Hungarian mustard or hot mustard

2 cups (300 g) drained sauerkraut, ½ cup (120 ml) juice reserved

2 teaspoons Hungarian hot paprika

1 teaspoon sweet paprika

2 teaspoons tomato paste

1 hot Hungarian pepper

3 quarts (3 l) lamb or chicken stock

For the garnish

Sour cream

Fresh dill sprigs

Finely chopped fresh flat-leaf parsley

1. Rub the neck chunks with the salt and pepper.

2. In a large heavy-bottomed pot, heat the oil over medium-high heat. Brown the neck pieces nicely all around, about 5 minutes per side.

3. Using your trusty tongs, remove the necks from the pot and set aside. Add the sausage and cook for 30 seconds, then stir in the onion slices. Sweat for 2 minutes, then add the garlic slices. Stir in the Vegeta, caraway seeds, and thyme. Reduce the heat to medium.

4. Stir in the mustard, combining well, and cook for a further 2 minutes.

5. Add the sauerkraut and reserved juice. Stir in both paprikas along with the tomato paste. Simmer for 4 minutes.

6. Add the hot pepper. Return the lamb necks to the pot along with the lamb stock. Bring to a boil, reduce the heat to low, and cook for 2½ hours, uncovered. Using a slotted spoon, remove and discard the hot pepper before serving. Adjust the seasoning to taste.

7. Keep the bones in the soup—we like picking up the bones with our hands. Serve piping hot with sour cream and a generous shower of fresh herbs.

Note Ask your butcher to chop the lamb necks into even-size pieces for stew.

Tater Tot Galette

Serves 8

~

You will need

Meat grinder or stand mixer with
a grinder attachment

6-inch (15-cm) ring mold

Deep fryer or heavy-bottomed,
tall-sided pot

Perhaps the biggest impetus for Fred to learn to cook was years of living off frozen tater tots cooked in the microwave with plum sauce from an army-size jug. As he improved at microwaving (see page 136), he added a thick slab of stretchy pizza cheese and pickled jalapeño. This, plus a couple of martinis, was the nightly routine and reason enough for future exclusion from the centenarian club.

The taste here is those tots, but in patty/galette form, suitable for the deer belly (page 167) or individual consumption.

---

6 russet potatoes

3.5 ounces (100 g) kosher salt

1 cup (130 g) cornstarch

Neutral oil for frying

Salt and freshly ground black pepper

1. Peel the potatoes and cut into medium dice. Place in cold water so that they don't oxidize.

2. Bring 4 quarts (4 l) water to a boil in a large pot, and add the salt.

3. Set up your meat grinder with the medium die. Grind the potatoes into a stainless-steel bowl.

4. Pour the boiling salted water onto the ground potatoes and let the water cool down to room temperature, about 20 minutes.

5. Strain the cool potatoes into a bowl, discarding the water, and stir in the cornstarch.

6. Working on a large sheet pan, use a 6-inch ring mold to form 8 individual potato patties, pressing firmly as you pack the potato into the mold (the patties should be about 1 inch/2.5 cm high). Refrigerate to set for at least 2 hours or overnight.

7. Heat your oil to 350°F (180°C).

8. Working in batches, fry the potato patties until golden brown, 3 to 4 minutes. Transfer to a paper towel–lined platter. Season with salt and pepper.

Note The potato galettes need to set for 2 plus hours or overnight.

Squash Sticky Buns

Makes 1 dozen buns

~~~

You will need

Offset spatula

9 x 13-inch (22.8 x 33-cm) Pyrex dish,
generously buttered

For the dough

1 cup (240 ml) whole milk

½ box (50 g) instant vanilla pudding

¼ cup (55 g) margarine

¼ cup (60 ml) water

2 teaspoons instant yeast

2 large eggs

2 tablespoons sugar

¼ teaspoon kosher salt

4 cups (480 g) all-purpose flour,
plus ¼ cup (30 g) for rolling out the
dough

For the filling

¾ cup (170 g) soft butter

1¼ cups (200 g) packed light brown sugar,
plus ½ cup (80 g) for sprinkling

1½ tablespoons ground cinnamon

1 tablespoon ground ginger

2 teaspoons ground nutmeg

½ teaspoon ground cloves

Pinch of ground star anise

2 teaspoons kosher salt

For the shredded squash

4 cups (960 g) coarsely grated
butternut squash

⅓ cup (80 ml) unsalted butter, melted

½ cup (70 g) pumpkin seeds, roasted
and unsalted

These are incredible when served with a generous dollop of quark and a dousing of very green pumpkin seed oil and freshly ground black pepper.

1. Make the dough: In the bowl of your stand mixer, whisk together the milk and instant vanilla pudding, beating well for 2 minutes. Switch to the dough hook attachment, then add the margarine, water, instant yeast, eggs, sugar, salt, and flour to the bowl. Knead for 3 to 4 minutes at medium-low speed. Transfer the dough to a nicely buttered mixing bowl, cover with plastic wrap, and leave in a warm place for a minimum of 2 hours, or until it doubles in size.

2. Preheat the oven to 350°F (180°C).

3. While the dough is resting and proofing, in a large bowl, combine the filling ingredients: the butter, brown sugar, cinnamon, ginger, nutmeg, cloves, star anise, and salt. Set aside.

4. For the squash: In a large bowl, mix the grated squash with the melted butter until well coated. Using your hands, spread the mixture on a sheet pan lined with parchment paper and bake for 30 minutes. Set aside to cool.

5. Once the dough has doubled in size, lay a sheet of parchment paper (12 x 17 inches/30 to 43 cm) down on your work surface and sprinkle with the remaining flour. Roll the dough out with a rolling pin to cover all of the parchment paper—the dough should be about ¼ inch (6 mm) thick. Brush off any excess flour on the top of your dough.

6. Using an offset spatula, spread the cooled butter/spice mixture evenly across the dough. Next, spread the cooked squash evenly, followed by a sprinkling of pumpkin seeds and the reserved ½ cup (80 g) brown sugar.

7. Now, starting at the bottom edge of the dough, roll it upward, trying to maintain an even log shape throughout. When you come to the end of the roll, make sure you rotate the roll so that the seam is positioned toward the bottom. Transfer to a cutting board, and, using a sharp serrated knife, cut the log into 1½-inch-(4-cm-) wide sections. Carefully pick up each roll and lay it sideways (cut side up) into the Pyrex dish, leaving a thin space between each one.

8. Cover the dish with buttered plastic wrap and move to a warm spot in your kitchen or inside the microwave. Let the buns proof for 1 hour, until doubled in size.

9. Preheat the oven to 350°F (180°C). Bake the buns for 45 minutes, until golden and bouncy when you press on their centers.

Note Count on a minimum of 2 hours for proofing the dough.

Omar's Dungeness Crab Curry

Serves 2

You will need

Spice grinder

Ice bath (for the crab)

Two 12-inch (30-cm) karahi pots
or flameproof clay pots

We knew Omar Zabuair from around town. He could do all the French cooking, all the Italian cooking, all the desserts, and he was terrific at reproducing his mother's Pakistani cooking. When he took over the reins at Liverpool House, we pushed him to make the curries he would make at home. "But Omar got stuck in a rut like I did," says David. "I knew he was closing down the bar across the street. Every night. I could see he was burning the candle at both ends. One day I came to work and decided we had to fire him for his own good: he had gone as far at LPH as he could go; there was no management job available for him; and, financially, we weren't able to open a new restaurant with him. We love Omar. We love Omar's wife. He was at the stage in his career where he could no longer work for other people."

So he found a space in the East End of Montreal, and went all *Field of Dreams* on it. If you're talented at cooking and your shit is delicious, you don't need a busy corner. Serve food you would eat yourself. Now, people travel across town to eat Omar's food. Omar would serve this curry at LPH, and it quickly became *a thing*. Locals loved it. Anthony Bourdain loved it. And we asked Omar for his recipe for this cookbook and he graciously said yes. On the day we visited to take his picture, he also made us nine other things, including improvised tandoori chicken made in a garbage can. It was fucking delicious.

For the tandoori masala

3 tablespoons coriander seeds

3 tablespoons cumin seeds

1 tablespoon black mustard seeds

One 2-inch (5-cm) piece cassia bark

3 bay leaves

1 small piece mace

1 tablespoon ground ginger

1 tablespoon amchoor (mango) powder

1 tablespoon smoked paprika

For the crab

1 large (about 2.2 pounds/1 kg)
Dungeness crab

2 large eggs, beaten

3 tablespoons cornstarch

3 tablespoons rice flour

½ tablespoon each minced fresh ginger and garlic, combined

1 teaspoon salt

1 teaspoon white pepper

1 teaspoon ground turmeric

1 tablespoon ground cumin

1 teaspoon ground coriander

2 tablespoons tandoori masala (from recipe at left)

Canola oil for frying

20 curry leaves

1 teaspoon cumin seeds

For the curry sauce

½ cup (120 ml) canola oil

4 dried red chiles

½ teaspoon fenugreek seeds

½ teaspoon black mustard seeds

6 garlic cloves, minced

2 onions, finely diced

1 teaspoon ground cumin

4 green chiles, seeded and julienned

3 medium tomatoes (1 pound/454 g), puréed

Salt

To serve

1 tablespoon julienned fresh ginger

1 tablespoon julienned green chiles

Lime wedges

Steamed plain basmati rice →

I. **Make the tandoori masala ahead of time:** In a small frying pan, toast each of the spices, one at a time, until fragrant. Set them aside to cool for a few minutes. Finely grind all the spices in a spice grinder, and store in an airtight container until ready to use.

2. Break the crab down however you feel comfortable. We are in favor of a quick 5-minute plunge into boiling salted water, followed by an ice bath.

3. Separate the claws and legs, and crack into them to retrieve the crabmeat. Remove the top shell to save for garnish. Remove and discard the gills, and cut the abdomen in half.

4. Combine the crab pieces with the eggs, cornstarch, rice flour, ginger/garlic mixture, salt, white pepper, spices, and the masala, then refrigerate for no more than 2 hours: you want to still be able to taste the crab at the end.

5. **Proceed with the curry sauce:** Heat the oil in the karahi pot over medium heat. Add the red chiles, fenugreek seeds, mustard seeds, and garlic, and stir-fry until they change color, about 1 minute. Add the onions, and cook, stirring frequently, for 4 to 6 minutes, until just golden. Reduce the heat as needed to prevent the spices from burning.

6. Stir in the ground cumin, green chiles, and tomato purée. Simmer for 10 for 15 minutes, adding water to adjust the consistency, until the oil starts to float to the surface. Season with salt. Remove from the heat and set aside.

7. Heat enough oil in another karahi to shallow-fry the crab pieces. Cook the curry leaves and cumin seeds until they start to pop. Add the crab and fry for 2 to 3 minutes. Transfer to a paper towel–lined plate.

8. Return the sauce to a boil, adjusting the seasoning and consistency as needed. Add the crab to the sauce and simmer for 3 to 5 minutes, until the crab is done.

9. Garnish with the julienned ginger and green chiles, and serve with lime wedges on the side and steamed basmati rice.

Note Before you come home from the fishmonger's with a large live crab that needs to be cooked stat, we recommend you make the tandoori masala for the crab marinade ahead of time. Then count on 2 hours to marinate the crab.

Carbonnade of Deer Necks

Serves 4 to 6

People have a conviction that cool dishes should be eaten in the summer and warm dishes in winter. Not true. This dish, along with a savory Tarte au Chou (page 186), is a perfect summer feast.

The carbonnade treatment applies wonderfully to pickled deer necks or any other brined "bony" meats.

12 to 16 pickled deer neck chunks (The Cellar, page 10)

¼ cup (57 g) bacon fat or butter

6 bacon slices, cut into thin matchsticks

4 onions, cut in half and thinly sliced

1 tablespoon all-purpose flour

2 tablespoons black currant jelly

3 juniper berries

1 tablespoon chopped fresh flat-leaf parsley

1 tablespoon chopped fresh tarragon

1 tablespoon chopped fresh thyme

4 garlic cloves, finely chopped

2 teaspoons ground black pepper

Two 12-ounce (350-ml) bottles of tasty ale (avoid very hoppy beers)

2 tablespoons apple cider vinegar

1 carrot

Kosher salt

I. Soak the neck bones in a bowl of fresh cold water, changing the water every hour. Do this for 4 to 5 hours.

2. Preheat the oven to 300°F (150°C).

3. In a large Dutch oven (the oval kind) over medium-high heat, melt the bacon fat, then cook the bacon until crisp, about 3 minutes. Stir in the onions, and cook until brown, stirring every minute or so.

4. Stir in the flour, coating the bacon and onions evenly.

5. Add in all the remaining ingredients, except the salt, adding water as needed so that the meat is almost but not quite covered. Bring to a slow simmer.

6. Cover and braise for a total of 3 hours. After 1 hour, remove the pot from the oven and check that the meat is still almost covered in braising liquid. Add salt to taste, cover, and return to the oven for a further 2 hours.

7. Remove from the oven. If the sauce seems too runny for your liking, remove the meat and set aside, then reduce the sauce over medium-high heat, adjusting the seasoning. Reunite the deer with its sauce and serve.

note This recipe assumes you pickled some deer neck (The Cellar, page 10) prior to the apocalypse. You will now need 4 to 5 hours' lead time to soak the pickled deer neck. Start the process morning of.

Tarte au Chou

Serves 6

You will need

Ice bath

12-inch (30-cm) pie plate

Skip the carbonnade and make this one for a country lunch, with a few terrines and pâtés, mustard, and *vin rouge*.

1 Savoy cabbage

4 tablespoons (57 g) unsalted butter

1 garlic clove

4 onions, thinly sliced

6 russet apples, or any kind that will sustain cooking, peeled, cored, and thickly sliced

¼ cup (60 ml) cider vinegar

A few fresh thyme sprigs

Salt and pepper

18 bacon slices

1 bay leaf

Store-bought pie dough, rolled out to a 14-inch (35-cm) circle and an 18-inch (46-cm) circle

1 large egg yolk, whisked with a bit of water

1. Preheat the oven to 375°F (190°C).

2. Remove the outer leaves of the cabbage. You will need enough to line and top the inside of the pie. Remove the stems and chop the core into matchbook-size squares.

3. Bring a large pot of salted water to a boil and briefly cook the outer leaves of the cabbage until pliable. Plunge into an ice bath and pat dry.

4. Over medium heat, melt 2 tablespoons of the butter and proceed to cook the chopped cabbage with the whole garlic clove. Add a bit of water to keep it wet. You want wilted but not mushy, because it will continue to cook inside the pie. Set aside.

5. Wipe the pan and sweat the onion in the remaining 2 tablespoons butter until lightly browned. Add the apples and cook for 5 to 6 minutes, then add the cider vinegar and thyme, and season with salt and pepper. Set aside.

6. Place the larger dough circle in the pie plate and line with the cabbage leaves, staying clear of the edges.

7. Layer most of the chopped cabbage, the apple mixture, and bacon on the top. Place the bay leaf in the center, top with the remainder of the cabbage, and add the top dough circle. Brush with the egg wash and bake for 45 minutes. The result should be a golden crust.

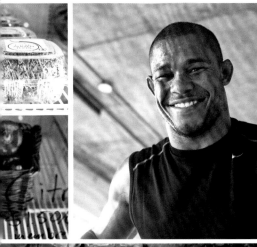

Five

Chicken Kimura[*] or the Healthful Side of Joe Beef

If Paradox were a religion, restaurants would be its temple.

Take the case of chefs, driven to go on epic sourcing quests (helping small farms remain organic), shunning food that's from more than a few paces away, sending an army of *stagiaires* on their days off to pillage the free resources of neighboring woods, and who will then flaunt a prizewinning wine list replete with factory-made dark and oaky gems! Protein bars are made with more care than most of the wines on those lists (more on this later).

How often do you overhear customers and chefs speaking monologues at one another about the health virtues of organic food, quoting the Internet like the book of Psalms, claiming that thyroid dysfunction is caused by the herbicides and insecticides in our food, all while puffing away on a cigarette, one of many that evening, one of thousands in a lifetime? And then, inevitably, one day, you pull the STOP trigger—curbing your consumption of alcohol, junk food, drugs, or time on the couch.

Dietary choices have become the new cool brand: you will sport that paleo label the way we wore our fake Lacostes in the nineties. We have nothing against doing what is right for you: everyone's story is complicated; it often

---

* Kimura: the segue for many into the dark arts of submission locks, named after a famed Japanese wrestler who fought the Original Gracie, Hélio, the main engineer of Brazilian jujitsu. No other move has triggered more enthusiastic and passionate comments from early days MMA announcers! If or when you have butchered enough chicken legs and wings, you will truly understand that articulation can be altered for the worse with a simple flexion in another direction.

involves a cloudy past, new children, and a case of stress disorder (cooks, chefs, all restaurant people are bruised—years of cooking feasts for others take their toll on a person). But your story is your story. Treat your dietary choices as your own secret urban garden! And that's what you will *not* find in this chapter, no quick tips to see your abs, no secret to make redemption taste like a martini, and no thumping of dietary principles—there are enough podcasts on the topic, and we would just be unconsciously repeating their schlang.

What you will find here are recipes we've doctored up to be tasty. Recipes that are made from some of the best ingredients, those found at your local indie seventies' health store, and tried and tasted by Fred, a lifelong celiac, and his band of merry mixed martial arts fighters.

→ Gluten-Free and MMA

I remember little from my school days: aside from being ostracized for eating hard-boiled eggs on the ski bus, my most vivid memory is repeatedly missing the bus because I had to go to the bathroom.

I have celiac. I ignored it for a long time, but after it became unbearable and my doctor told me I was being "really stupid" for not doing the diet, I had no choice. Overnight, I was propelled to the other side: I was that bill on the pass, written in red, the one the cooks roll their eyes at. Be it shellfish or gluten, any food allergies and food intolerances are no fun—I haven't met one person who tells me otherwise! When we can avoid it, in this chapter, most recipes contain no gluten. Turns out plenty of traditional French food is very simple gluten-free fare.

My life can be described as a series of brief but intense obsessions—which is great when you need material for a book, but otherwise it starts to look and feel a bit dysfunctional. When you pair that obsession with a staunch determination—a compulsion, really—to acquire the specific equipment for said interlude (diving, hunting, Lionel model trains, mixed martial arts . . .), you wind up with a house that's more like a storage locker for shin pads, diving watches,

and wood planers. So, if that apocalyptic shit were to hit the fan, I'm the guy you want to be with.

As for my brief plunge into the world of MMA, it has been a happy surprise (with a slipped disk or two). Turns out most boxers and fighters are dedicated, thoughtful, analytical, and skilled athletes. We've built solid friendships with a few of them: Georges St-Pierre is a good soul we at Joe Beef are blessed to count as a near-weekly customer; Olivier Aubin-Mercier is another sweetheart, and when he's not strangling people in a cage for a living, he's a good dad and friend. Lately, we have started following him to the fights. Having no knowledge of nutrition science and weight loss, we opted for the task we are skilled at: the weight gain! The day before the fight, pugilists are required to weigh in at a set low weight (and the efforts to get there are painful and dangerous, and involve extreme caloric restriction and dehydration), but after, they are free to gain weight until the fight, generally eating "bodybuilder" food or hotel food—neither tempting nor appetizing. This is how our sideline of cooking snapper and tacos in hotel rooms started. Not only is the food delicious, the routines, the tableware, and the meal overall have a calming effect on the eve of a fight.

—F. M.

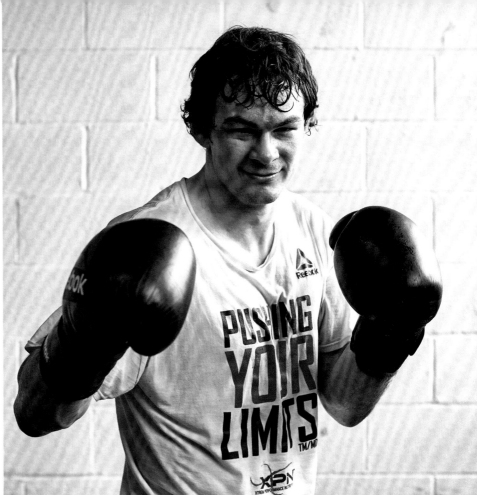

When I'm Fighting

I'm on his back. It looks a bit like the pottery scene between Patrick Swayze and Demi Moore in *Ghost.* The only difference is my uncontrollable urge to wring his neck. Let me do it! Don't resist! I promise, you won't feel any more pain!

I slip my forearm under his neck; the hardest part is over. All that's left is to secure the stranglehold by placing my hand in the crook of my elbow as if I were giving the finger to the ref, who's watching us intently.

He tries to break free. He wriggles like a worm. But it's useless; the hold is secure. I squeeze his neck forcefully and wait for the gentle taps that tell me he's giving up and that all my sacrifices these last few months have been worth it.

There they are! *Tap, tap, tap.* The ref jumps on us to show that I've won. Now I can take my vacation. *Bon match.*

—Words and image by our friend Olivier Aubin-Mercier,
translation by Catherine Macpherson

Rye Crisps and Cottage Cheese

Makes about 18 crackers
and 1 to 1½ cups (225 to 340 g)
cottage cheese

You will need

Instant-read thermometer

Fine-mesh sieve lined with several
layers of cheesecloth

Food processor

4-inch (10-cm) ring mold/pastry cutter

1¾-inch (4.5-cm) ring mold/pastry cutter

Alone, binge watching *Iron Chef* on your laptop, waiting for regret to slowly trickle away from your sad soul, the only joy you feel, in the drawn-curtains, midday darkness, is knowing that in your cupboard is a box of rye crisps, pumpkin seeds and all, waiting to soak up your sins. We've all been there. Don't add to your depression by buying these, no, no, no. Make your own, and treat yourself to a little jam or smoked fish and cracked pepper.

For the cottage cheese

1 quart (1 l) whole milk

¼ cup (60 ml) white vinegar

½ cup (125 ml) heavy cream
(35 percent butterfat)

¼ teaspoon kosher salt

For the crackers

½ tablespoon flaxseeds

½ tablespoon whole grain kasha/buckwheat

½ tablespoon millet

½ tablespoon whole grain amaranth

½ tablespoon quinoa

½ teaspoon sesame seeds

1 tablespoon pumpkin seeds

1 cup (150 g) all-purpose flour,
plus more for dusting

¾ cup (90 g) rye flour

3 teaspoons baking powder

2 teaspoons kosher salt

5 tablespoons (70 g) cold unsalted butter,
diced into cubes

⅔ cup (150 ml) water

2 tablespoons olive oil

2 tablespoons honey

1. In a heavy-bottomed saucepan, heat the milk to 170°F (77°C). Remove from the heat, stir in the vinegar, and let sit, covered, for 10 minutes.

2. Place cheesecloth-lined sieve over a bowl. Carefully ladle the curdled milk and whey into the sieve. Cover the top of the sieve tightly with plastic wrap. Discard the whey that has passed through the sieve into the bowl, then refrigerate the sieve and emptied bowl, letting the rest of the whey drain for 1½ to 2 hours.

3. Meanwhile, make the crackers:
Combine all the seeds, grains, flour, and dry ingredients in the bowl of your food processor. Process for 10 seconds, until finely ground.

4. Add the cold butter and pulse 6 to 7 times, until the mixture has the consistency of sand.

5. Add the water, oil, and honey, and blitz for 10 to 15 seconds, until a moist dough has taken shape.

6. Using a spatula, transfer the dough from the bowl onto a sheet of plastic wrap; use moistened hands to shape the dough into a disk, then wrap up in the plastic and refrigerate for at least 1 hour.

7. Preheat the oven to 350°F (180°C).

8. Remove the dough from the refrigerator, cut it in half, and place one half on a floured work surface. Dust your rolling pin with plenty of flour. Roll the dough out to a thickness of ⅛ inch (2 mm), and dust the pastry cutters/ring molds with flour before using the large one to cut out 6 or so circles, then the smaller one to cut circles out of the larger circles, creating flat doughnutlike shapes. Transfer the rings to a parchment-lined sheet pan and dock them with a fork or a rolling device. Gather up the ring centers and the trim, and roll this dough out again to cut 3 or so more circles. →

9. Bake the crackers until golden, 16 to 18 minutes. While the crackers are baking, roll out the second half of the dough, as outlined in the previous step. Bake the remaining crackers. When cool, transfer all of the crackers to an airtight container—they'll keep for 1 week.

10. Remove the cottage cheese from the fridge. Transfer the curds into a bowl, discarding the whey, and stir in the cream and salt. The cottage cheese will keep for 1 to 2 days.

Notes When transforming dairy products, sanitizing utensils and washing your hands as much as possible are key to a safe result. The cottage cheese recipe relies on your sourcing the most high-quality milk and cream. If this results in your driving through the hills of Vermont, so be it.

You can use the leftover whey from the cottage cheese to make your own lacto-fermented mustard, which we recommend serving with the All-Star Cabbage Diet Soup (page 201).

Halifax Lobster Curry and Marrow Pilaf

Only a few pages ago (page 181) you were reading about Omar's infamous crab curry. We know. But we had to include this curry too, as it is a very delicious dish, taught in precise detail by a lovely taxi driver we met in Halifax. The man had a passion for cooking *and* mixed martial arts (which was why we were in Halifax in the first place). This is a French-inspired curry—a roux-thickened stock that's then lightly creamed—with the faintest whiff of box store spice-aisle curry.

Serves 2

You will need

Ice bath

Sea salt for the water

Two 1½-pound (680-g) lobsters

1 tablespoon olive oil

1 small onion, diced

1 to 3 tablespoons curry powder

2 tablespoons minced fresh ginger

1 small bay leaf

1 yellow apple, peeled and diced small, tossed in a squeeze of fresh lemon juice

1 garlic clove, minced

1 chile pepper

1 heaping tablespoon all-purpose flour

1 tomato, seeded and roughly chopped

1 tablespoon unsalted butter

1 cup (240 ml) heavy cream (35 percent butterfat)

Salt and pepper

2 tablespoons currants, soaked in water for 1 hour

Marrow Pilaf (page 196)

For the garnish

2 tablespoons unsweetened coconut flakes

2 tablespoons slivered almonds

1. Bring a large pot of water to a boil and add a generous handful of salt to it, tasting it to ensure it's "salty like the sea." Boil the lobsters for 3 minutes, then carefully transfer them to a large bowl filled with ice and cold water.

2. When the lobsters are cool enough to handle, break into them and extract the maximum amount of meat (tips in Book One, pages 27–28), and refrigerate. Using an old knife/cleaver or kitchen shears, chop up the leftover carcass, legs and body, into 1-inch (2.5-cm) pieces.

3. Heat a large saucepan over medium heat, add the oil, and when it's nice and hot, add the carcass pieces and cook for 1 to 2 minutes, stirring often.

4. Add the onion and cook until translucent, then add the curry powder to taste, the ginger, bay leaf, half the apple, all of the garlic, and the whole chile pepper. Cook for about 1 minute, then add the flour, and stir well. Add the tomato and 2 cups (480 ml) water next.

5. Cover and simmer for 30 minutes, then add the butter and cream, simmering a further 10 minutes.

6. Strain into a medium saucepan, large enough to fit the lobster meat. Over medium heat, reduce the sauce down to 1 cup (240 ml), seasoning with salt and pepper as needed.

7. Add the lobster meat, the rest of the apple, and the soaked currants. Warm through over gentle heat, stirring carefully. Serve in the center of a marrow pilaf crown (recipe follows), and garnish with the coconut and almonds. →

MARROW PILAF

Serves 4 as a side

——— ~~~ ———

You will need

Clean, unscented dish towel

2 tablespoons olive oil

Six to eight 1-inch- (2.5-cm-) tall marrow bones, rinsed and soaked in cool water for 1 hour, then patted dry

¼ cup (40 g) chopped onion

1 garlic clove

1 small bay leaf

Salt and white pepper

1 cup (200 g) plain basmati rice, rinsed

1 cup (130 g) freshly shelled peas or awesome frozen peas

French cuisine, as classified but not "invented" by the famed "British" chef and writer Auguste Escoffier, always had rice dishes broken down into two distinct categories, *riz au gras* and *riz au maigre,* fat rice and skinny rice. This is fat rice.

I. Preheat the oven to 350°F (180°C).

2. In a large Dutch oven over medium heat, warm the olive oil. Add the bones and onion, and sweat while stirring occasionally, about 2 minutes. Add the garlic, bay leaf, 2 cups (500 ml) water, and season with salt and white pepper. Simmer for 2 to 3 minutes, then add the rice and cover. Transfer to the oven and bake for 10 minutes. After 10 minutes, remove from the oven and stir in the peas. Cover and bake for another 5 minutes.

3. Remove from the oven. Take off the lid and stretch a clean, unscented dish towel over the top of the Dutch oven, then cover with its lid again, and set aside for an additional 10 minutes.

4. Take the bones and the bay leaf out and discard. Fluff the rice with a fork, and return the bones to top the rice or, alternatively, scoop out the marrow from the bones and stir it into the rice, discarding the bones.

Power Franks

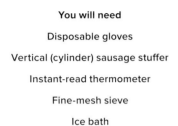

Makes 2.2 pounds (1 kg) franks

You will need

Disposable gloves

Vertical (cylinder) sausage stuffer

Instant-read thermometer

Fine-mesh sieve

Ice bath

If you like to know what you're eating and exactly how much of it, for athletic or health reasons, sausages are likely the last thing you're going to put into your body. You're probably more inclined toward a bare breast of fowl, with steamed vegetables and prepared with little to no love. However, should you combine the magic of a mail-ordered sausage maker with minimal culinary skills, you can enclose the right amount of macro- and micronutrients with healthy meats and fats in a tidy package to achieve peak performance.

This recipe is, in fact, more of a technique than a recipe: grind lean meat, balance it with a set ratio of a high-quality fattier cut, season it, condiment it, and supplement it!

One 4-foot (1.2-m) length natural sheep sausage casing or synthetic hotdog casing

1¾ pounds (800 g) lean meat, such as bison shoulder, cubed

7 ounces (200 g) fatty pork belly (skin removed), cubed

2 teaspoons sea salt

½ teaspoon beet powder

1½ tablespoons Chien Chaud Spice (The Cellar, page 5)

½ teaspoon celery seeds

¾ cup (100 g) hulled hemp seeds or sunflower seeds

1 cup (125 g) ice cubes

1. Wash your hands well. Rinse the casing by placing one end under the water tap and letting cold water run through the casing, pulling up on the end that you filled up, until the water comes out the other end—this removes the preserving salt from inside of the casing. Repeat two or three times. Place the rinsed casing in a bowl of clean cold water and refrigerate until ready to stuff. For synthetic casings, proceed according to the manufacturer's instructions. →

2. If you have not done so already, freeze the meat grinder and large die attachment as well as the cubed meats for at least 1 hour prior to grinding.

3. Set up your meat grinder and, working in batches, grind the lean meat and pork belly.

4. In a medium bowl, wearing gloves, mix the ground meat by hand with the salt, beet powder, spice, celery seeds, and hemp seeds. Freeze for 1 hour.

5. Working with one batch of the ground meat mixture at a time, pulse the meat mixture with a proportionate amount of the ice until combined and the ice has been "absorbed." Transfer to the refrigerator and continue with the rest of the batches.

6. Clamp the sausage stuffer to your kitchen counter, and install the smallest stuffing tube. Place the chilled meat mixture into your stuffer, and thread the sausage casing onto the stuffing tube.

7. The easiest way to proceed is to work with a friend, who cranks the stuffer while you handle the shaping of the sausages as they emerge from the stuffing attachment. Try to work consistently and evenly (practice makes perfect), keeping some looseness to the overall sausage to allow for twisting of the links. With a needle sterilized with the flame of a lighter, pierce through any air pockets, then roll into a big sausage spiral and refrigerate.

8. See steps 9 through 11 of the Base Sausage recipe (page 89) for instructions on shaping and cooking. These sausages are best refrigerated for 2 to 3 hours once you finish shaping them, before they are grilled. They will keep for 1 week, refrigerated, and 2 months if frozen.

Notes Similar to the Base Sausage recipe (page 89), a few things to remember: work clean; wash and rinse everything often, including yourself; keep all your tools and, most important, bowls and sausage stuffer parts in the freezer until you are ready to proceed.

This recipe contains no nitrates or nitrites, so if you want to achieve a smoky wiener, use liquid smoke or hot-smoke the wieners as directed by the manufacturer of your smoking device.

All-Star Cabbage Diet Soup

Makes 10 to 12 cups
(2½ to 3 l) soup,
serves 4 to 6

——— ⁓ ———

You will need

Large stockpot

One of our old associates from Globe Restaurant showed up one day with a brochure for "The Emergency Weight Loss Diet from Victoria Hospital." The diet consisted of one soup, which had only the following ingredients:

2 cabbages	1 turnip
1 celery stalk	1 can (28 ounces/796 ml) tomatoes
1 carrot	1 quart (1 l) water

These were to be boiled all together. The soup could be eaten hot or cold. Up to five cups a day. But *nothing* else. We made four gallons of it and ate nothing else for five days.

It made us extremely hungry, pissed off, and the flatulence was nuclear. This is not that soup.

---

1 beef shank bone, cut into pieces to fit your stockpot, rinsed

1 turkey neck or 4 chicken necks, rinsed

1 calf hoof or 2 pig's trotters, cut into 3 pieces each, rinsed

4 cups (about 600 g) ice

3 tablespoons apple cider vinegar

4 postcard-size pieces dried kombu

2 pounds (900 g) grass-fed flat-iron steak, rolled and tied (like a roast)

2 cups (120 g) thinly sliced Savoy cabbage

1 cup (100 g) thinly sliced Brussels sprouts

2 cups (110 g) packed thinly sliced kale

1 cup (110 g) shredded white turnip

2 cups (100 g) thinly sliced Napa cabbage

1 cup (250 ml) freshly extracted carrot juice

1 cup (250 ml) freshly extracted celery juice

French gray sea salt and freshly ground white pepper

For the garnish (optional)

Cold unsalted butter

Sunflower seeds

Beef or horse jerky (The Cellar, page 8)

1. Under cold running water, rinse all of the bones well. In a good stockpot, combine the beef bones, poultry neck(s), and calf hoof or pig's trotters and cover with cold water. Add the ice (the slower the water gets to a simmer, the better the collagen extraction from the bones) and cider vinegar.

2. Place on medium heat and slowly bring to a simmer—the process shouldn't take less than 30 minutes (more like 45 to 60 minutes). Maintain a slow simmer, remembering that any vigorous boiling will not help to extract the beneficial collagen and flavors.

3. Simmer very slowly for 6 hours, then add the kombu and steak, maintaining a slow and gentle simmer until the meat is no longer resilient, about 2 hours. Remove and reserve the beef, strain the stock carefully, discarding all bones and aromatics, and refrigerate both the clear stock and the steak overnight.

4. Remove the fat cap from the stock; feel free to reserve it for any frying use of your own devising. Then, in a large pot, warm up the stock over medium heat to return it to a liquid state.

5. In a separate large pot, combine all the sliced vegetables and vegetable juices. Add 4 cups (1 l) stock. Bring to a simmer over medium-high heat. Once the cabbage and kale have wilted and revealed their true size, top with another cup or two of stock (or an amount closer to your liking). Season with sea salt and white pepper to taste and simmer for another 20 minutes. You should have 1 to 1½ quarts →

(1 to 1½ l) stock left over—rejoice and freeze for future use!

6. While the soup is simmering, dice the cooked steak into bite-size pieces, and add to the soup 2 to 3 minutes before serving.

7. Ladle 2 cups (480 ml) of soup into each bowl. Optional: Place a pat of butter melt into each soup, then add a sprinkle of sunflower seeds and a dynamic grating of beef or horse jerky, as we do. We would also suggest serving a little fermented mustard on the side to go with this restorative potage.

Notes Ask your butcher ahead of time to save the poultry necks and assorted bones you'll need to make the soup stock.

You'll find kombu (dried seaweed) in the Asian section of any good grocer or at your local health food store.

This soup will require refrigeration overnight, so plan ahead.

A Note on the Seventies' Health Food Store

There is beauty and peace to be found in old-school health food stores: the seventies washed-out green of the walls, the creaking floors, the shelves full of bee pollen and dulse flakes, the compound aromas. This is where the hippies went to heal, spending their dough on a nice Champion juicer when the Man gave them a job.

We find inspiration in the oddest bits of history, and we've always loved the quaint idea that a few idealists could make such stores work. For the longest time, that's where we had to go for quinoa or specialty nut oils, and to this day, many of those health food stores, unlike small conventional grocers, are *still* open for business. A quick trip to one of them will likely convince you of the need for something flax-related. (Let's not forget that health food stores also stand for the dark era of any sugar-free childhood, where millet molasses and flax balls were considered holiday treats.) Take a look at *The Sunny, Munchy, Crunchy Natural Food Shop,* an old short film!

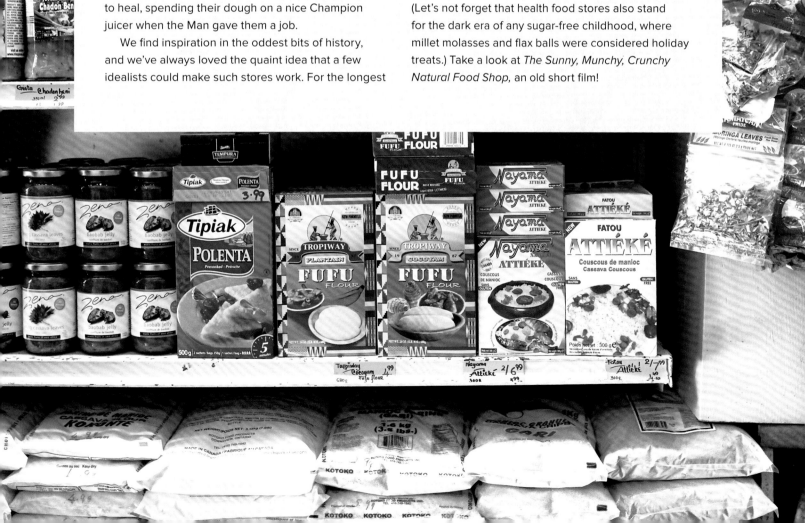

Mouflet aux Mulberries

Makes 10 muffins

You will need

12-cup muffin tin

Paper liners

The brochures still tout the Olympic Stadium, the Old Montreal horse carriages, and the "Underground Montreal" as pinnacles of the city's tourism. Though we cannot tell you the entire city is connected via underground tunnels, we can tell you there is a Mmmuffins in Place Ville Marie in Montreal's downtown that comes up in conversation between Meredith and Fred way too often.

David hates muffins. He even hates the word *muffins*. But these are good!

We suggest eating this one with local (from wherever you are) goat cheese and mulberry or blackberry jam.

Note: There was, and is, a bureau whose mission is to French the English words commonly used in Quebec, hence hamburger became *hambourgeois*, a t-shirt a *gaminet*, and a muffin a *mouflet*. We agree that whispered with a French accent imbued with cigarettes and aperitifs, Mouflet aux Mulberries sounds quite nice.

⅔ cup (60 g) hazelnut meal/flour

¾ cup (80 g) confectioners' sugar

1 teaspoon vanilla sugar (store-bought or homemade, see page 142)

¼ cup (30 g) all-purpose flour

5 large egg whites

1 tablespoon apple jelly

½ teaspoon gingerbread spices

¼ teaspoon salt

¾ cup (170 g) unsalted butter

½ cup (50 g) dried white mulberries

¼ cup (30 g) caramelized hazelnut praline bits (optional)

For serving

Local goat cheese

Mulberry or blackberry jam

I. Preheat the oven to 350°F (180°C).

2. Combine the nut meal, confectioners' sugar, vanilla sugar, flour, egg whites, apple jelly, spices, and salt in a mixing bowl, using a wooden spoon or spatula.

3. In a saucepan over medium-high heat, cook the butter until hazel in color. Transfer immediately to a metal bowl and let temper.

4. Whisk the butter slowly into the dough. Distribute the batter evenly among paper-lined muffin molds, filling up two-thirds of the way. Add the mulberries to the top of each muffin, and push delicately into the batter. If you managed to find hazelnut praline, divide it equally over the muffins. Bake for 17 minutes.

5. Eat at room temperature with the goat cheese of your choosing, and mulberry or blackberry jam.

Note We use a ewe's milk cheese that is soft-ripened, but a soft-ripened goat cheese is great too.

Insta Risotto

Serves 4 as dinner sides
or a modest breakfast

Many cooks enjoy an enviable culinary heritage full of their nonna's risotto. Not us. We grew up eating instant rice and Costco egg rolls. Writing this is not intended as a therapy breakthrough we're hoping to subtly convey to our parents, but as mere statement of fact.

Now, before you drag us to the public square where you lapidate cooks for their sacrilegious treatment of risotto, let us just say that by using the Minute rice below, the dish keeps itself entirely clear of the traditional Venetian's rice turf. You can pack this risotto and cook it on a hike when combustibles are scarce, but also serve it next to a roasted veal loin for a nice dinner.

---

1 cup (90 g) Minute rice, the instant version

½ cup (15 g) freeze-dried muskmelon (honeydew or cantaloupe), cut into tiny cubes

½ cup (55 g) speck slices, crisped and crumbled by hand

3 tablespoons freeze-dried onions

2 tablespoons olive oil

2 to 3 cups (475 to 720 ml) water or clear stock, as needed

2 tablespoons unsalted butter

½ cup (55 g) great local Cheddar cheese, grated

Salt and pepper

4 teaspoons dark forest (buckwheat) honey

1. Using a sturdy mixer or food processor, break the rice in brief yet confident pulses—each grain will need to be fractured in three or four parts.

2. Combine the rice with the melon, speck, and onions. Add the oil and toss well.

3. If this is intended as camp food, add the cheese and the rest of the ingredients in smaller Ziploc bags inside a larger Ziploc containing the rice and aromatics. Pack the honey, stock, and butter separately. Proceed as below whether cooking over an open fire or the open flame of your stove top.

4. Bring 2 cups (475 ml) water or stock to a slow boil, then stir in the rice/melon/speck/onion mixture.

5. Add liquid as needed over the next 4 to 5 minutes of total cooking time. Remove from the heat, and stir in the butter and cheese, taste and season with salt and pepper as desired, then drizzle a bit of honey at serving time.

Notes You'll find freeze-dried or dried melon online, or cube and dry your own—your call.

If you're actually hiking when making this, opt for a drier, less perishable cheese such as pecorino.

Fig Bars

Makes 6 biscuits

꙳

You will need

Blender

Offset spatula

This was one of the first desserts we had on the menu, back when Joe Beef—the space—was small and it was four of us in the front—Allison, Vanya, Meredith, and Julie—and one dishwasher who never showed up. Though the restaurant has grown and multiplied, dessert offerings remain limited, as we still don't have a proper pastry station. Hence the lack of a sweets chapter in this book. As described in Book One, marjolaines, financiers, panna cottas, éclairs, ice cream, and Dutch Babies (page 35) are still very much the order of the day. Here, with these fig bars, we're including a whipped blue cheese topping, for the people who just can't decide between cheese and dessert. We say both.

These bars are GF.

For the fig purée

1¾ cups (230 g) dried black figs, roughly chopped

¾ cup (175 ml) water

1 tablespoon plus 2 teaspoons fresh lemon juice

2 tablespoons plus 1 teaspoon honey

For the cookie dough

½ cup (113 g) unsalted butter, softened

½ teaspoon sea salt

¼ cup (40 g) confectioners' sugar

Pinch of ground cloves

½ teaspoon ground cinnamon

¼ teaspoon ground nutmeg

1 large egg, beaten

¼ cup (27 g) tapioca flour

⅓ cup (60 g) rice flour

2 tablespoons potato starch

⅔ cup (60 g) hazelnut meal/flour

For the whipped blue cheese (optional)

1 cup (240 ml) cold heavy cream (35 percent butterfat)

3½ ounces (100 g) blue cheese, room temperature, crumbled into small pieces

2 tablespoons honey

I. In a small pot over medium heat, combine the figs, water, lemon juice, and honey, and cook until almost all of the water has evaporated, about 25 minutes. Transfer to a blender and purée until smooth.

2. Line a small baking sheet or pan with plastic wrap. Using an offset spatula, spread the fig paste into a 12 x 2 x 2½-inch (30 x 5 x 6-cm) rectangle (the purée should be about ½ inch [1.5 cm] thick) on the plastic wrap—you can spread it along the bottom edge of the pan to create an even border. Cover the fig filling with the wrap and transfer to the freezer to chill for at least 1½ hours.

3. For the cookie dough: In a stand mixer fitted with the paddle attachment, combine the butter, salt, confectioners' sugar, cloves, cinnamon, and nutmeg on medium speed until well creamed. Stop the mixer and scrape down the sides of the bowl with a spatula. Add the egg, and continue to mix, on medium-low speed now, for 20 seconds or so. Reduce the speed to low and add the flours, potato starch, and hazelnut meal, mixing until just combined.

4. On a large sheet of parchment paper (large enough to line a sheet pan), trace a 12 x 7-inch (30 x 18-cm) rectangle. Using a moistened offset spatula, spread out the dough to cover the surface of the rectangle. Lay a sheet of parchment on top of the dough, then use a rolling pin to gently even out the surface. Refrigerate for 45 minutes or more.

5. Preheat the oven to 350°F (180°C).

6. Remove the dough from the fridge and the fig paste from the freezer. →

Let the dough thaw for 5 to 10 minutes so that it softens up enough to be folded without cracking. Remove the top layer of parchment. Unwrap the fig paste and lay it in the center of the dough rectangle. Using the bottom parchment paper for support, carefully fold one of the long sides of the dough over the fig paste, then fold the other long side over, pressing down gently to create a seal—you can use your offset spatula to smooth out the seam. Move the wrapped fig roll to the side and line the sheet pan with a fresh sheet of parchment. Transfer the fig roll to the sheet pan, making sure the seal rests on the parchment rather than facing up. Refrigerate for 30 minutes before baking.

7. While the fig roll is chilling, make the blue cheese cream (if using): Whip the cream until medium peaks form, and add the blue cheese and honey. Refrigerate until ready to serve.

8. Bake the fig roll for 25 to 30 minutes, until the roll looks golden and the edges start to brown.

9. When the fig roll comes out of the oven, let cool for 30 to 60 minutes, then cut into 6 large cookies. Serve one dollop of the blue cheese cream per cookie.

Galettes au Sucre de Mammie

Some might find a sense of nostalgic comfort in looking through old pictures. I never liked the outfits I was made to wear, so instead of reminiscing fondly while perusing pictures of young Fred in lederhosen, I opt for the few recipe cards my mom still has lying around. Much better. The example below, distributed by ITT Nova, is one of my favorites, with its simple, utilitarian design.

My mother made these in a pizzelle/galette maker (the name depends if you buy it in Italy or Belgium) that a great-aunt smuggled from Belgium, along with smoked ham and shellfish-shaped chocolates. My father swiftly conceived a strategy to adequately power the device with our feeble North American electrical current. It consisted mostly of an octopus of cords to plug in in perfect sequence—otherwise, both the house *and* the galette maker would have suffered total shutdown. She still makes them the same way, but now gluten-free for the latest generation (my kids), who seem to have inherited that wheat thing.

—F.M.

¾ cup plus 2 tablespoons (180 g) granulated sugar

3 large eggs

Pinch of salt

Two 0.32 ounce (9 g) packs of vanilla sugar

⅞ cup (200 g) unsalted butter, melted

1½ cups (275 g) gluten-free flour (we like Bob's Red Mill Gluten Free 1-to-1 baking flour)

1. Using a stand mixer, whisk the granulated sugar and eggs in a mixing bowl until the sugar has dissolved and the color turns to white, about 4 minutes.

2. Change from the whisk to the paddle attachment. Add the salt, vanilla sugar, and melted butter. Then, in three batches, add the flour. Incorporate well, until the dough is soft yet not runny, 2 to 3 minutes.

3. Cook in your pizzelle maker according to the manufacturer's directions. Note that when the cookies are hot, they can easily be shaped to fit a bowl and later be filled with buttercream, or (as we do at Joe Beef) with soft-serve.

suikerwafeltjes

verhoudingen

500 g bloem
400 g fijne suiker
3 pakjes vanille-suiker
5 eieren
400 g boter
1 snuifje zout

bereiding

De bloem in een kom gieten - de suiker, het zout en de vanille-suiker er in mengen - een kuiltje maken - er de geklopte eieren in gieten, de bloem er geleidelijk in verwerken en de gesmolten boter toevoegen - het deeg bewerken tot het glad en homogeen is - het tenminste 2 uren laten rusten op een koele plaats - er langwerpige worstjes van rollen en bakken in het vorm 16 x 28.

fijne wafeltjes

verhoudingen

180 g fijne suiker
3 eieren
200 g boter
2 pakjes vanille-suiker
250 g bloem
1 snuifje zout

bereiding

De hele eieren kloppen met de suiker tot deze volledig gesmolten en het geheel een wit-schuimende massa geworden is - het zout, de vanille-suiker en de gesmolten boter toevoegen - vervolgens de bloem er bij kleine hoeveelheden in mengen tot een mals, doch niet vloeibaar deeg bekomen is - breken de wafeltjes tijdens het bakken, dan een weinig bloem toevoegen - bakken in het vorm 16 x 28 - om gerolde wafeltjes te bekomen, ze vlug rond de steel van een houten lepel draaien, zo gauw ze uit het ijzer komen - vullen met boterkreem met vanille-, mokka- of chocoladesmaak.

galettes de sucre & galettes fines - suikerwafeltjes & fijne wafeltjes

Good Ketchup

Makes a good 2 cups
(550 to 575 ml)

—⁓—

You will need

Handheld immersion blender

Considering its association with fast food, and its sweetness, perhaps no other food embodies nutritional and culinary evil better than ketchup. Here in Canada, the second leading brand of ketchup made significant market gains when Heinz stopped buying tomatoes from Leamington, Ontario, proving that some things, though not many, can be stronger than brand association.

Our version of ketchup is tasty and not too bad for you: just tell your kids it's the kind of ketchup that makes Pikachu appear.

2 tablespoons maple syrup

½ cup (125 ml) apple cider vinegar

10 medjool dates, pitted and coarsely chopped

One 4½-ounce (127-g) tube organic tomato paste

1 teaspoon sea salt

¼ teaspoon garlic powder

Tiny pinch of cayenne pepper, or more to taste

Tiny pinch of ground turmeric, or more to taste

1 small onion, very finely chopped

1. In a heavy-bottomed pot, combine 1 cup (120 ml) water, the maple syrup, cider vinegar, and dates. Bring to a boil and cover. Set aside for 1 hour at room temperature.

2. Into the mixture, stir in the tomato paste, salt, garlic powder, cayenne, turmeric, and onion. Over low heat, bring to a simmer and cook very gently for 30 minutes, stirring frequently to avoid scorching toward the end, adding water as required.

3. Blend with an immersion blender until smooth, and transfer to an airtight glass container immediately. Refrigerate. This will keep for 1 month.

Irish Moss Coconut Drink

Makes one 12-ounce
(350-ml) drink

Whether the stuff of legend or not, it's said that Bob Marley had a pint of Irish moss drink a day—though for what perceived health benefits, we will never know. Popular in Jamaica and the Caribbean, Irish moss is also used in a traditional Irish dessert known as carrageen pudding, included in the great Fergus Henderson's first book. This seaweed's ability to thicken smoothly and its very faint ocean taste are quite pleasant, we admit. Here, it's simply used for a delicious rum-based beverage.

FYI: If you Google Bob Marley and Irish moss, you'll see that Marley had a lot to say about how it makes bodily fluids more fragrant.

For the Irish moss base

¼ cup (15 g) packed Irish moss

For 1 drink

2 to 3 heaping tablespoons Irish moss base (see above)

2 heaping tablespoons sweetened condensed milk

½ cup (120 ml) coconut water

1 tablespoon maple syrup

2 tablespoons old and mellow rum

1 teaspoon juice from a jar of maraschino cherries

3 dashes Angostura bitters

1 teaspoon minced fresh ginger

Ice as needed (start with a few cubes)

For the garnish

1 maraschino cherry

Pinch of ground mace

I. **To make the base:** Rinse the Irish moss under cold running water, then place in a bowl of clean water and refrigerate overnight.

2. Drain the moss, then place in a small saucepan with 3 cups (720 ml) water and simmer gently over medium heat until tender and melting (the seaweed will have mostly dissolved), being careful not to scorch, 30 to 40 minutes. Stir well and transfer to a glass container and refrigerate until cold and set, about 2 hours. You should have 1½ cups (375 ml) of Irish moss base, which can be used to make 6 or 7 of these drinks. The base will keep refrigerated for up to 5 days.

3. **To make one drink:** In a blender, combine 2 to 3 heaping tablespoons of the Irish moss base and all the remaining ingredients. Blend until smooth, then taste: do not shy away from adding more of any one ingredient you favor. Transfer to an appropriate tall vessel and garnish with a cherry and a pinch of mace. If you wanted to make a less debauched and more elevated version of this drink, omit the sweetened condensed milk and the rum, replacing them with coconut cream and a very conservative amount (5 mg) of CBD hemp oil concentrate or 1 capsule ginkgo biloba extract.

Note This recipe makes enough Irish moss base for six or seven of these drinks. The base does require steeping overnight. Enjoy.

Vitality Shake

Makes 2 shakes

This is not a panacea.

This is not going to get you ripped.

This will not erase any wrinkles.

This will not accelerate recovery.

This will not affect inches on or below your waistline.

This will not get you high.

This will not bring you closer to God.

This will not save any puppies.

This is perhaps sustainable.

This is delicious.

---

1 greeting card–size sheet macro kelp, rinsed and soaked for 10 minutes in cold water

1 tablespoon cashew butter

½ teaspoon ground ginger

1 teaspoon ground turmeric

1 teaspoon chaga powder

Dash of pure vanilla extract

Pinch of ground cinnamon

Pinch of ground nutmeg

2 teaspoons hemp oil

½ cup (120 ml) cooked squash or sunchoke purée

2 to 4 tablespoons maple syrup

Pinch of sea salt

1 cup (240 ml) filtered water, plus more as needed

1 cup ice

Drops of CBD hemp oil concentrate (optional)

1. Squeeze the water out of the soaking kelp.

2. Combine all the ingredients in a blender and blend at high speed until smooth.

3. Serve in tall tiki glasses of your choosing.

Note Kelp can be found in most health food stores. We order ours from Canadian Kelp Resources in Bamfield, British Columbia.

Cactus Pear Limeade

Makes 2 cups (500 ml) syrup

David walked into Joe Beef one morning looking like a man whose fundamental thirst had been quenched. He had a glow. The cause of said glow was *a dream he'd had* about drinking cactus pear limeade . . . and we thought the idea was amazing. Cactus pears are good and so is limeade; the aloe makes curative hydrating promises and the green tea quenches one's fundamental thirst.

1 lime, sliced

1 lemon, sliced

3 cactus pears, peeled (2 smashed into pulp, 1 crumbled and reserved)

One 4- to 5-inch- (10- to 12.7-cm-) long fresh aloe vera leaf, rinsed and smashed, plus a few slices of leaf per glass for garnish

1 cup (100 g) sugar

½ cup (120 ml) agave syrup

1 cup (240 ml) freshly squeezed lime or key lime juice

3 to 4 cups (750 ml to 1 l) unsweetened green tea

Crushed ice

1. Place the lime and lemon slices, the cactus pear pulp, and the smashed aloe leaf in a medium heat-resistant bowl. In a small saucepan, bring the sugar, agave syrup, and lime juice to a boil. Pour into the bowl, cover with plastic wrap, let the mixture cool to room temperature, then refrigerate overnight.

2. Strain the syrup into a pitcher, pressing to extract all the goodness out of the citrus, the aloe, and the cactus pears.

3. Add some, not all, of the green tea into the syrup, tasting and adding as you go to attain your preferred proportion. Stir in the crumbled cactus pear and some aloe slices. Serve over crushed ice. Mescal would be the spirit of choice should you wish to elevate this elixir to the level of nectar.

Notes Wear rubber gloves or use a thick cloth to hold cactus pears when peeling them. Their tiny thorns will otherwise kill your hands.

The base for this drink needs to be refrigerated overnight. Plan accordingly.

Curried Bean Curd

We used to think that we needed tempeh (cooked and fermented soybeans) like we needed a spoiler wing on a pickup truck, until Fred bought a slab of it at the local health food store and cooked it into this tight and intense curry. It was delicious; the texture is unique; it might even be nutritious.

For the garnish/accompaniment

¼ red cabbage (165 g), cut into thin strips

1 tablespoon minced fresh ginger

2 tablespoons apple cider vinegar

¼ cup (35 g) hemp seeds

½ teaspoon sea salt

4 slices (150 g) ripe pineapple

Juice of 1 lime

Squirt of Sriracha sauce

Dash of fish sauce

4 small sweet potatoes

Kosher salt

1 pound (454 g) good-quality tempeh, cut into bite-size pieces

2 dashes Worcestershire Sauce (page 106)

1 to 2 tablespoons Jamaican curry powder

¼ cup (75 g) Napa cabbage kimchi

1 tomato, peeled and seeded

¼ cup (60 ml) coconut oil

4 scallions, thinly sliced

3 tablespoons minced fresh ginger

3 garlic cloves, minced

Peel of 1 lime

Salt and pepper

2 tablespoons Sriracha sauce

¼ cup (30 g) raw cashews

1. One hour or more before serving the curry, prepare the red cabbage garnish: In a bowl, combine the cabbage with the ginger, cider vinegar, hemp seeds, and sea salt, massaging the cabbage with your hands. Let the topping sit for 1 hour at room temperature before serving.

2. Toss the pineapple slices in a bowl with the lime juice, Sriracha, and fish sauce. Set aside until ready to serve.

3. In a bowl, toss the tempeh with the Worcestershire sauce and curry powder. Set aside.

4. In a blender, combine the kimchi and tomato and blend briefly until coarsely ground.

5. In a heavy-bottomed pot set over medium-high heat, sweat the scallions, ginger, and garlic in the coconut oil until fragrant, about 5 minutes. Add the lime peel and tempeh, and sweat for another 2 minutes. Season with salt and pepper and add the kimchi/tomato blend, adding a splash or two of water as required, but keeping the sauce tight overall. Cover and simmer for 20 minutes.

6. In the meantime, cook the sweet potatoes: Rinse them under cold water, salt them generously, then wrap each in paper towel. Microwave whole (and wrapped) for 5 to 6 minutes, until soft (or continue to microwave in 1- to 2-minute bursts, if needed). If you don't have a microwave, you can steam them whole in a steamer on the stove top, allowing for longer cooking time. Peel the potatoes by hand and slice as you desire.

7. Add the Sriracha to the curry (it will round out the spiciness rather than add to it), and adjust the seasoning to taste. Stir in the cashews. Serve over the sweet potato slices, and top with the red cabbage and spicy pineapple slices.

Interlude

Are You There, God? It's Me, David.

"Every time I drink Burgundy wine, I feel like I'm part of a secret club of people who know things. The best things. Like Star Trek *things. Did you know that Burgundy was drunk in space? Yep, it was Nuits-Saint-Georges, to be exact.*

If I scrape my knee I immediately consider pouring Burgundy on it. I'm sold on its healing qualities. If I see someone with acne, I want to rub it on his or her face."

—*Us, Book One*

Perhaps in the first book we were a tad bombastic. Indeed, I personally may have gone overboard with the "I love red Burgundy so much I want to pour it into my eyes" bit.

Burgundy will always have a place in my heart and on our wine lists, but I don't really drink it much anymore. There's a lot of mundane wine, and I feel that Burgundy is in a funk, a victim of its own success. Is it because of a failure to embrace organic viniculture? A fear of change? A reliance on tradition? Whatever it is, it feels like the safe game. I want to try new things, new grapes, and discover new flavors.

I have taken the controversial plunge into the cursed world of natural wine. Like *Dungeons and Dragons,* role-playing in medieval gear, or Civil War reenactors, I've embraced an alternate reality. We find one another in Brooklyn, Paris, London, or Rimouski on an app called Raisin: The Natural Wine and on WineTerroirs.com. We're the ones incessantly posting bottles with nonsensical esoteric labels, exchanging pathetic group texts. Can you believe this shit? It's like collecting Pokémon. We are everywhere.

I've found truth and meaning in a glass. No bottle of conventional wine has given me pleasure like this. It gives me a physical energy similar to a tonic or elixir. And a kind of cerebral stimulation that's more intoxicating than when I heard the Grateful Dead for the first time in 1985.

I am engaged in the eternal struggle to drink without any added SO_2, or the least amount possible, anyway. I will not drink wine that's not organic/bio/sans sucre/unfiltered/un-fucked with. All wine lovers agree: we want the best possible wine, made the best possible way. And when it's natural *and* delicious, that's the best ever. Ever, ever. Stars aligned, rivers parting.

What, Dave? Are you nuts?

Listen, drink whatever you feel like. Finish your day with a factory-farmed little critter Cab Sauv 150 percent new oak, 15 percent alcohol (which nutritionally makes cola a more intelligent beverage). I would sooner drink moat water.

Some people say, "David, aren't you being a little extreme?"

Yes, I am.

I have worked in this business for twenty-five years, and am still working with Vanya, our sommelier for fifteen of those years. We run tiny restaurants that serve food from tiny producers, cheese farmers, fishermen, bakers, et cetera. We have relationships with all of them. We want to have the same relationship with winemakers, so we buy from small wineries. I want to get the truth. We are your emissaries.

You're coming to the restaurant to put things in your mouth. It's our job to make sure what you're putting in your mouth is the best that we can get.

Conventional wine doesn't fit that bill any longer, because it's too easy with chemical additives to get it right. There are too many scientific safety nets in the wine world, and it's easy to make perfect wine from a formula. Having reread our first book, we stand by most of what we thought. But some of what we said, the producers we admire and so forth, has evolved. And now, we're asking a lot from you, but: *Drink* vin nature.

A lot of loving wine is about nostalgia and memories—and I have great moments of love with natural producers of all regions. The only thing that's certain is my disdain for craft beers or how Donna Jean Godchaux fucked up a lot of the Grateful Dead live recordings between 1972 and 1979.

Natural wine wasn't always this good though. It takes a couple of vintages, at least, to get the hang of wild, awful-smelling fermentations and funky gassy wines in the cellar.

Winemakers everywhere were caught off guard for many years, and are now learning to let go and trust the process. They are learning to do longer elevage, bottle on descending moons, rack less, and sulfur less or only at crucial moments. These

instincts are much to our benefit. If you were once traumatized by a horrible bottle of natural wine that oxidized before you could enjoy the second sip, try again. It's only going to get better, I promise.

I'm blown away by the youth. Kids today are sharper. They work hard and buy quality goods. Kids drink cleaner. They buy magnums and share the bottle at one a.m., instead of guzzling four vodka sodas. We are showing our age. I'm forty-six, and I'm the oldest person working at the restaurant, generally. The young people in the restaurant (the heavy lifters, the bar backs, the busboys) drink much better than I ever did. Ganevat Y'a Bon the Canon was the first wine one of our employees ever tasted. Think about that for a moment. It's a beautiful thing. They aren't easily marketed to, as they have so much information at their fingertips. That Veuve Clicquot

orange isn't enough for this new generation of drinkers.

Classic wine pairings will always remain, but it's not good enough anymore to just have "Muscadet with oysters" or "Rosé and aioli." We must remember to seek out new producers, terroirs, and natural viticulture. With this in mind, a world of possibilities opens up. All of a sudden, a Picpoul de Pinet that has finished malolactic fermentation is better with cheese than with seafood. All of a sudden, we have oxidative Sauvignon Blanc from the Loire, which sings with roast piglet but isn't so great with whitefish. With this new way of looking at wine, we are always on our toes, and we really have to *taste* things together and start over in the pairing game. Wine is alive again. How fun.

There are some things, however, that you can't fuck up. The below pairings will always have a place at Joe Beef:

- Garlic snails and Aligoté
- Jambon Persillé with classic Chardonnay
- Comté and Savagnin
- The wines of Bandol with lamb and artichokes
- Rosé and aioli
- Quebec seafood pie and grower Champagne or Pét-Nat
- Lapin à la Moutarde with Pinot Noir
- Riesling with asparagus

Vanya could easily walk over to Atwater Market and put cases of anything in a cart. But every day, from ten to five, she is at the restaurant

tasting forty-eight different wines, which most of our diners will never have tried before. She goes to the source. She travels all over to vineyards, tasting, tasting, tasting. Getting answers, inspiration, and information. Better doesn't mean more expensive, better means better made. That's what we are looking for.

The general public assumes grapes are picked and fermented, and then we drink the wine. The fact is there are a lot of steps today: fining, filtration, super purple color adjustments, chaptalization, deacidification, reacidification, enzymes, sulfur, and a variety of other tricks we're not even aware of. But it doesn't have to be that way. The good news for you is you can make wine in a YETI cooler. Yep, it's true. Guys make tomato wine in prison. If there is sugar and if there is yeast, then you can make wine.

Nonetheless, I read recently in some wine journal that when the apocalypse hits one of the first things to go will be wine. Vines have to be nurtured and tended to—pruned, soils plowed, et cetera.

We could MacGyver pears, apples, crab apples. Perhaps the end of the world will lead to a dumbing down of elite beverages. And this would be good. Less wood, less sun, and fewer chemicals equal better drinkability. Less really is more. Also, a return to biodiversity (as, indeed, there are not too many pear trees in vineyards in Bordeaux or Champagne these days).

We suggest using our wine pairing device to help you meander through the complexities of divinatoire science!

I could build a second Joe Beef out of the corks we go through at the restaurant. We have often asked ourselves: *Why doesn't someone find the courage to sell fine wines from a Tetra Pak?* One cardboard box vs. twelve glass bottles. (With twelve labels. Twelve corks. Twelve foils.) The cost of the packaging outweighs the product in most cases. In some instances, as with cosmetics, the wine is the cheapest thing in the box.

Where's the romance? The tradition? The apocalypse is near.

We asked Chianti producer Michael Schmelzer if it's possible to change from bottling to Tetras. He said: "Tetras are great packages for wine, but they are for immediate consumption, with a shelf life of two years. Whilst a bottle is what works for wine that is meant to be aged, more than 90 percent of wines are consumed within twenty-four hours of purchase,

faster than the milk in our fridge, so, yes, the majority of the wines we drink should come in Tetra Paks. I make Chianti Classico that expresses a very specific place that will continually evolve in a glass bottle, and I make Sangiovese, Grillo, and Nero d'Avola (Rosato) that are ready to drink, in their prime, and filled into Tetra Paks.

"There are hurdles: such as bureaucracy with DOCG traditions. With a push from the customer, though,

and readers like you, this could become more and more feasible in the future."

See? We told you.

Box wine equals bad wine in our collective minds but also in reality, sadly. Most boxed wine is probably not even made from grapes, let alone organic ones. But, pretense in wine is the enemy of wine. As soon as pretense appears, you'll find me drinking fizzy water instead.

I understand the historical significance and weight of old vineyards in Burgundy and Bordeaux. The history of the region, its traditions have fascinated me for a long time, and in many ways continue to. But pretense is not a friend to anyone in this day and age. Life is short. The idea is simple; more people should drink better wine. Wine and food have become more of a casual affair. When I think Château Latour the word *fun* doesn't come to mind. But, when I am face-to-face with an ancient selection planting of Garrut from northern Spain made into a red Pét-Nat, my brain wants to explode with excitement. *This* is the future of wine.

✦ Musings from Vanya (Joe Beef and Vin Papillon BOSS)

- Every bottle on the Joe Beef list has to have an element of authenticity and surprise.

- At any given moment we have approximately 150 offerings on our list, which is written on a smallish chalkboard where real estate counts. Every line has a purpose, and every wine is there for a reason.

- People are incredibly well read. One thing that's changed since Book

One, for example, is the wine nerds come because they know that we at the restaurants have older vintages of their favorite producers. What's fun is, we are nerds too, and we pride ourselves on knowing what's available in your market, and what isn't. Talk to us; we'll make sure to take you on a ride.

- A well-written wine list is a beautiful thing. If ever we travel and we want

to drink well, we look for a sensible list with wines that are full of life. We hope for some surprises as well! This is what we want our own list to convey.

- Our cellar is a maze below us. If a wine is not on the menu, it doesn't mean we don't have it. It's just not ready yet. Cellaring is important. Patience!

- We know the food we are serving, and we know how eating a five-course meal will make you feel. Trust us, you will be thankful. That "full-bodied" wine you want is not what your body needs.

- Drink by the glass. Get the Pét-Nat instead of the Champagne. Have a Calvados before dessert, not the 1872 Armagnac. Don't break the bank. We aren't here to rob you blind. We are on your side.

- Look at your waiter's face when you tell him, "Just bring me something delicious." You just won the lottery. Everyone is excited for you!

- A good list should have something for everyone. We will open bottles until you find the one. We might steer you away from Napa Cab. But *we will find something you love.*

- Drink wine that comes from magical gardens. At the end of the day, you can be sure that we are looking at all the details, smelling, tasting . . . so that when you picture the vineyard where the wine came from, you can be sure there are birds and flowers there.

Merci, Terroir! Parcels and Why We Love Them

Visiting vineyards is really boring. I know you're horrified. But it's true. Being in a winemaker's cellar and drinking twenty-seven wines is exhausting and mind-numbing. I always walk out not really sure what just happened. I would much rather have one bottle of wine with a winemaker and get the historic lowdown, asking, *What do you know that I don't know? What are your desert island wines? What do you drink with your family? If you could make wine anywhere in the world, where would you make wine?*

In the past, when I drank a wine that Vanya didn't approve of, she would say to me in her motherly, disapproving, yet always gracious voice, "David, those vineyards are dead." "What do you mean," I would say. "David," she would respond, "The vineyards look like the surface of the moon."

I've admitted to being extreme, so let's talk about some of the most extreme wine-making places in the world. If you haven't been, you can Google Earth this and prepare to be blown away.

Some of our favorite apocalyptic vineyards!

1. The vineyards of the Canary Islands. The vines grow in black volcano soil, and each vine is dug into ash and sand. The locals have to build a circular stone wall around each vine. Just to protect it from the wind! The work of madmen!

2. What's more apocalyptic than Mount Etna's wild vines growing on the slopes of a live volcano? Hot in temperature, as well as trend.

3. The basket-trained Assyrtiko on Santorini. People weave the vines into basket formations to protect them from critters, the wind, and the sun. How is it that wines in Santorini have such vibrant acidity in such a sunny, hot island climate? Those baskets!

4. The vertical terraces of wines of the Cinque Terre and the wines of Liguria are the work of the insane.

5. In Colares, Portugal, where they harvest gooseneck barnacles. It's literally on the edge of a cliff, where location scouts should be filming *Game of Thrones.*

—D.M.

✦ Grateful Dead and Hospitality

David on the Dead

I was a late bloomer.

My first show was July 2, 1989, in Foxborough, Massachusetts.

I am not sure but I think Edie Brickell opened for the Dead. It was an epic hot day.

There were eighty thousand people in the parking lot (okay, we didn't fact-check this, but it *felt* like it). I was so high I was considering going to the hospital. But everything was all right.

There were people there who had been on tour since the seventies. Complete strangers, a couple in matching Guatemalan pants sat me in a lawn chair and gave me a glass of orange juice. The woman told me to sit and relax and have a good time. On subsequent trips, people made me veggie burritos, drank my beer, shared hash. The acceptance and the brotherly love were warm and enveloping. Even years later, when we are meaner, colder, and broken, when the Dead plays, we get sweet again.

You will spend time and money, and perhaps have to travel to eat at Joe Beef. Thus it is our moral and near-religious obligation to fulfill our role as a host, and, at least some of that is owed to the Dead.

One of the greatest quotes from the Dead is "Be kind."

Fred on the Dead

Only recently it became clear to me that the influence the Dead had on us was perhaps greater than I previously suspected. Unlike most touring acts, the Dead actually permitted the taping of live shows now and then, and the establishment of temporary cities (and their parallel economies) alongside show venues. Looking back, it's a great lesson in how to treat customers, diners, or fans, whatever you call them. Morphed into a hospitality philosophy, it means a restaurant where you are welcomed and listened to.

Fred on the Dead

Another, less obvious influence of the Dead (perhaps more of a special kinship) is found in David's menu-writing skills. Robert Hunter wrote songs for the Dead so perfectly that they felt like ancient traditional chants; you never felt there was a word missing or a sentence that didn't serve its purpose. When Jerry sang his words, you felt like they were the humble tales of heroic feats: short, coherent, and percussive verse that made for plausible stories you became immersed in.

Similarly, every chef has his beat, or his shtick; at Joe Beef, we favor the comma-ampersand style. Some chefs are boldly stoic, stopping at one or two ingredients—like the late Nicolas Jongleux. Riad Nasr is a classicist relying on terminology tried and tested by the likes of Ali-baba and Alain Chapel, and for Normand Laprise, it's a shout-out to farmers and techniques.

We don't want to sound like the old folks who found Elvis Presley too provocative and The Beatles' hair girly, we are not denying the value of modern phone photography, but there is merit in paying attention to menu writing. Twenty years back you would wait eagerly for your buddies' return from Paris or NYC eating trips, and for the pile of menus looted from the very houses of the culinary heroes of our generation. You got those menus and you wondered what could go in there? What was black rice used as? The verbena mentioned was used where? How did it look; how did it taste?

I remember the pre-Internet phone recon missions: if you wanted to see Jean-Georges's menu, *you* had to drive to New York and take a picture of the menu with a real pre–phone camera and then decipher what we thought it was because we couldn't afford to eat there. The menus had cadence and rhythm, there was a grammatical skill that took years to elevate to an art form.

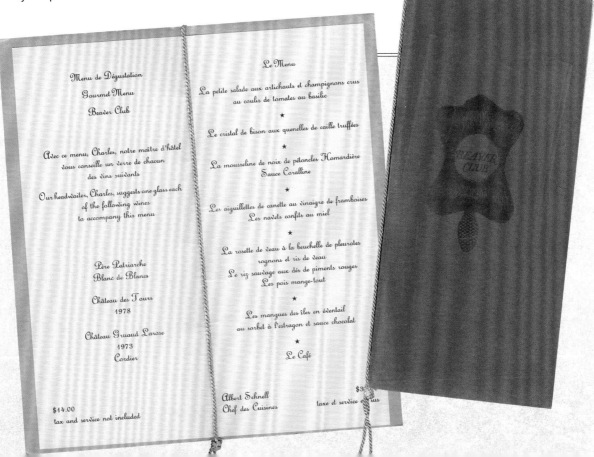

Wine Gums

Makes about 50 wine gums,
1½ teaspoons (7.5 ml) each
or 1½ cups (375 ml) total
pourable syrup

You will need

One or more silicone chocolate/jelly/
candy molds

8½ sheets (17 g) leaf gelatin

1 cup (250 ml) wine

⅓ cup (70 g) sugar

⅛ cup (25 ml) liquid pectin

Natural food color (optional)

We grew up on Maynard's wine gums (favorite flavor: cassis).

Wine gums are on our dessert list, mostly at Vin Papillon but sometimes at Joe Beef: a little plate of six to eight wine gums per table to end the meal. We have experimented with many different wines and all have worked. It seems reducing wine with sugar is fail-proof.

Vanya was once dared by a tedious wine fan to blind taste our wine gums: she nailed three out of five.

I. Plunge the gelatin sheets into a large bowl of cold water and let sit for 10 minutes until softened.

2. In a small saucepan, combine ½ cup (125 ml) of the wine and the sugar. Warm until the sugar has dissolved, about 5 minutes on medium heat. Do not bring to a boil.

3. Pick up the gelatin and gently squeeze it, removing the excess water. Place the gelatin in the pan, whisking until dissolved. Remove the pan from the heat. Add the pectin and whisk some more.

4. Pour in the remaining ½ cup (125 ml) wine and stir. Transfer to a small jug or other pouring vessel.

5. Place your wine gum mold(s) on a sheet pan. Carefully pour the wine gum mixture into the individual cavities all the way to the top. Transfer to the refrigerator and chill for 6 to 8 hours.

6. When ready to serve, take a toothpick and carve around the top edges of each gum, as you would with a knife to unmold a cake, then push the individual cavity inside out to release the gum. This enables you to get that true wine gum form, perfected. Keep refrigerated in an airtight container. Best eaten fresh.

Note Tasting jokes aside, we suggest these varietals for your gum-making adventures: Pinot Noir, Chardonnay, Riesling, Merlot, and Savagnin.

Six

In Praise of PBS

We learned the joy of having friends over for dinner by watching Jacques Pépin. The joy of gardening watching James Crockett tend to his *Victory Garden*. The joys of carpentry and essential shelter by watching master carpenter Norm Abram on *This Old House* and *The New Yankee Workshop*.

In our world, the local affiliate was always Plattsburgh, New York's Mountain Lake PBS, because that's what we could tune in to from Montreal. We've talked about our personal Potato Chips Road Map (page 115), and, for us, the local appointment of PBS stations is just as fascinating. Perhaps these stations remain at the vanguard of what's truly local. *This Old House* doesn't have to remind you that they're produced by WGBH Boston's PBS station: they *are* Boston.

We can remember doing, or not doing, our homework upstairs at our desks, with snow falling outside, while the PBS telethon/fund-raiser was broadcasting downstairs. True, you may have witnessed too many pan flute concertos or Saratoga Springs horse show pageants. But PBS has brought us a multitude of shows celebrating human dexterity and gumption. And it should come as no surprise that we've grown up striving for this (subconsciously, perhaps, when we were teens, and more definitively as adults). We needed to create our own small world with our own hands. Both at home and at the restaurant.

Day to day, it goes like this: David will text Fred a link to a big oven grill in Texas and say, "We should order this" to use as an idyllic bread oven. Because they've worked together for twenty years, David knows Fred will bite the juicy worm. Plans will be drafted on grid paper. There'll be talk of never having to

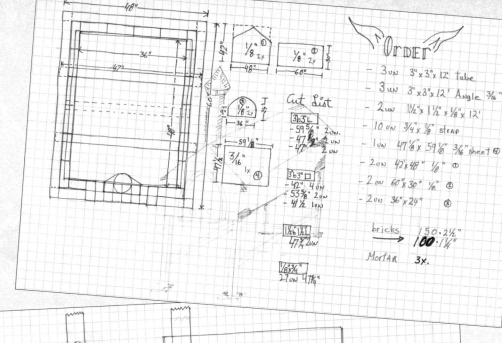

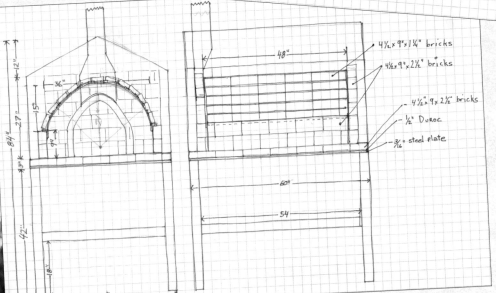

cook inside again, finally breaking free from the shackles of the six-burner Garland stove. Fred will buy tools he doesn't need. A concrete guy will show up. Then a steel guy will come to the restaurant. Trucks will clog up the back alley.

And then . . . Voilà. The bread oven stands by the back fence of Joe Beef. The workstation lies at a right angle to the oven. It's a simple monolith made of steel, refractory bricks, and perlite. It operates twelve months of the year (in outdoor temperatures ranging from −30°F [−35°C] to +95°F [+35°C]), and, depending on the time of year, it can be used for braising lamb shoulder, cooking earthenware bowls of shellfish, searing rib steaks in cast iron, roasting whole vegetables

overnight. Name it and it can cook it. This left just enough room for us to channel our inner James Crockett.

We are still wringing as much produce as we can from our 1,000 square feet (93 m) of junkyard turned garden. Since we started the gardens at all three restaurants, we've narrowed down our choices to a few varietals that work for

supplying the kitchens: Behind Vin Papillon, we have a monumental tomato garden that grows up, up, up like a TV tower. We have Brassicaceae, aka the cabbage family, in raised beds at JB. We grow Russian red kale, cavolo nero, spigarello kale. We have Swiss chard, and lettuces like green and red oak leaf, red buttercrunch,

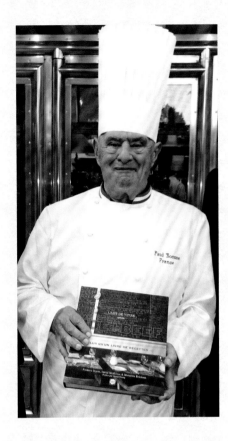

green and red coral, green and red romaine. (Did you know that because of the milky liquid that comes out of the plant when cut, we know lettuce as *laitue* because *lait* is "milk" in French? Fact.)

We also have sorrel, which we harvest as soon as the leaves are big as a spoon. Another perennial we have is lovage: we use it for our green croissants (see page 259), and also the hollow stalks make excellent straws for bloody Caesars.

We also grow hydroponic watercress, which leads us to the trout pond: in creating the garden of our dreams, there was David's love of fishing to consider. That's how the trout pond came to be. In hindsight, perhaps this was a project for Norm, the master carpenter, a professional. Because no one on our team had any experience building an urban pond. We created our own personal purgatory with 6 x 9-foot forms. Then we poured concrete into the forms. Then we added a water chiller, clay filter, and a backup pump. The result: one instant pond!

Our thinking here: a cook working the bread oven could just shuffle over to the pond, net a trout, pick a few chive blossoms in the garden, and voilà! The essence of true farm-to-table cooking. Initially, it was all going swimmingly. The water was cool and clean and the levels were where they had to be. The parameters were optimized for speckled trout to thrive. But we couldn't find any trout. After six weeks of frantic searching, Marco found a guy who sold us a few tiny fish. But then, when it rained, the extension cord that was powering the various pond life-support machines would short and the trout would go belly up. We couldn't serve electrified trout. JC Rainville, our original Groundskeeper Willie, would pull up net and dispose of the evidence. Marco would get into the car to go meet Trout Man to get new fish. In the end, JC turned out to be more of a grave digger than a fisherman. So what about the pond now? Sometimes there are fish in it. Sometimes there aren't. Like whale watching. But not at all. Perhaps the best thing that came from our trout experiments was the Watercress Soup with Trout Quenelles (page 54) and the Quenelles de Truite (page 121).

Most important, you should know: *All of these endeavors have been made possible by the generous contributions of viewers like you.*

—M.E.

Mirepoix Bolognese

Makes 3 quarts (3 l) sauce

You will need

Meat grinder with medium die or food processor

We do love giving vegetables the royal meat treatment (Loin of Squash, page 281), right down to passing them through a meat grinder. This recipe provides a way to use those vegetables in your fridge that are beginning to run out of steam—like that rutabaga that's been staring at you the last couple of weeks. We like to serve this Bolognese atop shellfish like razor clams or hard-shelled clams, but it also works marvelously on hanger steak, pasta, or just crusty Italian bread.

1 whole fennel, roughly chopped

1 large onion, roughly chopped

4 shallots, roughly chopped

3 large carrots, roughly chopped

1 leek, just the whites, thinly sliced

4 celery stalks, roughly chopped

6 garlic cloves

1 fresh rosemary sprig

4 anchovy fillets

Salt and black pepper

Pinch of red pepper flakes

2 tablespoons tomato paste

2 cups (475 ml) tomato passata (tomato sauce)

Parmesan rind

2 cups (475 ml) olive oil

I. If you don't have a slow cooker, preheat the oven to 225°F (110°C).

2. Using a meat grinder, process the fennel, onion, shallots, carrots, leek, celery, and garlic directly into the bowl of a slow cooker or a Dutch oven (alternatively, pulse them in a food processor until they look coarsely ground).

3. Top with the rosemary sprig, anchovies, salt, black pepper, red pepper flakes, tomato paste, and the passata, Parmesan, and olive oil. Stir to combine. It won't look like anything special at this point, but trust us.

4. Cover with a lid or aluminum foil and braise for 8 hours. If you're using a slow cooker, set it to 225°F (110°C) and cook for 8 hours.

Serves 4

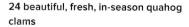

MIREPOIX BOLOGNESE ON BAKED CLAMS

24 beautiful, fresh, in-season quahog clams

1 pound (454 g) coarse salt, to nestle the clams while baking

1 heaping tablespoon of Bolognese for each clam, 2 cups (480 ml) total (recipe above)

4 heaping tablespoons (60 g) of good bread crumbs

A wedge of lemon per person

3 to 4 tablespoons of good olive oil for a drizzle, plus more to serve

2 tablespoons chopped parsley

I. Scrub and rinse the clams.

2. Preheat the oven to 450°F (235°C).

3. Steam the clams in ¼ cup (60 ml) of water in an appropriately sized saucepan with a lid. Shake the pan occasionally but cautiously so as to not shatter the clams. After 3 or 4 minutes, remove the lid and transfer the clams as they open to a clean plate.

4. Remove the meat from the open clams, and split the shells in two.

5. Place the salt on a sheet pan.

6. In each half shell, place a clam topped by a spoonful of the Bolognese, followed by a sprinkle of bread crumbs.

7. Bake for 5 to 6 minutes until sizzling and serve immediately with a wedge of lemon, a drizzle of good olive oil, and a scattering of the parsley.

Little Ghosts

Serves 8 or more

You will need

Cheap mandoline or long sharp knife

Handheld immersion blender
or mortar and pestle

One of the most unexpected weapons in David's parenting arsenal is the NBC television show *30 Rock*. When his daughter Dylan was at the age where glitter and finger paints should have been the priority, she was quoting Jack Donaghy and Liz Lemon. So when you have a dish of thinly sliced propped-up sheets of celery root, David's first thought was to call it Ghost Meat, a tribute of sorts to the episode where Tracy Jordan mentions eating ghost meat in an homage to Pac-Man's diet. Whilst obviously not PBS-oriented, this dish has been a staple at Vin Papillon since we opened. Goes well with anchovy paste (obviously), romesco sauce, and a sharp mustard.

2 nice big celery roots, or 3 smallish ones (¾ pound/350 g each)

¼ cup (60 ml) extra-virgin olive oil

One 2-ounce (55-g) can anchovy fillets in olive oil

6 garlic cloves

Dash (or more) of hot sauce

Salt and pepper

For the sauce (our bagna cauda dip from Book One) (makes 2 cups/500 ml)

1 cup (240 ml) heavy cream (35 percent butterfat)

Two 2-ounce (55-g) cans anchovy fillets in olive oil, oil drained and reserved

3 or 4 garlic cloves, finely chopped

1 cup (240 ml) olive oil

1 cup (225 g) cold unsalted butter, cubed

1 or 2 ice cubes, as needed

Salt and pepper to taste

To serve

Small jar of capers, drained

1 teaspoon lemon zest

Cherries (optional)

1. Preheat the oven to 375°F (190°C).

2. With a clean brush, carefully brush away the dirt from the celery root; then, using a vegetable peeler, peel the orbs completely.

3. Make the marinade paste for the celery roots using an immersion blender, or if you are living off the grid, a mortar and pestle: Blend the oil, anchovies and their oil, garlic, and hot sauce, adding salt (if you feel it needs it) and pepper to taste. Rub the orbs with the paste as an elite bowler would polish his cherished ball.

4. Bake on a parchment-lined sheet pan for 35 to 40 minutes, until al dente. Remove and chill completely.

5. While the celery roots are baking, make the bagna cauda: In a small saucepan, combine the cream and anchovies and simmer over medium-low heat until the cream is reduced by one-third, 8 to 10 minutes. Off heat, use an immersion blender to slowly blend in the garlic first, then the oil.

The sauce will thicken as the emulsion forms. (Should the emulsion break or split, strain the sauce, reserving the oil, then return the strained "solids" back to the saucepan and slowly add the oil back in.) Next, whisk in the butter manually, a few cubes at a time. If the sauce breaks now, add an ice cube or two and keep whisking. Season generously with salt and pepper and serve warm. The bagna cauda will keep 3 days refrigerated.

6. If you have a large budget and a passion for meat slicers, then use the machine to carefully slice the celery roots into thin slices. If you are not, use a sharp mandoline or a long, clean, very sharp knife.

7. Pinch each slice and prop it up on a plate to make it look like a small ghost, pop a caper onto each slice, and drizzle the delicious dressing, adding some lemon zest here and there. Enjoy with a bowl of cherries.

Ham on the Radio

Makes one 6.6-pound
(3-kg) ham, serves 10 to 12,
plus sandwiches the next day

You will need

Piglet leg: there is no alternative
or other options. It is *the* recipe,
and your butcher will surely be able
to procure the leg.

Meat brine injector

Small bag (2 pounds/0.91 kg) of
applewood chips and a small bag
(2 pounds/0.91 kg) of maple wood chips

Spray bottle filled with water

Instant-read digital thermometer

For the ham brine

4 quarts (4 l) water

2½ cups (340 g) kosher salt

½ cup (120 ml) unflavored corn syrup
or maple syrup

¾ cup (170 g) sugar

1 tablespoon black peppercorns

1 bay leaf

3 cloves

1 garlic clove, smashed

1½ teaspoons pink curing salt
(helps for preservation and color,
but optional)

1 fresh leg of piglet, 6.6 pounds (3 kg)
more or less, excess skin trimmed

It's occurred to us that a lot of what we have built—the smoker, the wood-burning oven, the small rotisserie—is essentially us devising new ways to cook a ham. There has been the oft-attempted ham in hay, the fall Easter ham, the corncob smoked ham, the bread-oven Prague ham, and even the ham-under-the-ashes-in-a-metal-wheelbarrow! None of them quite as successful as the jambon blanc that Marco makes at Vin Papillon, but that's a gentlemen's agreement (and it's for another book)!

This ham is easy—it requires some basic tinkering skills to fit a rotisserie in front of your fireplace or in your BBQ. And after that you need enough space in your fridge to cure a piglet hind leg for a week. Then you're golden.

---

1. For the brine: Put half the water in a pot, bring to a simmer, then add the rest of the ingredients minus the other 2 quarts (2 l) water and the pork, obviously. Simmer until the salt and sugar have dissolved.

2. Simmer for 2 minutes, then add the other half of the water. Let temper before placing in the fridge until cold, or, for faster cooling, make a mark on the pot at the 4-quart (4-l) mark with a Sharpie, and fill up with ice until the mark.

3. In a plastic container or a roasting pan, place the pig leg. With the syringe of the brine injector full of cool brine, inject at different locations while trying to avoid overpiercing the skin. Witdhdraw the needle as you push the plunger in order to spread the brine through the needle hole. Do that about 20 times.

4. Place the leg in a Ziploc bag, in a container that will fit your fridge. Add the remaining brine and seal.

5. Every day, lightly massage the meat through the bag; flip the bag every second day.

6. After 7 days, remove the leg from the bag, discard the brine, and rinse the leg under cool running water for 5 minutes. Dry the leg with a paper towel. Refrigerate in a clean bag for 2 days, which will let the salt settle through the meat uniformly.

7. If you do not have a rotisserie, preheat the oven to 300°F (150°C) and cook for 1½ to 2 hours. If you have a rotisserie: you want a low, undirect heat of around 275°F (135°C), applewood or maple wood chips on the fire. Cook until a core temperature of 150°F (65°C) registers on an instant-read thermometer, spritzing occasionally with a spray bottle filled with water. It should require 2 to 3 hours in total.

8. Refrigerate overnight before slicing as thinly as needed.

Notes This is a nine-day brining process plus one night of refrigeration (ten-day total) before ham enjoyment.

As this is the how-to-build-it chapter, this is a rotisserie ham, which means it includes a rotisserie to cook ham. That said, we have also given oven instructions.

Burnt-End Bourguignon

Serves 4

The idea of simmering the charred, smoked, dried-out end bits of the brisket is not new; but it occurred to us that these bits would then probably make the best boeuf bourguignon!

10 bacon slices, cut into matchsticks

1 large onion, finely diced

1 tablespoon chopped fresh thyme

1 garlic clove

1 teaspoon black pepper

2 tablespoons all-purpose flour

2 cups (480 ml) red wine

2 tablespoons red wine vinegar

1 cup (240 ml) veal stock or water

¼ cup (57 g) salted butter

2 pounds (900 g) brisket burnt ends

1 cup (130 g) peeled pearl onions

Salt and pepper

1 cup (150 g) sautéed mushrooms of your choice, from 10 ounces (285 g) raw

¼ cup (20 g) chopped fresh flat-leaf parsley

I. Preheat the oven to 325°F (160°C).

2. In a deep sauté pan or large Dutch oven over medium-high heat, sweat the bacon until it renders all its fat, then add the onion and cook until translucent. Add the thyme, garlic, and pepper, cooking for a minute.

3. Add the flour, stirring well, then pour in the wine, vinegar, and veal stock, stirring to combine.

4. Add the salted butter and stir in the brisket ends and pearl onions. Bring to a simmer and cover tightly with aluminum foil or the Dutch oven's lid, and braise in the oven for 1 hour, giving it a stir and checking on the braising liquid at the halfway mark.

5. Adjust the seasoning to taste, then stir in the mushrooms and the parsley. Serve.

Le Pavillon

My friend, the most talented musician Eric San (aka Kid Koala), called me one day to say there was a guy who had a train (a real one) in his basement and we could do dinner there. So we did. It was here I met Jörn Weisbrodt (who would be cast as the German art impresario in a *Simpsons* episode), a lover of Kraftwerk, old-school food, and trains.

A year later, I got a call from Jörn, at the time the artistic director for the Luminato Festival, to create a two-week pop-up restaurant in the decommissioned Hearn Generating Station (on Toronto's east side, on the edge of Lake Ontario), a location mostly used as a backdrop for dystopian movies. Since my mind is also decommissioned, I said yes too fast, only to be quickly seconded by John Bil, who also spoke too fast: John actually checked himself out of the hospital to take a look at the site. Back in Montreal, I'd already started

making fake French château props, including a plaster bust of Marianne, goddess of Liberty, for the classic French bistro of our dreams.

John Bil, whom you remember from the Fruit du Jour Cocktail (page 72) had, for the last few years, been afflicted with a disease that required long periods of rest, so in those times, we liked to watch two kinds of things together: shit we laughed at (*Chef's Table,* CrossFit documentaries) and any movie ever made that featured a restaurant. *The French Connection* has Les Copains, a dessert-trolley-and-all-the-French-classics den of opulence. You see Gene Hackman's character on a stakeout across the street, visibly unimpressed by his pizza slice and his New York deli coffee, while inside the bistro, the drug kingpins are feasting on éclairs and escargots. Frame by frame, the greatest movie moment of all time. →

But I digress. Before there was a French restaurant in the Hearn Generating Station, there was nothing. Only a dial-faced wall, giant operating consoles, and no running water—*everything else* had to be brought in and carried up several flights of stairs. We got unwavering support on that front and for manning the vintage hand-cranked slicer from David Dundas. Beyond that, it's amazing what a grove of indoor palms can do for a space.

I left my house for what was supposed to be three days. My partner in life and business, Allison, must have known that it would be more like three weeks, but as usual she didn't flinch.

All our loved ones came to pitch in: David, Allison, Meredith, Vanya, Samia, Ryan, Emma, Marco, Sheila Flaherty, Riad Nasr from New York City, even MMA fighter Olivier Aubin-Mercier showed up after a win. Michael Olson, Jesse Grasso, and the best of Toronto came out to help us.

I have fond memories of that time: sharing a pop-up tent trailer in the parking lot next to the generating station, with Benji at the plonge (dishwasher) and Garreth pushing his cart of refuse through bureaucratic barricades like an optimistic dung beetle. I definitely have less money, brain cells, and tent-trailer love than I did before, but, for two weeks, John and I got to run our very own Les Copains.

—F.M.

Thought from David on Le Pavillon

Fred vaguely told me he was doing a catering thing with John Bil in Toronto. Suddenly, boxes of antiques were showing up. Fred was ordering lights and meat slicers. John wasn't answering my texts. Suddenly Benji told us he was moving to Toronto to live in a trailer with Fred in a parking lot. I finally figured out this "catering thing" was actually a pop-up restaurant in a power building. I flew there. I was amazed. It was the best restaurant in Canada for the weeks it was open. We never talked about how much money we lost and we never will. Magic is magic.

Le Pavillon

Carte du Vendredi 24 Juin

Caviar:
Truite $32
Whitefish $22
Esturgeon $122

Huîtres sur Glace   *prix du marché*

Escargots de Bourgogne, la demi-douzaine $16

Aïoli Classique, Clams, Crevettes $28

Confit de Foie Gras au Pain d'Épices $38

Tartare de Cheval $24

Salade Verte à l'Huile de Noix, Mimolette $14

Salade de Homard à la Parisienne   *prix du marché*

Salade de Haricots Fins, Confit de Thon $19

Vol-au-Vent à la Financière $21

Sabodet en Brioche, Sauce Morilles $18

Coquilles Saint-Jacques $20

Filet de Cheval au Poivre Vert $44

Asperges Vertes, Crème Fraîche & Whitefish Roe $18

Mousse au Chocolat $11

Tartelette aux Fraises de l'Ontario $14

Baba au Rhum $12

Cœur à la Crème, Melba $11

Oranges Rafraîchies au Rhum $8

Fromages de France   *prix du marché*

Biscuits et Chocolats $8

Greens Cheesecake

Serves 8 to 10

You will need

8-inch (21-cm) springform pan with
3-inch- (7-cm-) tall edges

Patrick Thibault, our gardener, is the James Underwood Crockett (erstwhile *Victory Garden* host) of Montreal: he dutifully tends to the daily greens and produce we harvest from the Vin Papillon and Joe Beef gardens, while also leisurely providing the end-of-season greens we might use to create a torte like this one.

For the raisin/cherry soak

1 ½ cups (360 ml) water

Peel of 1 orange (large shavings)

2 tablespoons best-quality honey

½ cup (75 g) raisins

1 cup (125 g) pitted Bing cherries mixed with 3 tablespoons honey

For the cheesecake

2 bunches Swiss chard
(stems diced small, leaves chopped fine)

1⅔ cups (400 g) fresh ricotta

2 large eggs

8 large egg yolks

¼ cup (100 g) honey

1 teaspoon sea salt

1 teaspoon ground cinnamon

½ teaspoon ground nutmeg

Zest of 1 lemon

For the garnish

½ cup (200 g) honey

½ cup (70 g) toasted pine nuts

I. Preheat the oven to 325°F (160°C).

2. In a small saucepan, combine the water with the orange peel and honey. Bring to a boil over high heat, then immediately turn off the heat. Add the raisins and cherries and cover, letting the fruit soak for 25 minutes or so.

3. In the meantime, in a large pot of salted boiling water, blanch the Swiss chard, both the stems and leaves. Transfer the chard to a large bowl filled with cold water, then strain and use paper towels to press any excess water out of the chard.

4. Strain the raisins and cherries, discarding the soaking liquid and the orange peel.

5. In a large bowl, whisk together the ricotta, eggs, honey, salt, cinnamon, nutmeg, lemon, raisins, and cherries, and then the chard.

6. Butter the springform pan generously. Pour in the batter and bake for 35 minutes, or until golden, and a knife inserted into the center comes out clean. Serve at room temp or cold the next day.

7. To serve, unmold the torte and top with a generous drizzle of honey and a scattering of pine nuts.

Note The taste here is neither a traditional dessert nor a main course. But do serve it as a dessert option or a side.

Munster Mash

You will need

Potato ricer

2 pounds (900 g) fingerling potatoes, unpeeled

1 tablespoon sea salt

½ cup (125 ml) whole milk

1 small wheel (3- to 4-inch- or 10- to 13-cm-diameter) munster cheese

½ cup (113 g) cold unsalted butter, cubed, plus more as needed

1 teaspoon cumin seeds

2 tablespoons chopped fresh chives

Black pepper

Another recipe to prove that bad puns sometimes trump Instagram for inspiration. This washed-rind cheese from Alsace is traditionally served as is, with cumin seeds, but warm on mash, it's quite fragrant and very delicious.

1. Place the potatoes in a saucepan. Add water to cover by 1 inch (2.5 cm) and the salt, and bring to a boil over high heat. Reduce the heat to medium and cook for 15 to 20 minutes, until you can press against the potatoes with a spoon and feel them yield under pressure.

2. In a small saucepan, bring the milk to a boil with one-quarter of the cheese, then remove from the heat. Drain the potatoes and pass them through a potato ricer into a large bowl. Add the butter and half of the hot milk mixture to the bowl. Using a wooden spoon, stir gently until silky. Add the rest of the milk mixture and more butter, if you deem it necessary. Season to taste with salt.

3. Preheat the oven to 300°F (150°C).

4. Push the potato mash through the ricer again (if you're going for that look) straight onto plates. Top the mash with the remaining cheese, cut into slices, and transfer to the oven for 4 minutes. The cheese should melt a bit. Sprinkle the cumin seeds, chives, and black pepper atop and serve.

Le BBQ Français

When walking through the outdoor aisles of Montreal's Jean-Talon Market, especially in the autumn when the wind starts to feel a little bitter, and I'm surrounded by all those end-of-summer greens, gourds, and apple pyramids, and the bounty's just as good as any market in France, I can get overwhelmed and unfocused. When this feeling strikes, I think, "What would Jacques Pépin do?" Jacques doesn't need a plan: the market takes care of the plan. Cool and calm in a denim shirt, smiling at purveyors at the Bourg-en-Bresse market—or Arles, or Avignon, or Antibes—his recipes reflect both his open state of mind and produce at its best.

The idea for French BBQ came about when our American chef friends Riad Nasr and BBQ master Adam Perry Lang were visiting us in Montreal. David was suggesting that traditional American BBQ had perhaps been overplayed—and why couldn't we just do a French barbecue with lapin, whole duck, rack of lamb, all in a French rub (and what's more French than tarragon and white pepper)? You could accompany those meats with little légumes, some salad and rémoulade sides, a cassoulet, and an Arlésienne mayonnaise. Once the joking around subsided, in true Joe Beef fashion, the idea had to be realized *now,* not a week from now. And so, there we were in the Joe Beef garden: Marco butchering rabbit and checking the smoker; Fred lying on the ground, plating each dish meticulously on a tray; me polishing silver and dabbing away meat drippings; and photographer Jen May, high atop her ladder, collecting the visual evidence. Please note all recipe components are provided below, with no expectation you will make them all, but do sub your favorites in and out per your mood (and the size of your tray).

—M.E.

A Very French Salade Composée

Boston lettuce, same-day radishes, hard-boiled egg, chunks of Comté or Gruyère cheese, a few slices of French-cooked white ham draped nonchalantly over the edge of the plate, a simple dressing of wine vinegar and walnut oil. A proper *salade composée* is nothing more than what the garden had to offer that day, with some of what your local charcutier excels at, be it *foie gras au torchon, jambon blanc,* or rabbit terrine.

Betteraves à la Cendre, Girolle Pickles

As the fire is dying off, you will be left with a thick layer of hot embers, perfect for slow-cooking beets. Simply wash red or yellow beets, oil them a little, salt them generously, and wrap them in aluminum foil before burying them in the smoldering ashes. Keep an eye on them and give them a poke to check for doneness after 30 minutes. Peel while still warm, slice or cube them, and dress them with a splash of vinegary pickle (in this case, we had pickled chanterelles on hand).

Cassoulet Rapide

Braise some canned flageolet beans, fresh garlic, crushed tomatoes, lard, and fresh flat-leaf parsley with bits of cooked quail and rabbit, until the top is brown. Push lightly on top with the back of a spoon to submerge it before returning it to the broiler. You may need to do this 3 or 4 times in order to build up a more substantial, concentrated layer.

Cornichons

Very French, very tiny sour gherkins, usually pickled with fresh tarragon, and never sweet.

Mayonnaise Arlésienne

¼ cup (35 g) chopped shallots

2 tablespoons chopped fresh tarragon

2 tablespoons chopped anchovies

1 cup (240 ml) dry white wine

2 tablespoons white wine vinegar

1 teaspoon white pepper

Good pinch of cayenne pepper

1 plum tomato, seeded and diced

2 tablespoons tomato paste

2 cups (480 ml) mayonnaise

Salt and black pepper

A favorite of Geek Chef Quiz Night! Arlésienne sauce is a béarnaise variation, elevated by tomatoes, anchovies, and cayenne pepper. We make this as a mayonnaise rather than a butter-based sauce.

I. In a small saucepan, combine the shallots, tarragon, anchovies, wine, vinegar, white pepper, cayenne, diced tomato, and tomato paste. Simmer on medium heat until almost dry.

2. Refrigerate the reduction until cool to the touch, then stir into the mayonnaise and season with salt and black pepper to taste.

Rémoulade de Carottes, Cerfeuil, Câpres, et Ciboulette

¾ cup (180 ml) heavy cream
(35 percent butterfat)

¼ cup (60 ml) mayonnaise

¼ cup (60 ml) (or more) Dijon mustard

2 tablespoons walnut oil

2 tablespoons chopped capers

2 tablespoons finely chopped fresh chives

¼ cup (20 g) finely chopped fresh chervil

Sea salt and white pepper

4 cups (400 g) grated carrots

1. Combine the cream, mayonnaise, mustard, walnut oil, chopped capers, and herbs. Season with salt and white pepper to taste.

2. In a medium bowl, coat the carrots generously with this rémoulade sauce.

French-Smoked Rack of Lamb, Whole Duck, Blood Sausage, Beef Brisket, Rabbit, Chicken, and Whole Veal Shank

You will need

Smoker

Charcoal and vine cuttings

Spray bottle filled with cold dry white wine

→ *Tried and True Digits*

- *Aim for 275°F (135°C) in the cooking chamber of the smoker; note the bottom is cooler than the top!*

- *Tougher cuts, such as brisket and shank, are cooked to a 195°F (90°C) internal temperature, often wrapped before they reach that temperature to prevent surface evaporation.*

- *Ducks, other birds, and rabbits are cooked to 165°F (75°C) in their meatiest part and should not be wrapped.*

Our friend Dylan Kier, from Blackstrap BBQ in Montreal's Verdun neighborhood, offered us some crucial guidance on good and simple BBQ as well as a fantastic France-inspired rub. He has a simple and instinctive approach to meat cooking that doesn't clash with the dogmas of French cuisine.

The French twist calls for a non-Southern rub and the banishment of all sugar. The wood to use as a complement to the lump charcoal could be vine cuttings (*sarments*) or French oak barrel staves. Keep the chamber temperature in your smoker at 275°F (135°C) for all of the meats. As a general guideline, the collagen-rich cuts like shanks or brisket will need to be moistened and wrapped in aluminum foil before they reach an internal temperature of 195°F (90°C) (this method is referred to as the Texas Crutch and is meant to prevent drying of the meat in tougher, leaner cuts).

During cooking, regularly spray the meats with cold white wine to keep them and yourself adequately hydrated.

Of course, these are not exhaustive guidelines, but following these tips and respecting the tried and true digits at left will definitely save your behind.

For the French rub (do your own math on this one; multiply it roughly per your own needs)

8 tablespoons (130 g) sea salt

8 tablespoons (65 g) ground mustard seeds

6 tablespoons (10 g) dehydrated shallots

4 tablespoons (35 g) garlic powder

4 tablespoons (10 g) dried tarragon

4 tablespoons (10 g) dried thyme

6 tablespoons (45 g) white pepper

One hour prior to cooking: In a small bowl, combine all the spices well. With clean hands, rub the meat. The bigger pieces receive a more generous dusting.

Lovage Croissants

Lovage, used here to flavor the butter and the hydration water in the puff pastry, is a divisive herb. Croissants are not made from scratch in a day, but you can make the flavored puff pastry in several steps over the course of one day, go to bed, and wake up to shape, proof, and bake the croissants. Courage!

We like our lovage croissants with a side of sliced smoked sturgeon.

Step One

3 packed cups (100 g) fresh lovage leaves

1 garlic clove

1 tablespoon Sriracha sauce

½ teaspoon sea salt

½ teaspoon white pepper

1 tablespoon spinach powder

1. Combine all the ingredients in the bowl of a high-speed blender and purée completely.

2. Strain the purée through a fine-mesh sieve into a small bowl, letting the sieve and bowl sit for 30 minutes or so. Press down gently on the pulp to extract the last bit of juice, and reserve. Divide the purée in half, one part for the butter and another part for the dough.

Step Two

2¾ cups (330 g) bread flour

¼ cup (50 g) sugar

2 tablespoons milk powder

1 tablespoon fleur de sel

¼ cup (57 g) unsalted butter, softened

2 packets (5 to 7 g each) active dry yeast

1 cup (240 ml) water plus reserved lovage juice

1. Combine all the ingredients in the bowl of a stand mixer fitted with the hook attachment, mixing on low speed for 5 minutes, until the dough is sticky and uniform.

2. Turn the dough out onto a lightly floured work surface (do not wash the mixer bowl!), and shape into a 4 x 10-inch (10 x 25-cm) rectangle. Wrap it in plastic wrap and refrigerate for 2 to 4 hours.

Step Three

1¼ cups (250 g) salted or unsalted cultured butter, softened

Reserved lovage pulp

2 tablespoons bread flour

1. In the unwashed bowl of the mixer now fitted with the paddle attachment, combine the butter, lovage pulp, and flour. Mix on low speed until well combined and the green hue is uniform throughout.

2. Lay a sheet of plastic wrap on your work surface. Spread the butter mixture onto the plastic wrap, using an offset spatula or ruler to shape it into a 7-inch (18-cm) square of even thickness. Transfer to a flat plate or small pan and refrigerate next to the dough from Step Two.

Step Four

1. Working on a lightly floured and cool surface, and rolling in one direction only, roll the chilled dough rectangle into a 7 x 14-inch (17 x 34-cm) rectangle, making sure you get the edges as straight and even as possible—it's okay to roll a little larger, then trim down to size with a knife. →

2. Lay the chilled butter square directly over one half of the dough rectangle, then fold the rest of the dough over the butter, pressing the edges together gently to seal.

3. Roll this package out into a new 7 x 14-inch (17 x 34-cm) rectangle, again rolling in one direction only, trimming to size as needed. Fold the top third of the dough down toward the center, then fold the bottom third of the dough over the flap you've just created (like a business letter) and wrap this square of dough in plastic wrap. Make a note on the plastic that reads "Turn 1" and the time. Refrigerate.

4. Every hour, remove the dough from the fridge, unwrap, and position it on your counter like it's a book you're about to open, with the "spine" to your left. Repeat step 3, then mark "Turn 2" and the time. Repeat this every hour for a grand total of 4 turns, then go to bed!

Step Five

Egg wash made from ⅓ cup (80 ml) whole milk and 1 large egg yolk

1. Preheat the oven to 400°F (200°C). This will warm your kitchen and help the croissants rise prior to baking.

2. Roll the dough out to a large rectangle about ½ inch (1 cm) thick, working to maintain as rectangular a shape as possible.

3. Cut 6-inch- (15-cm-) wide strips horizontally across the width of the rectangle (rather than the length).

4. Cut each 6-inch (15-cm) strip into 2 triangles.

5. Roll each triangle up onto itself, starting at the base of the triangle and tucking the point under. Transfer to a large parchment-lined sheet pan. Brush each croissant with the egg wash.

6. Let the croissants rise in a warm spot for 1½ to 2½ hours.

7. Bake for 20 minutes until golden brown.

Bee Pollen Gâteau Basque, Buckwheat Honey Parfait, and Apricot Sauce

Serves 8 to 10

You will need

8-inch (20-cm) cake ring set on a parchment-lined sheet pan

Semifreddo mold, or a vessel of your choosing—or individual molds

People believe it prevents gangrene, cures strep throat, and, in some parts of the world, serves as barter currency for marijuana—honey is the true panacea. Honey doesn't cure all, however. In one of Fred and Meredith's self-prescription experiments, it was concluded that honey application doesn't alleviate shingles. You will just be sticky. With shingles.

Bee pollen enjoys its own share of attributed virtues, but it's actually great for its almost meatlike flavor, unique in today's pantry staples. A word of caution: try it slowly at first and build up a tolerance to it before you go all Joey Chestnut on that gâteau Basque.

For the apricot sauce

One 14-ounce (400-g) can apricot halves in light syrup

3 tablespoons apricot jam

Juice of ½ lemon

2 tablespoons brandy

For the parfait

4 large egg yolks

4½ tablespoons (37 g) sugar

3 tablespoons buckwheat honey

¼ cup (60 ml) apricot sauce (see above)

1½ cups (360 ml) heavy cream (35 percent butterfat)

3 large egg whites

Tiny pinch of salt

For the gâteau Basque

¾ cup (75 g) almond flour

½ teaspoon sea salt

¼ cup (60 g) bee pollen, plus more for garnish

1 cup (200 g) plus 2 tablespoons sugar

1 tablespoon water

½ cup (113 g) unsalted butter, softened

1 large egg plus 2 large egg yolks

¼ teaspoon almond extract

1 tablespoon brandy

1⅔ cups (250 g) Bob's Red Mill Gluten Free 1-to-1 baking flour

2 teaspoons baking powder

¼ cup (80 g) apricot jam

1. Make the apricot sauce: Combine the ingredients for the sauce in a small saucepan over medium-high heat, and bring to a sustained boil for 2 minutes. Carefully transfer to a blender and blend into a uniform purée.

2. Focus on the parfait next: In the bowl of a stand mixer fitted with the whisk attachment, whisk the egg yolks on slow speed until lighter in color.

3. In a small saucepan over medium high heat, bring 3 tablespoons of the sugar, the honey, and the apricot sauce to a boil, and maintain the boil for 90 seconds before pouring this hot

syrup very slowly over the yolks, having increased the speed of the mixer to high. Mix until the egg/syrup mixture turns whitish and is significantly thicker in texture, and continue to whisk until the side of the mixing bowl registers as lukewarm to the touch, about 5 minutes. Transfer the parfait base to a small bowl or container and refrigerate.

4. Rinse the mixing bowl and whisk, then use the stand mixer to whip the cream to soft peaks. Transfer the cream to a bigger mixing bowl and refrigerate.

5. Wash the mixing bowl and whisk, then whip the egg whites, salt, and the remaining 1½ tablespoons sugar to stiff peaks. Set aside.

6. Gently but thoroughly mix the egg yolk mixture into the bowl of whipped cream.

7. Working in batches, whisk in the whipped egg whites, but switch to a spatula to fold in (rather than whisk) the last of the egg whites. Transfer →

the parfait base into the mold(s) of your choosing and freeze overnight.

8. Make the cake: In a food processor, combine the almond flour, salt, pollen, and 1 cup of the sugar, and pulse a few times to obtain a fine uniform texture. Sift the mixture into a bowl and set aside.

9. In a small saucepan or using the microwave, bring the remaining 2 tablespoons sugar and the water to a quick boil: that's your basting syrup. Set aside.

10. In the bowl of a stand mixer fitted with the paddle attachment, cream the butter on medium-high speed, then add the pollen mixture and continue to paddle until light in color.

11. Add the egg, egg yolks, almond extract, and brandy, and mix for an additional minute on high.

12. Reduce the speed to low, add the gluten-free flour and baking powder, and mix well. Transfer the dough onto a sheet of plastic wrap, shape into a ball, wrap tightly, and refrigerate for 2 hours.

13. When ready to bake, preheat the oven to 350°F (180°C).

14. Unwrap the dough, and lay it between two fresh sheets of plastic wrap. Roll the dough out into a large rectangle, to a thickness of ½ inch (1 generous 1 cm), large enough to accommodate two 8-inch (20-cm) circles.

15. Using the ring mold, cut out 2 cake circles. Butter and flour the ring mold, lay it on the parchment-lined sheet pan, then nestle one circle of dough into it. Cover the surface of the dough with the apricot jam, leaving a border of about 1 inch (2.5 cm) around the perimeter. Cover with the remaining disk, pressing

lightly to seal the edges. Using a sharp knife, score the surface of the cake lightly in a diamond/crisscross pattern.

16. Bake the cake for 22 minutes, remove from the oven, and baste with the syrup, then return to the oven and bake for another 6 minutes, until the top is golden brown. Let the cake cool for a few minutes before removing the ring mold.

17. When the gâteau Basque is at room temperature, unmold the parfait, then sprinkle bee pollen over the top. Serve with the apricot sauce.

Notes The parfait needs to be frozen overnight. Plan accordingly.

Naturally, Fred built his own beehive parfait mold. You don't have to do any such thing.

Pumpkin Natas

Makes 12 natas

━━━━━━━━━━━━━

You will need

12-cup muffin tin

Paper liners

4⅓-inch (11-cm) ring mold/
pastry cutter or bowl

Fine-mesh sieve

Ice cream scoop (the kind with a spring
release) for portioning the batter

1 pound (454 g) puff pastry, thawed
but chilled

1 cup (250 g) pumpkin purée

1 cup (240 ml) whole milk

½ cup (125 g) sugar

2 tablespoons honey

¼ cup (30 g) cornstarch

½ teaspoon ground cinnamon

¼ teaspoon ground nutmeg

¼ teaspoon ground cloves

¼ teaspoon ground ginger

¼ teaspoon pure vanilla extract

½ teaspoon sea salt

Pinch of black pepper

1 large egg

3 ounces (85 g) large egg yolks
(5 to 6 yolks)

There was a time when there were more shops selling *pastéis de nata* on the Plateau than there are vape shops now—Montreal has a big Portuguese community. These little custard tarts were part of a classic picnic on the Mountain along with Portugalia's grilled chicken and a bag of chips. Rumor has it these natas came about as a delicious way for Portuguese nuns to use leftover egg yolks after having used the whites to starch their habits . . . or clarify their wine.

---

1. Preheat the oven to 425°F (220°C) and lightly grease a 12-cup muffin tin.

2. Roll out the puff pastry to a thickness of ⅛ inch (2 mm). Using a round cutter or bowl, cut out 1 round of puff pastry—check that it fits nicely in the muffin tin (and adjust the size of your mold or bowl) before cutting the remaining 11 circles.

3. Delicately press a pastry round into each muffin cup. Refrigerate for 1 hour.

4. In a blender, mix all the remaining ingredients at medium speed, adding the egg and egg yolks at the end. When well blended, transfer this custard base to a medium saucepan.

5. Cook the custard over medium-high heat, whisking constantly, until it starts to thicken and bubble. Pass through a fine-mesh sieve into a bowl.

6. Portion the custard into the 12 cups, ideally using an ice cream scoop, or a soupspoon and a small spatula. Don't overfill the cups: two-thirds full is great.

7. Bake for 10 to 12 minutes, until the crusts are nicely golden. Allow the natas to cool slightly before unmolding. To get that distinctive burnt crust atop the tarts in a home oven, pass them under the broiler for 2 to 3 minutes, keeping a vigilant eye on them.

Seven

Beyond Roadblocks
and Bannock

In the winter of 2012, we received the following e-mail:

Shé:kon skennenkowa, greetings Brothers,

I recently bought a copy of your book, The Art of Living According to Joe Beef, *and am writing to ask you a question about it, as a Kahnawake Mohawk and as a (now) fan of your work.*

First, I want to say that I think the book is masterful in its presentation of the culture of our beloved city. Congratulations to you both and Ms. Erickson on its well-deserved praise and popularity.

But, I read through the book a few times and was left wondering this: How can these people write a whole book about Montreal and not mention Mohawks? Don't they know that the Kanien'kehá:ka, Mohawks, have been here for millennia, that Hochelaga is not just a street name? Our peoples' cultures and histories have been intertwined throughout the ages, and we are still here today as rightful owners of Kawennote Tiohtià:ke, the island of Montreal. If you are going to tell people about Montreal, you should not be excluding the original people of this place from the story.

It's frustrating that as the world comes to know and appreciate Montreal better through your voices, the deeper history of the people and the land and the relationships that form this place will, once again, not be heard.

If you ever want to talk about this, let me know.

Skennen, peace,
Taiaiake

We couldn't argue with this letter. Tai was right.

Fred and David both grew up and still live near the Mercier Bridge, which leads directly to the Mohawk land of Kahnawake. They drive by the land every day on their way to the restaurants. Looking over from the Montreal side, it's a beautiful view: the river narrows where the bridge is; to the east lie the busy seaway lanes of the mighty St. Lawrence; to the west, the river becomes Lac Saint-Louis.

So we invited Tai, an Indigenous Governance scholar, professor at the University of Victoria, and former marine, to Joe Beef. We spoke about Mohawk life, corn seed saving, the Halal goat farm/slaughterhouse, Club Rez. We talked about his dad, an ironworker who often took off to work on the building of New York City skyscrapers, a common job for men in Kahnawake (so common, in fact, we hear there is a corner in Brooklyn referred to as Little Caughnawaga—the colonized spelling—where the local tavern would serve traditional corn bread and gravy). Tai then invited us to his house, where his mom made us her corn soup and even let Tai say it was his (see page 277). We went fishing with Tai and his lovably fierce and bombastic friend Eric "Dirt" McComber, who caught us sturgeon, from which we made Jamaican patties (see page 275), and who schooled us on the ways of the old Kahnawake fisheries. We talked about how cities repossessed the land when the seaway was being built in the 1960s. We talked about Saint Kateri, the Mowhak saint, the miracles attributed to her, and her role in Leonard Cohen's *Beautiful Losers.*

We talked about Montreal and the hot-blooded tension between the First Nations peoples and the French four hundred years ago and how you see it in Quebecers today. We talked of the *filles du roi*, and we imagined what it must have been like back then for the hungry Scots, Brits, French, and Irish arriving on the island—a virtual all-you-can-eat buffet of natural resources—looking for a fresh start.

Mostly we shared our own frustrations with the modern-day city of Montreal: in the fall of 2015, 2 billion gallons of raw sewage were knowingly dumped into the St. Lawrence River while a major city sewer connector was being repaired and updated. The mayor at the time declared that damage to the environment was "minimal," and the work was "progressing at record speed." Our children were being told to drink bottled water as a precaution. Unlike the 1990 Oka Crisis, when Mohawks put up roadblocks—including one on the Mercier Bridge to protest the expansion of a golf course on disputed land (and Fred was a pudgy teen focused on ham radio, drinking the blue Kool-Aid from Télé-Métropole)—this time we were old enough to understand what was happening all around us. The St. Lawrence is a river people eat from, an actual, legitimate source of food. It's something we all share.

p. 569

p. 513

On that day we remembered the rage, felt it deeply, and wanted to park a truck across any roadway to protest. But news upon news mounted over the CBC, kids had

to be picked up, calls made, and restaurants run. And so the fever-pitch anger fizzled, and we kept following the ever-changing right side of the road.

We asked Tai to give us a few words of his own, thoughts beyond roadblocks and bannock—the OG of native bread—for this book. He obliged with the following.

WE WERE ALWAYS HERE

by Taiaiake Alfred

The river runs from lake to shallow shore and beyond the rapids to the deep water. I stand beside it with my eyes closed feeling light emerge in the sky and ancient prayers rise from the ground. The river flowing sounds like an ancestral song from a time when kindness flowed through the generations. The river runs and the ancestors are there with me and I can hear their words. As long as the earth exists, and grasses, trees, and plants grow wild, as long as springs emerge from the ground and as long as rivers flow, and the sun journeys across the sky, the moon turns in her phases and there are stars guiding us at night, as long as winds stir the land, the earthly world and the heavenly world will be in harmony.

The world knows this place as Montreal, an island-city in the middle of a river called the St. Lawrence, the city and its valley the spiritual heart of a nation, whether that country is Canada or Quebec. It's been this way for 375 years. But the country looks different when you see it through Indigenous eyes. To us, this place is Kawennote Tiohtià:ke, "the island that divides." It sits in the middle of Kaniatero'wane:ne, "the great flowing majesty." And all of this, on the prairie we call Kentá:ke, is the heart and home of the Kanien'kehá:ka, "the people of the flint." It's been this way for thousands of years.

Our people and our relatives lived and worked and warred; governed, planted, and hunted; feasted; were born and raised their children and died and buried in this land, in these waters, on these islands, for countless generations before a lost sea captain named Jacques Cartier got stuck and sick at Kahnawà:ke—this wasn't China, as he believed. It was Kanien'ke, Mohawk territory, and it was a paradise of nature—we Indigenous Nations lived here for thousands of years using the land. The land itself was so strong and verdant that you could walk from Montreal to Florida under a tree canopy so thick that it blocked out the sun just like it still does in the Amazonian rain forest today.

Our special connection is to this place, and it is not only named, it is deeply storied, embodied; we feel it in our bones. To be Indigenous is to be of this place in all senses. As Onkwehonwe people, our culture and spirituality and language are drawn right from this land and these waters, and we are inseparable from the web of relations that make up the

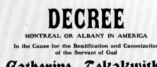

natural environment and landscape here. This is the difference between Mohawks and other people who have come to live in this place. This is our ancient, true, and only home. Our names and ancestral memories, our religion and epics, have all risen from this place on earth.

It was our people who saved Jacques Cartier and his crew from scurvy with corn bread and the gift of *onenta,* medicine from the pine tree, so that he could go back home to France. Our men worked as fishing guides, taking these visitors out on the river to catch walleye and yellow perch and eels and especially *teionatienitare*, sturgeon, showing them all of the best fishing spots and teaching them about the river. Women would earn money by smoking eels and cooking meals of river fish and sharing their knowledge about the plants and medicines found in this

area; there were great tunnels of strawberries and delicacies like *tarakwi*, which is a kind of date that tastes like wild candy.

But it has been many years since our people made treaties with the Europeans who followed Jacques Cartier here, a peace made of sacred promises of mutual respect and sharing of knowledge of the foods and medicines so that people from Europe could make a life here. In those years, treachery, waves of newcomers, and apocalyptic winds of change bent us low and overwhelmed us and swept our stories from the land. As Canada grew and industry replaced land-based culture, our gifts were forgotten and our knowledge discarded. We were forgotten, yet we have always been here. Kahnawake is only six miles (ten kilometers) from downtown Montreal, on the

we have left of our land, culture, and community. This is what underlies our fierce independence and drives our self-determination, to build our own schools, to teach our language, and to stand up to protect the land and our rights as we did in the summer of 1990. We know that we are the spiritual owners of this land, even if we are currently outnumbered. This is still Kanien'ke, and this place will always be Mohawk territory.

In terms of our relationship to Canadians, we are told that we are in the Era of Reconciliation, a project that has recently been proclaimed and seems to be embraced enthusiastically by people in this country. Reconciliation at its core is a search for authenticity. But, as we've witnessed, it can easily turn into window dressing for colonialism. In its deepest sense, reconciliation means respecting the rights of the original people, the spiritual owners of the land, to live our culture in our homeland and working with us to create new ways to allow us to do that and to restore a regime of peaceful coexistence and respect between our peoples. We don't need governments to do this. This is the work of people, like us. Individuals reaching out across racial and cultural divides and remaking relationships is key to true reconciliation. It is everyday action, getting to know the original people

south shore of the St. Lawrence river, and hardly anyone in Montreal knows where it is. Fewer have taken the time to go there.

Yet we remain. The stories we tell our children are of our creation and ancient presence in this place. We remind ourselves and teach our children about our loss and the pain of colonialism too. We are angry, but we are not consumed by the past, because we know that we have a responsibility to our children and future generations, the faces that are yet to emerge from the earth, to continue to live. This is the spirit of survival and resurgence, adapting to the new reality of this place while staying true to who we are as Onkwehonwe. It is tenaciously holding on to and defending what

and the history of the place that you live by sharing knowledge of the land and food. Changing attitudes and behaviors through friendship, undermining colonial assumptions and arrogances by talking together, arguing with one another . . . this is the real work of decolonization.

The dawn feels like a homecoming as the wind off the wide water caresses the land. Nations of insects throbbing in the grass are ready to rise too on the heat, and the air is moist, colored by buzzing cicadas, crickets, and the tsi-rap konk-ah-reeee *of red-winged blackbirds. I move through a patch of milkweed and mustard grass, feeling the sharp edges of plants against the thin skin of my ankles. The shore is shimmering water and huge flat rocks lying in a natural steppe, the scent of marsh marigold, dark clay, crayfish, and fish life. On my knees on the mossy carpet, I lift the river onto my face and splash it on my eyes, into my ears, and onto my lips. I bend into the river and drink the water; it is sweet and alive and cool. Turning my face to the wind, I feel the harmony of earth and heaven and I am in love with this desecrated majesty. The sun rises above the horizon, the river runs, and I reach into the massive flow and drink it in again and again.*

SUGGESTED READINGS

Alfred, Taiaiake. *Wasáse: Indigenous Pathways of Action and Freedom.* Toronto: University of Toronto Press, 2005.

Dickason, Oliva P. *A Concise History of Canada's First Nations.* Toronto: Oxford University Press Canada, 2006.

Kimmerer, Robin Wall. *Braiding Sweetgrass: Indigenous Wisdom, Scientific Knowledge, and the Teaching of the Plains.* Minneapolis, MN: Milkweed Editions, 2013.

King, Thomas. *The Inconvenient Indian: A Curious Account of Native People in North America.* Toronto: Anchor Canada, 2013.

Saul, John Ralston. *The Comeback: How Aboriginals Are Reclaiming Power and Influence.* New York: Viking, 2014.

Weatherford, Jack. *Indian Givers: How the Indians of the Americas Transformed the World.* New York: Crown/Archetype, 1988.

Jamaican Sturgeon Patties

Makes 4 patties

You will need

8-inch (20-cm) bowl or cake pan

Our families have deep roots along the Fleuve area, which includes Lac Saint-Louis, where David's house sits, just across from Kahnawake. Thus the St. Lawrence has tremendous influence on what we eat. In these waters, sturgeon, the prehistoric and slightly terrifying monster, looms large (an odd morphology for the fish also associated with caviar).

Our favorite local spice shop at Atwater Market, Les Douceurs du Marché, had a warm box always filled with lava-hot patties. The scalding meat paste inside the crumbly, salty crust seemed to be waiting for sturgeon to show up to the recipe!

For the dough

1⅔ cups (200 g) all-purpose flour

½ teaspoon kosher salt

1 tablespoon ground turmeric

¼ cup (60 g) cold unsalted butter, cubed

2 ounces (60 g) pork lard or beef tallow, cold and cubed

⅓ cup (80 ml) ice-cold water

1 teaspoon white vinegar

For the filling

2 tablespoons vegetable oil

1 small onion, diced

1 garlic clove, minced

2 fresh thyme sprigs

½ habanero pepper

1 teaspoon ground ginger

1 tablespoon Jamaican curry powder

1 pound (454 g) smoked sturgeon, pin bones removed, shredded with your fingers

1 teaspoon kosher salt

1 teaspoon black pepper

¼ cup (30 g) bread crumbs

¼ cup (60 ml) chicken stock

1. Make the dough for the patties: In the bowl of a food processor, combine the flour, salt, and turmeric. Pulse 1 or 2 times to combine. Add the butter and the lard, and pulse a few times until the mixture has become sandy and a few pea-size lumps of fat remain. Add the ice-cold water and vinegar and pulse again until the dough starts to come together. Wrap the dough in plastic and let it rest in the refrigerator for at least 1 hour.

2. For the filling: In a large pan, warm the oil over medium heat. Add the onion, garlic, thyme, habanero pepper, ginger, and curry powder, stirring well to coat and cook until the onions are translucent, about 5 minutes.

3. Stir in the shredded sturgeon, mixing well, and continue to cook for 1 to 2 minutes. Season with the salt and pepper, then stir in the bread crumbs and chicken stock. Warm in a nonstick pan and then immediately remove from the heat and transfer the sturgeon mixture to a bowl and refrigerate for 30 minutes.

4. Once the dough has rested and chilled for 1 hour, roll it out on a lightly floured surface, to a thickness of ¼ inch (2 mm). Use an 8-inch (21-cm) bowl or cake pan as a guide for cutting out 4 circles of dough. →

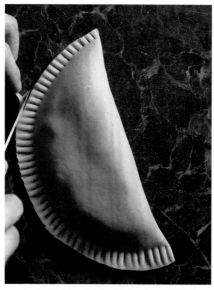

5. Spread a quarter of the filling (about ½ cup) on one half of each circle, leaving a ½-inch (1-cm) margin. Wet your finger or a pastry brush with water to moisten the edges of each circle. Fold the empty half of each circle over the filling to form a half-moon-shape patty. Using the tines of a fork, press the dough all around to seal it, then use a knife to trim any errant edge. Poke the top of each patty 3 times with the fork to allow for steam release. Refrigerate the patties for 30 minutes.

6. While the patties are chilling, preheat the oven to 350°F (180°C).

7. Bake the patties for 25 minutes until golden brown. Serve with Good Ketchup (page 214).

Mohawk Corn Soup

Serves 8

This is how Tai describes his soup: "A thick soup of corn, beans, and squash, flavored with meat, is traditionally the staple food of all Iroquois people. It is very simple, but the coming together of the ingredients makes for a unique taste. There is some variation in the dish between communities, with a definite French influence in the Kahnawake and Akwesasne versions. Some families in these communities add cabbage, turnip, or other vegetables. As for meat, it is standard now to use salt pork for flavoring, though of course, traditionally, game meat and even sturgeon would have been used. This recipe is my own version, and though it is fairly faithful to my mother's soup, it is self-consciously traditionalist in its use of moose."

1 pound (454 g) dried Iroquois white corn

1 pound (454 g) dried red beans

2 moose marrow bones, with meat still on the bone

Vegetable oil for sautéing

1 medium butternut squash, peeled and cubed

Sea salt and freshly ground black pepper

I. In separate bowls, soak the corn and beans in plenty of cold water overnight.

2. In a large Dutch oven or heavy-bottomed pot, sear the meaty bones in oil until deeply browned, then add the drained corn and beans and the cubed squash to the pot. Add enough water to cover everything by 3 inches (8 cm).

3. Bring the liquid to a hard boil, then lower the heat, cover, and simmer for at least 2 hours. Toward the end of cooking time, use a spatula to press the softened squash pieces against the side of the pot to cloud the broth. Season with salt and pepper to taste and serve.

Notes   The beans and corn will need to be soaked overnight.

Substitute canned white hominy and kidney beans for the Iroquois corn and red beans.

Moose Stew and Chips

You will need

This stew can be cooked in a
Dutch oven or canned in mason jars,
using an immersion circulator
(4 jars, 16 ounces/500 ml each).
It's optional.

If Jeremy Charles from Raymonds Restaurant in St. John's, Newfoundland, takes you hunting near Buchans, there is a good chance that the lunch he packs will be bottled moose, a simple stew of moose meat, lard, and potatoes, cooked and kept in a mason jar. Same if you stop by for dinner at an Ulkatchot'en pal's house in Anahim Lake, British Columbia. Maybe moose should be our reconciliatory common denominator. Our mutual love of chips is now known fact.

(Obviously, a bag of chips with a good stew is a winning combination. That said, we will admit we thought about a Frito-pie, but, like stretch limousines and unicycles, this idea should be left to fantasy.)

For the épices à boudin

1 tablespoon ground cloves

1 tablespoon ground cinnamon

2 tablespoons ground allspice

¼ teaspoon cayenne pepper

For the stew

6 bacon slices, finely diced

2 tablespoons olive oil or pork lard

2 large onions, finely diced

1 cup (240 ml) strong black tea

1 tablespoon red or black currant jelly

2.2 pounds (1 kg) moose shoulder meat, cut into playing dice–size cubes

¾ teaspoon épices à boudin (see above)

1 cup (135 g) finely sliced parsnip

2 tablespoons golden raisins

3 tablespoons apple cider vinegar

1 teaspoon sea salt

1½ teaspoons black pepper

Small veal marrow bones to include in the mason jars (optional)

To serve

A (big) handful of plain potato chips

12 or so shavings of mature Canadian Cheddar

A few shavings of Microwaved Foie Gras (page 136) (optional)

1. Make a batch of épices à boudin by mixing all the ingredients together. Set aside.

2. In a large skillet over medium-high heat, sauté the bacon in the oil until almost crispy. Add the onions and cook over medium heat until definitely browned, 15 to 20 minutes, stirring occasionally. Deglaze the pan with the tea, add the currant jelly, and transfer to a bowl or sheet pan to cool quickly.

3. In a large bowl, combine the meat with the épices à boudin, then stir in the parsnip, raisins, cider vinegar, salt, and pepper. Once the bacon and →

onions have cooled, stir them in to make a stew. Cover and refrigerate overnight.

4. To cook the moose stew: Preheat the oven to 300°F (150°C).

5. Transfer the stew to a Dutch oven, cover, and braise for 3 hours, or until tender. We know it doesn't seem like enough braising liquid. Trust us.

6. Transfer the stew to mason jars, including some small marrow bones if you have them. Cover with the lids, and cook fully submerged in a hot-water bath with an immersion circulator set at 150°F (65°C), for a total of 16 hours. The cooking method is not 100 percent faithful to canning precepts, so we can't advise you to store in a cool, dark place that is not your refrigerator. The stew will keep refrigerated for 2 weeks.

7. To serve, spoon the warm stew over plain potato chips, with some shaved Cheddar and foie gras (optional) as a garnish.

Note The meat needs to marinate overnight. Plan accordingly.

Loin of Squash

Serves 2

You will need

Swiss-style Castor peeler for the squash

Large oval Dutch oven big enough to contain a full loin of squash

One 2- to 3-pound (1- to 1.5-kg) butternut squash

1 tablespoon maple syrup

2 tablespoons yellow mustard

3 to 4 tablespoons (45 to 60 g) Chien Chaud Spice (The Cellar, page 5)

1 teaspoon sea salt

½ teaspoon black pepper

2 small red onions, finely sliced

2 cups (480 ml) whole milk

At Joe Beef and Vin Papillon, no mise en place is complete without squash, one of the Three Sisters (along with corn and beans). We smoke it; we pot-roast it; we grill it; we even flavor it with Chien Chaud Spice (The Cellar, page 5). It's a welcome change happening in metropolitan kitchens everywhere: treating vegetables like meat.

1. Slice off the very bottom of the squash. Use a spoon to hollow out the seed cavity from the bottom.

2. Using a Castor peeler, peel the squash but keep the stem on.

3. In a large bowl, combine the syrup, mustard, spice mix, salt, and pepper to make a paste. Coat the squash with the paste, cover, and refrigerate (overnight, preferably).

4. Preheat the oven to 350°F (180°C).

5. In an oval Dutch oven, place the squash, and add the onions and milk. Cover and transfer to the oven.

6. Bake, covered, for 1 hour, then uncover. Add water as needed to avoid the bottom of the pot from drying out. Cook for another hour, and baste in regular intervals, every 15 minutes. Increase the heat to 425°F (220°C). Bake for a final 10 to 20 minutes, until the squash looks roasted and meaty.

Note   This will taste even better if you can marinate the squash overnight before cooking.

Polentamales

You will need

Butcher's twine to wrap the tamales

For the veal-mushroom filling

2 shallots, diced small

2 tablespoons olive oil

½ pound (225 g) ground veal

¼ pound (110 g) ground white ham

¼ cup (10 g) morel mushrooms (fresh or rehydrated), finely chopped

Pinch of ground nutmeg

¼ cup (60 ml) dry sherry

½ cup (120 ml) chicken stock

½ cup (120 ml) heavy cream (35 percent butterfat)

½ cup (70 g) small green peas

Salt and pepper

For the polenta

2 ears of corn, husk and all

1 cup (120 ml) water

2 tablespoons unsalted butter

¼ cup (45 g) fine cornmeal

Salt and pepper

For the cheese sauce

½ cup (120 ml) whole milk

½ cup (120 ml) light cream

1 cup (80 g) grated Gruyère or a local Gruyère-like cheese

2 tablespoons grated Parmesan cheese

2 teaspoons all-purpose flour

Salt and white pepper

Black truffle (optional)

Just as the culinary fabric of Montreal has been built and woven from the threads of many origin stories and cultural traditions, this recipe could have found a home in any of the chapters of this book—we had to choose one! This dish is best prepared between late August and October, when corn is at its best.

1. In a sauté pan over medium heat, sweat the shallots in the oil until fragrant, 4 to 5 minutes. Increase the heat to high, stir in the ground veal, and cook until browned. Reduce the heat to medium and add in the ham, mushrooms, nutmeg, sherry, and chicken stock. Cook until almost dry, then stir in the cream and peas. The consistency of the mixture should be sticky, not runny. Season with salt and pepper to taste and refrigerate.

2. Shuck the corn. Set aside the husks, and discard the silk. Using a sharp knife, cut the kernels off the cob in long sheets.

3. In a medium saucepan, bring the water and butter to a boil. Add the corn and whisk in the cornmeal. Cook over medium-low heat, while stirring often with a wooden spoon, until the polenta becomes thick and cohesive, about 15 minutes. Season with salt and pepper.

4. Select 12 of the biggest corn husks and lay them flat on your work surface. Into each husk, place a few tablespoons of the polenta mixture, then create an indent in the middle of the polenta. Spoon in one generous spoonful of veal mixture, then fold the husk back onto itself. Use a bit of twine to fasten the leaves around the polenta/stew morsel, as you would a tamale.

5. In a double boiler or a sieve set up over a pot of simmering water, steam the tamales for 10 minutes.

6. In the meantime, make the cheese sauce: In a small saucepan, bring the milk and light cream to a simmer. Toss the Gruyère and Parmesan in the flour. When the milk mixture begins to boil, stir in the cheese and flour mix, and simmer for 2 to 3 minutes, until melted and thickened. Season with salt and white pepper to taste.

7. Prior to serving, open one of the corn parcels—if the consistency of the polenta seems a little loose now, zap the remaining parcels in the microwave for 30 seconds or so until set.

8. Open up the corn parcels, ladle some cheese sauce over the top, and, perhaps, shave a little truffle over each.

Notes These tamales can be prepared a day ahead and refrigerated until it's time to steam them.

To "grind" the cooked ham, cut it into cubes, then pulse a few times in a food processor until it looks coarsely ground.

A Proper Corn Syrup

You will need

Large nylon mesh grain bag
(the kind used for "Brew in a Bag"
home brewing)

Digital or candy thermometer

2-cup (500-ml) sterilized jar

Before our beloved maize was altered to its genetic core, it was a cornerstone in the diet of generations of hungry ancestors. Just as you would extract sap from maple or birch trees and boil it down to syrup, if corn was your staple crop, we reckon you'd have made a delicious and nourishing syrup. It took the insight and engineering/brewing mind of Fred's brother Benoît to help us crack this one. The corn is Mohawk, of course.

4½ pounds (2.1 kg) dried white corn kernels (whole or coarsely ground)

3⅓ cups (600 g) six-row malted barley

1⅔ cups (300 g) malted rye

1. Using a high-speed blender, grind the corn kernels into a coarse meal.

2. Line the interior of a large pot with the mesh bag, and add the ground corn and 5½ quarts (5½ l) water. Give the corn a stir to break up any clumps.

3. Over medium heat, heat the mixture to 170° F (77° C), then cover the pot with a lid and remove from the heat.

4. Wrap the pot with a blanket and let it sit for 1 hour, occasionally removing the lid to give the corn mixture a stir.

5. In a high-speed blender, grind the barley and rye into a coarse meal.

6. Stir the barley, rye meal, and 1 quart (1 l) water into the pot. If the temperature is higher than 150°F (65° C), progressively add cold water while stirring until the mixture reaches the desired temperature.

7. Cover the pot and let it sit for another hour, occasionally stirring and re-covering.

8. Remove the blanket, then slowly and carefully lift the mesh bag to strain. Lift and hang the bag for a moment while it drains. When most of the liquid has drained through, discard the pulp.

9. Bring the corn/barley/rye water to a simmer over medium-high heat. Let the water cook out until the liquid reaches a temperature of 230°F (110° C) (aka "thread stage"), about 1 hour. The syrup should now be about 20 percent water, 80 percent sugar. Transfer the syrup to a sterilized glass jar. The corn syrup will keep in a cool, dry place for up to 1 month.

Note All ingredients should be at room temperature before you proceed.

The Beaver
MAGAZINE OF THE NORTH
Editor: Malvina Bolus

SUMMER 1964
OUTFIT 296
$2 A YEAR

CONTENTS

COVER

(is shown on this page) drawn by Ronald Searle

PEMMICAN
AND HOW TO MAKE IT

WHEN THE WHITE MEN set out across North America, a reliable supply of portable provisions was one of the major problems. It was doubtful that they could live off the country. They knew something about preserving food, a necessity for sailing ships, but it was on the lines of salting and pickling. The resultant salt pork and hardtack were unappetising fare but they kept life in a man.

The Plains Indians had a better solution to the problem, and one on which the fur traders and explorers came to depend. The answer was pemmican. The Cree word *pimikan* meant, roughly, manufactured grease, but there was a lot more than that to it.

Basically it was buffalo meat, cut (with the grain) in thin slices or strips and dried in the sun or over a slow fire. A smoking fire added flavour and was useful for keeping the flies off though if meat racks were high they tended to be clear of flies. It was then spread on a hide and pounded by stones or mallets to become 'beat meat' which was tossed into a rectangular rawhide container (hair on the outside) about the size of a flour sack. To the dehydrated, crumbled meat was added one-third or more of melted fat and the bag was sewn up. The fat might be mixed with the meat before or after it was bagged. While the pemmican was cooling the bag was turned from time to time to prevent the fat all settling on one side. Compressed in a skin bag that was greased along the seams to eliminate air and moisture it would keep for years.

In the best pemmican, which was limited in quantity, the meat was very finely pulverized and only marrow-fat, from boiled broken bones, was used. For variety some-

which though better tasting was comparatively scarce and did not keep as well as ordinary tallow, would be preserved in bladders. The bags of pemmican weighed 80 to 90 pounds and it was estimated that each bag accounted for two buffalo (bison). So high was the food value that three-quarters of a pound was a reasonable day's ration but hard working voyageurs were more likely to consume between one and two pounds each in a day.

Moose and elk meat was sometimes treated similarly but the results were not so satisfactory. In some regions fish pemmican was made by pounding dried fish, mixed often with sturgeon oil, but it was more usual (as it is now among the Crees) for the pounded fish and fish oil to be kept separately, the oil in animal bladders.

David Thompson, in 1810, described pemmican in detail: ". . . dried Provisions made of the meat and fat of the Bison under the name of Pemican, a wholesome, well tasted nutritious food, upon which all persons engaged in the Furr Trade mostly depend for their subsistence during the open season; it is made of the lean and fleshy parts of the Bison dried, smoked and pounded fine; in this state it is called Beat Meat: the fat of the Bison is of two qualities, called hard and soft; . . . the latter . . . when carefully melted resembles Butter in softness and sweetness. Pimmecan is made up in bags of ninety pounds weight, made of the parchment hide of the Bison with the hair on; the proportion of the Pemmecan when best made for keeping is twenty pounds of soft and the same of hard fat, slowly melted together, and at a low warmth poured on fifty pounds of Beat Meat, well mixed together, and closely packed in a bag of about thirty inches in

---

gluttonous french canadian [the voyageurs] that devours eight pounds of fresh meat every day is contented with one and a half pound p' day: it would be admirable provision for the Army and Navy."

James Isham, writing fifty years earlier, comments on the quality of the marrow-fat, it being ". . . fine and as sweet as any Butter or fatt that is made, moose and Bufflow fatt they Reserve after the same manner in great Quantity's". He mentions that the meat, cut in slices, is dried on poles over a fire, which takes about four days, and then pounded or beaten between two stones till some of it is as small as dust. "Pimmegan" he claimed, was "Reckon'd by some Very good food by the English as well as Natives."

There were three ways of eating pemmican. There was the soup or stew called rubbaboo in which a lump of pemmican was chopped off and put in a pot of boiling water. If it was available, flour was added and possibly wild onions, sometimes a little sugar, occasionally a vegetable and a scrap of salt pork. Frying the pemmican in its own fat resulted in what was called rousseau (or rechaud or richot) and to it also might be added some flour or a suitable wild plant or berries. The third method was to hack off a lump and eat it raw, a slow process, since it dried extremely hard, but a satisfying concentrated food for the traveller with no time to stop.

Though they realised its worth, not everyone enjoyed pemmican, no matter how prepared. A party from Boston travelling to the Saskatchewan to see the solar eclipse in 1860 commented that "rousseau is by comparison with the others palatable, though it is even then impossible to so disguise it as to avoid the suggestion of tallow candles; and this and the leathery, or India-rubbery, structure of the meat are its chief disqualifications. But even rousseau may loose its charms when taken as a steady diet three times a day for weeks."

While it is known that pemmican lasts for a long period it is doubtful if there is any lying about now. At times a strange lump of organic matter is dug up and is claimed to be 'fossil pemmican'. This is a trap for the unwary for in all likelihood this 'relic' will turn out to be a fungus known as tuckahoe (*Polyporus tuberaster*) which is found in prairie black soils in conjunction with aspen.

There is now no more genuine pemmican made from the bison or buffalo, but the photographs here show how to make a modern version by the best Cree methods. A. B. McIvor who took the pictures of his wife making the pemmican offers the following advice:

The first step is to procure a moose, or other large animal. The meat of the animal is sliced, as thinly as possible, in sheets and strips.

A rack is built to hang the sheets and strips of meat on and this rack is enclosed in a canvas shelter, or a lumber smoke-house is built. (The McIvors have a smoke-house for preparing their meat and fish.)

A slow fire of dry poplar, willow, or other hardwood is made under the meat and kept going till the meat is completely dried and smoked. This takes from forty-eight hours up.

The dried meat is then partially enclosed in a moose hide or a strong canvas bag and pounded with a heavy instrument such as an axe or a wooden mallet made for the purpose till the meat is in very small pieces or, for the best pemmican, completely powdered. In these days, after pounding the meat might be put through a grinder.

The best parts of the animal fat are taken and rendered. The bones of the animal are broken up and boiled for their marrow-fat content.

The rendered fat is heated to boiling point and put in a container. Then as much of the pounded meat as can be absorbed is added to the hot fat.

This is now pemmican and it is put in animal hide bags, or, more probably, in moulds such as small dishes to set. Such is the food on which the western travellers of former years depended.

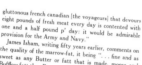

1. The first step in making pemmican: cutting the meat into thin slices and strips.

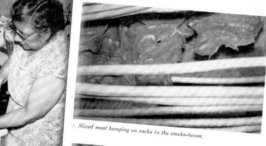

2. Sliced meat hanging on racks in the smoke-house.

3. Meat completely dried and smoked.

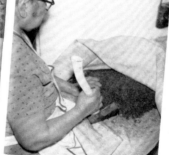

4. Pounding the dried meat with a wooden mallet

6. Fat and meat combined, placed in dishes to set.

5. Before pounding, and a bowl of 'beat meat'.

7. Fine pemmican, pulverized moose meat and marrow-fat. The copper kettle is 5½ inches high.

54

Pemmican Sticks

Makes 1 to 1½ pounds sticks

You will need

Meat grinder

Jerky gun, available online

Dehydrator

Small desiccant packets, available online

2.2 pounds (1 kg) horse, elk,
or bison shoulder meat, cubed small
(ask your butcher)

½ cup (60 g) dried ground cherries

½ cup (50 g) roasted cashews,
coarsely chopped

2 tablespoons flaxseeds

2 teaspoons sea salt

½ teaspoon black pepper

1 teaspoon ground turmeric

2 teaspoons Korean chili powder

6 green tea capsules, powder extracted

6 tablespoons (54 g) maple sugar

½ teaspoon Prague Powder #2
dissolved in ½ cup (120 ml) cold water

Traditionally, when heading out on any journey, the First Peoples in Canada used to take with them pemmican, a mixture of dried meat, berries, corn, and fat. If you're into hiking, trail running with a fully loaded flak jacket, or you work in covert surveillance—occupations that require on-the-go portable, nutritious treats—you will be thrilled with this recipe. Don't be deterred by the purchase of the necessary gear: once the global economy collapses, the person with the jerky gun is guaranteed to be the cornerstone of the postapocalyptic economy.

1. Wash all your equipment thoroughly and let it air-dry. Refrigerate or freeze the meat grinder parts and the jerky gun for at least 30 minutes.

2. In a large bowl, combine all the ingredients and mix thoroughly by hand.

3. Set up your meat grinder with the medium die. Grind the meat mixture in small batches, keeping the rest of the mix in the fridge while you work. Refrigerate every ground batch. When you've ground through the entire mix, combine it in one bowl, cover with plastic wrap, and refrigerate overnight. This allows curative and aromatic compounds time to meld.

4. Fill the jerky gun according to the manufacturer's instructions and pump out the sticks on the tighter-meshed tray of your dehydrator. Dehydrate at 155°F (70°C) for 4 to 6 hours, until fully dried.

5. Transfer to an airtight glass container—we recommend you include a few small packets of desiccant. If you're making these sticks for home use, we recommend you err on the side of utmost safety and refrigerate, because you can; they will keep for up to 2 weeks. But if you're off canoeing in the wild, you can confidently pack these and go.

Notes The size of these sticks will depend on the size of the nozzle on your jerky gun (and on how you cut them).

This recipe requires refrigeration overnight, so plan accordingly.

Wild Rice and Oyster Soup

The Canadian middle-aged chef has a love-hate relationship with wild rice; in fact, anytime and anywhere a menu is meant to sound Canadian, this remote cousin of oats gets trotted out. And for good reason.

Harvesting wild rice—specifically by canoe, because it grows in water—is as old as time, and was taught to settlers by the Ojibwa. The harvest couldn't look more bucolic: poling through shallow waters in a canoe, you bend and whip the fronds of this tasty grass against the gunwale to shake off its seeds directly into your canoe. At the shore, the wild rice is dried in the sun and then parched by either smoke-drying or blanching.

---

1 cup (170 g) wild rice

Salt and white pepper

2 tablespoons olive oil

1 teaspoon Old Bay seasoning

¼ cup (30 g) diced salt lard

4 to 6 tablespoons (60 to 80 g) unsalted butter

4 shallots, minced

4 celery stalks, finely chopped

One 3-ounce (85-g) can "artisanal" smoked oysters, drained

3½ cups (750 ml) store-bought vegetable or chicken broth

12 large, plump raw oysters, shucked, liquor reserved

1 teaspoon Worcestershire Sauce (page 106)

Dash of Tabasco sauce

4 individual packages of your favorite oyster crackers

1 tablespoon minced fresh chives

1. In a large pot, bring 2 quarts (2 l) water to a boil. Add the wild rice and a pinch of salt, and simmer, covered, for about 1 hour: the rice has to blow up and curl backward, as a threatened caterpillar would.

2. While the rice is cooking, preheat the oven to 375°F (190°C).

3. When the rice kernels have curled into a *C* shape, drain the rice in a sieve and rinse under cold water.

4. Set aside half of the rice. Coat the remaining half in the olive oil and Old Bay. Bake on a parchment-lined sheet pan until fairly crunchy, 15 to 25 minutes, tossing occasionally.

5. In a heavy-bottomed pot over medium heat, sweat the lard in 1 tablespoon of the butter. When the lard has rendered its fat and starts to brown, add the shallots and celery.

Lower the heat and sweat until tender, 7 to 10 minutes.

6. Add the smoked oysters and the cooked-but-not-roasted-in-the-oven rice to the pot, cooking for 2 to 3 minutes.

7. Add the broth and the reserved raw oyster liquor, and simmer for 5 minutes. Adjust the seasonings with the Worcestershire, Tabasco, salt, and white pepper.

8. Proceeding gradually and tasting as you go, whisk in the remaining butter. Bring to a simmer, then add the raw oysters, poaching them briefly, 1 to 2 minutes.

9. Serve in warm bowls, and top each portion with the roasted rice, oyster crackers, and some chives.

Eight

Christmas in July

This campground tradition, although well known, is poorly documented, even as opinions come aplenty about why and where this summer celebration of Christmas might have started. One theory, heard from our parents: given the oppressive shadows Catholic institutions often cast on a society (Quebec has more saints on its map than there is space in heaven. Don't believe us? Look!), a secular Christmas, where all the icons, incantations, and prayers are sifted out and only the *fun* is left would, of course, appeal to the Canadiens-Français.

There is also this: for many years, French Canadian factory and construction workers would be on holiday for the last two weeks of July, flooding campgrounds located along the newly built Quebec highways or the kitschy motels of Maine's coast. Given the daily grind they went through the rest of the working year, obviously they embraced any occasion to celebrate with a *caisse de 24*.

In the excitement leading up to the World's Fair in Montreal, aka Expo 67, some farmers saw an opportunity to convert their fields into easily accessible family campgrounds, where the patriarch could return to the city for work during the week while *madame et les enfants* stayed *au camping*. People started booking for coming years, and pension funds being what they were, trailers

fistfights by a solid half hour! And so obviously, we included a recipe (see page 295).

In keeping with the old ways, our three restaurants close for two weeks around the end of July. Shortly after reopening, when the summer is still in full swing, Marco usually sets up a freakishly amazing, not so traditional *épluchette de blé d'inde,* a corn boil, for the staff to enjoy. In true Joe Beef style, there is a plethora of far-out sides and condiments for the humble cobs, a long way from the tub of margarine, the shaker of salt, and the frozen cakes you would usually find in the campground incarnation of the corn boil.

—M. E., F. M., D. M.

replaced tents, but always decorated in a polychromatic, dreamy tropical way, one part Elvis's *Blue Hawaii* and another part Douanier Rousseau jungle. Every summer a new king and queen would be chosen, and it was a great honor to be Père Noël and Mère Noël. Invariably, there would be, and still is, a parade where the golf carts would be donned in the most magnificent sleigh attire.

Beers were drunk early, then le Gros Gin was called up (Geneva and De Kuyper gin); Export "A" green cigarettes were smoked with no filters; and punches were thrown over Montreal Habs coach Toe Blake or Conservative Catholic QC politician Maurice Le Noblet Duplessis. Punches are still thrown today, just Google Quebec camping

brawl (we are in no way condoning the Christmas in July brawl, but hey, it's part of the story).

The Christmas in July tradition is one you remember hearing about as a kid and then one day, as an adult, you are flabbergasted to discover it again. Only this time the trailers are bigger, and the golf carts more decked out. Sometimes, a real *debrouillard* (the clever tinkerer, resourceful guy) shows up with his *poêle à grillade.* FYI, grillade is fresh bacon, cooked over coals on a sliding grill to prevent flare-ups, stuffed between two puffy slices of *pain* Weston, with onions, a proprietary blend of épices à grillade and mustard. It does wonders on the metabolizing of alcohol, probably delaying the

Fred & David Margarita

Makes 2 large drinks

Fred and I don't drink margaritas. But since the first book we've had to travel. We've had to say yes to oddball dinners and oddball TV shows. So we've ended up at a couple of oddball airport hotels. In one hotel bar, a substandard wine list led to only one choice: tequila, lime, and salt. Now when we travel, the basic margarita is our drink of choice, followed by finding the airport hotel hot tub, Cisco Burgers, and bad chicken wings.*

—D.M.

---

* There are no bad chicken wings according to Fred.

4 ounces (120 ml) tequila

2 ounces (60 ml) Cointreau

1¼ ounces (35 to 40 ml) fresh lime juice

1 tablespoon coarse salt

4 limes

1. Order.

2. Drink it.

Grillades de Valleyfield, Épices à Grillade

Makes 4 sandwiches

En route to celebrate Christmas in July at Camping Rouville in the town of Saint-Jean Baptiste (told you there were a lot of "Saints"), Marco and I stopped in the quaint marina town of Salaberry-de-Valleyfield specifically to eat a grillades sandwich.

When we arrived, just off the road we (barely) spotted a sign with a little pig dressed in green fatigues engulfed in flames. This must be the place. A small trailer with *plancha*, pork belly, and a Tupperware container of spice resulted in the best sandwich of my life.

We were still talking about the sandwich when we pulled up to Rouville, where there were (according to officials) close to ninety thousand campers celebrating Christmas. Over soft-serve from the campsite dairy bar, we waved to Joseph, Mary, and baby Jesus as they cruised by on the back of a fourteen-wheeler with speakers playing Bruno Mars.

—M.E.

For the épices à grillade

¼ cup (35 g) paprika

3 tablespoons light brown sugar

1 tablespoon ground cumin

2 tablespoons dried oregano

2 tablespoons onion powder

¼ cup (35 g) kosher salt

2 tablespoons ground black pepper

½ teaspoon cayenne pepper

1 teaspoon Accent seasoning

2 teaspoons canola oil

2 tablespoons cracked coriander

2 tablespoons dried thyme

For the sandwiches

8 thick-cut slices fresh pork belly

¼ cup (35 g) épices à grillade (see above)

8 slices plain ole white sandwich bread

¼ cup (60 g) corn relish

8 slices white onions

8 slices summer tomatoes (ripe)

¼ cup (65 g) baseball (yellow) mustard

I. For the spice mix: Combine all the ingredients but the coriander and thyme in a bowl. With a whisk, mix gently to spread the oil. Push through a loose-mesh sieve, then mix in the coriander and thyme. Place in a jar with a tight-fitting lid, and store away from the light. The mix will keep for up to 6 months.

2. Preheat the oven to 300°F (150°C).

3. For the sandwiches: Coat the pork belly generously with the grillade spices. Keep a bit for seasoning post cooking.

4. Cook the belly strips for 30 minutes on a sheet pan lined with parchment paper in the oven, just enough to cook it through. You want to render most of the fat here, so the BBQ doesn't flare up.

5. On a grill preheated at low, finish the belly slices, about 1 minute on each side, moving them around to obtain a nice crisp while avoiding flames.

6. Make a regular sandwich. Really important: *Do not grill the bread.* The layers: bread, corn relish, pork belly strips, extra grillade spices, onions, tomatoes, mustard, bread.

Note The spice mix was taught to us by Francois "Réno," the *debrouillard*, a man who welds his own *poêle à grillade*.

Muffuletta à la Maïté
(La cuisine des mousquetaires)

Serves 4

Cable TV brought us PBS heroes and the cuisine of Maïté—a meridional, larger-than-life chef, who would prepare live eels and flame grouses with combusting pork drippings—another mentor of sorts.

If you found yourself binge watching episodes of *La Cuisine des Mousquetaires* in the nineties, this dish is going to bring back memories.

Consider this dish a French lunch buffet encapsulated in a loaf. Make this recipe, or just trust your butcher, aka French deli, for any of the layers. Only two rules: one, use a thick crusty bread to hold the filling; and two, alternate the progression of pâtés and charcuteries, and layer according to their softness. Put the harder terrine on the ground floor, otherwise, at the moment of serving, the first drag on your knife will squeeze everything in carton-like fashion, as the contents will be forcefully extruded by the pressure exerted by the cutting device.

Note The ingredients here are completely optional. This is a suggestion of how we build.

Layers

Pain de Campagne
(French Sourdough)
Hollow out a 2.2-pound (1-kg) bread, keeping *la mie,* all the crust, intact with ⅓ inch (1 cm) of soft bread all around, bread bowl style.

Mustard-Époisses Butter
Whip all together ½ cup (125 g) Dijon mustard, ½ cup (125 g) Époisses cheese, 1 cup (227 g) room temperature salted butter, 1 teaspoon ground black pepper, and ¼ teaspoon white pepper. (This is also great on any red-meat steak.)

Jambon Blanc

You can make the piglet ham from this book (Ham on the Radio, page 241) or ask your butcher for thick-cut jambon de madrange (a classic, commonly available French cooked ham).

Cheese

Use a sharp nutty cheese such as Comté. We use Louis d'Or, its local iteration, but really, any firm cheese will do, in thin slices, rind removed.

Terrine and Pâtés

Terrine is easy to make. Approach this just like a cold meat loaf, with more fat and more seasoning. Or buy the one from the guy who makes it better than you. We use either duck rillettes or foie gras confit. You can very easily use the Microwaved Foie Gras (page 136) for this layer or buy a good-quality duck or goose foie gras terrine at the butcher. →

Truffles

In season, use fresh truffles. Out of season, buy one of those beautiful cans of *truffes de Péybere*. Use the juice in the can to wet the bread a little bit with a very clean pastry brush (as it always should be).

Head Cheese

Trust us, buy the head cheese; they also make it better than you.

Pickled Quail Eggs and Cornichons

Smoked Beef Tongue

Omelet

A simple omelet—chives, truffles, chanterelles—it's up to you. Keep the color light, and the texture loose.

Seasoning Plus Chives

Smoked Meat Bolognese

**Makes 1½ quarts
(1½ l)**

Driving back from the campground, the cottage, or the coast of Maine, it's a tradition for most to stop at a favorite *casse-croûte* for a late lunch. For many, the pit stop is Orange Julep, Montreal's most delicious sphere for a smoked meat sandwich, poutine, and whipped orange drinks.

The *grosse orange,* as it's called here, attracts everyone from muscle car aficionados to George St-Pierre, the greatest of all time G.O.A.T. This dish, done right, brings a tougher cut of beef to utter deliciousness.

1 onion, finely diced

1 garlic clove, finely diced

1 carrot, finely diced

1 celery stalk, finely diced

2 tablespoons tomato paste

2 tablespoons olive oil

1 pound (454 g) lean ground beef

1 pound (454 g) Montreal smoked meat, medium-lean, ground in the food processor

½ teaspoon ground black pepper

One 14.5-ounce (428-ml) can whole, peeled tomatoes, puréed

Salt and pepper

1. Preheat the oven to 275°F (135°C). In a medium Dutch oven over medium-high heat, sweat the onion, garlic, carrot, celery, and tomato paste in the oil until translucent.

2. Add the beef and smoked meat, stir, and add the pepper and tomato purée. Fill the tomato can halfway up with water, swirl the water around, and add to the pot. Cover and place in the oven.

3. Bake for 2 hours, stirring occasionally. Season to taste, with salt and pepper. This will keep for 5 to 7 days refrigerated.

"Bar-Salon" Toast

Serves 2

There was a time in Quebec when taverns were beer drinking halls with tiny windows, male-only institutions where cabbies and train engineers would mingle with cops while waiting for the next shifts to start. The scent of sweaty Dacron polyester shirts, diesel fuel, and sticky beer was definitely not one of gastronomical excellence. So, they did what impaired and culinarily inept men do: they opened a bunch of jars and a bag of chips!

Joe Beef's paint-swatch DNA is made of burgundy, hunter green, and maroons, and our back of bars are stacked with bottles, torn photos, and tarnished mirrors. A subconscious yet suspicious nod to the Quebec tavern heritage.

2 slices bread

2 generous pats Chips "All-Dressed" Butter (page 60)

1 kosher pickle, thinly sliced

2 pickled eggs and/or 2 pickled quail eggs

1 karnatzel (long, thin smoked pepperoni stick), cut into rounds

8 ounces (225 g) fresh cheese curds

1 pig's tongue, pickled, sliced lengthwise

1 small bag (1½ ounce/42 g) BBQ or "all-dressed" potato chips

Salty fish eggs, caviar

Toast and butter the bread, arrange in similar fashion to what is depicted in the photograph, enjoy.

Corn Doughnuts with Corn Custard

Makes 20 doughnuts

You will need

Deep-frying thermometer

Ice bath

Handheld immersion blender

Doughnut cutter

Deep fryer

Piping bag (or if you're confident,
a spatula will do)

For the dough

6 tablespoons (90 g) unsalted butter

⅓ cup (90 g) sugar

6 large egg yolks

1¾ cups (450 ml) whole milk

6 cups (720 g) all-purpose flour

⅔ cup (80 g) fine cornmeal

1 tablespoon plus 1 teaspoon (14 g)
instant yeast

2 teaspoons sea salt

For the curd

4 large eggs

3 ounces (80 g) egg yolks (4 large eggs)

¾ cup (180 g) sugar, plus 1 cup (200 g)
to toss in at the end

Kosher salt

1 cup (240 ml) corn juice (about 5 ears of
corn, cut at the kernel of the cob with a
knife; juice in a blender and strain)

3 sheets leaf gelatin, bloomed in
cold water

¾ cup (180 g) butter at room temperature

Canola oil for deep-frying

2 cups (500 g) heavy cream
(35 percent butterfat)

The filling here is *crème pâtissière,* but instead of a typical lemon curd recipe, we've replaced lemon juice with corn juice. There is a deep corn flavor here, and you can taste it in the silky texture too! We make these upon reopening in mid-August after our summer holiday.

I. Make the dough: Mix the butter and sugar. Add the egg yolks. Add the milk and mix with the flour, cornmeal, yeast, and salt. In a stand mixer fitted with the hook attachment at low speed, knead until smooth, about 3 minutes. Proof until the dough doubles in size, 1 to 1½ hours.

2. While the dough is proofing, make the curd: Mix together the eggs, egg yolks, sugar and a pinch of salt. In a pot over medium heat, warm the corn juice. Add the warm juice to the egg mixture. Keep cooking while whisking until the mixture reaches 182°F (83°C). Stir in the gelatin.

3. Transfer to a bowl set over an ice bath, and let the custard cool down to 113°F (45°C). Using an immersion blender, slowly add the butter until the custard is smooth and silky. Let the custard set in the fridge for about 4 hours.

4. On a floured work surface, roll out the dough about ½ inch (12 mm) thick. With a doughnut cutter, cut out the doughnuts. (It's okay to gather up the scraps, roll out the dough again, and cut a few more doughnuts, though the finished product won't be as tender.) Let the doughnuts rise until nice and puffed, about 30 minutes to 1 hour.

5. Pour the oil to a depth of 3 inches (7.5 cm) into your deep fryer (or according to the manufacturer's instructions) and heat to 350°F (180°C). (Or, use a thick-bottomed, high-sided pot and a deep-frying thermometer.) Working in batches, add the doughnuts and fry for 2 to 3 minutes on each side, or until they are a nice light brown. Drain on paper towels. Toss in the remaining 1 cup (200 g) sugar.

6. To serve, cut the doughnuts in half. With a piping bag or a spatula, spread some corn custard on the bottom half of the doughnut and top with cream.

Bûche de Noël des Campeurs (Christmas in July Yule Log)

Serves 8 to 10

You will need

11 x 16-inch (30 x 40-cm) sheet pan lined with parchment paper

Piping bag fitted with a star tip

Pastry brush

Offset spatula

Clean, unscented dish towel

The worst part of Christmas, at least for me, is the unveiling of the bûche de Noël. The log lands on the table like the frozen dud that it is, and more often than not, it's not homemade. Why serve this at all and not a nice plum cake with a bit of orange zest? My disdain for bûche had never wavered until Fred and Guillaume, our pastry-inclined friend, made this, the bûche of my summer dreams, with flavors of cold Hawaiian pizza, coconut, and cheap cake. It's Christmas in July after all, and so this is meant to be carved out on a bed of AstroTurf or foil, served cold whilst you're in your swimsuit, drinking a Dr Pepper so fast it burns your throat. It takes a lot of real work to make a cake taste this fake and . . . fabulous.

—M.E.

For the cake

5½ ounces (160 g) egg yolks
(5 or 6 large eggs)

½ cup (50 g) confectioners' sugar, plus 3 tablespoons for dusting

1 vanilla bean, cut in half, seeds scraped and reserved

Zest of 1 lime

8½ ounces (240 g) egg whites
(8 large eggs)

¼ teaspoon sea salt

¼ cup (50 g) granulated sugar

1 tablespoon fine cornmeal

2 cups (200 g) all-purpose flour, sifted

1 cup (100 g) ham powder
(or if you can't find, per Note, 9 ounces [250 g] sliced fresh ham)

For the syrup

⅓ cup (75 g) granulated sugar

⅓ cup (75 ml) water

¼ vanilla bean, cut in half, seeds scraped

2 tablespoons Sailor Jerry or any spiced rum

For the filling

14 ounces (400 g) pineapple pieces, finely chopped, juice reserved

Juice of 1 lime

¼ cup (50 g) packed brown sugar

¼ vanilla bean, cut in half, seeds scraped and reserved

3 sheets (6 g) leaf gelatin, rehydrated in cold water

For the icing

1 pound (454 g) unsalted butter, at room temperature

14 ounces (400 g) Map-O-Spread (maple butter, source online if needed)

For the garnish

Large bag unsweetened shredded coconut

Fresh flowers

1. Preheat the oven to 325°F (160°C).

2. Make the cake: In a stand mixer using the whisk, mix together the egg yolks, confectioners' sugar, vanilla seeds, and lime zest until fluffy and doubled in volume, about 5 minutes. Transfer to a separate bowl and set aside.

3. Clean the stand mixer bowl and whisk attachment, then use it to whisk the egg whites with the salt. When the whites start to foam, slowly add the granulated sugar, and continue to whisk until soft peaks form. Working in batches, gently fold this meringue into the yolk mixture. Finish by stirring in the cornmeal, flour, and ham powder.

4. Spread the batter evenly in the parchment-lined sheet pan. Bake for 12 minutes, until it's all golden and bouncy when you touch the center. Remove from the oven and sprinkle 1½ tablespoons confectioners' sugar over the cake. Flip the sheet of →

cake over onto a clean, unscented dish towel and sprinkle the rest of the confectioners' sugar over this side. Roll the cake up with the cloth along its long side and let it completely cool down.

5. Work on the syrup: Bring the granulated sugar, water, vanilla bean, and rum to a boil in a small saucepan and set aside to cool.

6. Move on to the filling: In a saucepan over medium-high heat, bring to a simmer the pineapple with its juice, the lime juice, brown sugar, and vanilla seeds, and let it reduce and thicken for 10 minutes. Remove the vanilla seeds. Add the gelatin sheets and keep in the refrigerator until the mixture starts to set, about 45 minutes.

7. For the icing: In a stand mixer fitted with the paddle attachment, beat the butter until it gets very smooth, about

3 minutes, stopping the machine to scrape down the sides of the bowl a few times. Slowly add the Map-O-Spread and mix for another minute. Transfer to a large pastry bag fitted with a star tip.

8. To assemble: Carefully unroll the cake. Using a pastry brush, moisturize the cake with the syrup. Don't use all the syrup; it would get the cake too wet. With an offset spatula, spread the filling evenly. Roll the cake up again, tightly, without the towel. Refrigerate to set for 4 hours.

9. Unwrap the cake, lay it on an AstroTurf or aluminum foil–lined surface of your choice, then cut a piece at an angle from the end of the roll, and place it jauntily next to the main log to achieve the Y shape, using some of the icing as your glue. Cover with icing, then sprinkle generously with both toasted and raw coconut shreds and flower garnishes.

Notes Refrigerate the bûche for a minimum of 4 hours, but overnight is even better.

If you can't find ham powder, make your own: Take 9 ounces (250 g) sliced white ham, and place overnight in a dehydrator or for 2 hours at the lowest setting in the oven. Place on a sheet pan lined with parchment paper. Remove, let cool to room temperature, and blitz in the food processor.

We used edible and inedible fresh flowers on the bûche, but feel free to decorate to your taste: in keeping with the theme; a botched half-sleeve tattoo is a good place to start.

Rum Ball Croquembouche

It's the end of July and the peak of the construction holiday in Quebec, which means you can just walk out your front door and nab yourself a safety cone to use as a shape for building this *croquembouche,* a French dessert made of stacked choux à la crème balls.

For the rum-and-Coke currants

¼ cup (60 ml) rum

½ cup (125 ml) Coca-Cola

2 dashes Angostura bitters

¾ cup (100 g) Zante currants, immersed in boiling water, drained, then immersed and drained again

For the crème pâtissière

1 quart (1 l) whole milk

1¼ cups (250 g) sugar

1 vanilla bean, cut in half lengthwise

2 large eggs, plus 2.6 ounces (80 g) yolks (about 4 large eggs)

⅓ cup (50 g) cornstarch

3 sheets (6 g) leaf gelatin, rehydrated in cold water

For the rum balls

Updated Financier crumbs (page 314)

Rum-and-Coke currants (see above)

4 tablespoons (20 g) unsweetened cocoa powder

1¾ cups (400 g) crème pâtissière (see above)

For the coating

Colored sugar (suggested palette: orange, white, red, and pink, brown, moss, and Kelly green!)

Sparkly sprinkles

Cocoa nibs

For the buttercream

1¼ cups (300 g) crème pâtissière (see left), heated to 113°F (45°C)

¾ cup (150 g) unsalted butter, softened

For the spun sugar

½ cup (100 g) sugar

I. Make the rum-and-Coke currants: Combine the rum, Coke, and bitters in a bowl, then stir in the currants. Set aside to soak.

2. If you haven't already, make the Updated Financier (page 314) now. Set aside.

3. Prepare the crème pâtissière: In a medium heavy-bottomed saucepan, bring the milk, ¾ cup (150 g) of the sugar, and the split vanilla bean to a simmer over medium heat. In a large bowl, whisk together the eggs, egg yolks,

the remaining ½ cup (100 g) sugar, and the cornstarch. Whisk in a little hot milk over the mixture to temper, then gradually whisk in the rest of the milk and return everything to the saucepan. Cook over medium heat, whisking continuously while the mixture bubbles for 2 minutes. Squeeze the water out of the soaked gelatin, and whisk it into the crème pâtissière. Transfer to a bowl set over an ice bath and continue to stir until the custard cools to 113°F (45°C).

4. For the rum balls: In a large bowl, combine the financier crumbs, the drained currants, cocoa powder, and enough warm crème pâtissière (about 1¾ cups/400 g) to make a paste stiff enough that you can use your hands to shape it into balls. Use more crème pâtissière as needed. You will need 20 or so Ping-Pong-size balls for the first two rows of the croquembouche and then progressively smaller balls as you work your way around to the top of the cone, likely a total of 40 balls.

5. Set the balls aside on a large sheet pan. Now is your chance for whimsy as you toss the rum balls in →

different colored sugars, sparkles, or cocoa nibs.

6. Make the buttercream: Start by making sure the 1¼ cups (300 g) crème pâtissière are at 113°F (45°C) for the best possible buttercream texture. Reheat it as needed. Then, using a hand blender, combine the crème with the softened butter. Refrigerate the buttercream until you're ready to build the croquembouche.

7. To build the tower of rum balls, start by sticking the rum balls, largest ones first, one by one, against the cone using a good amount of buttercream. To improve the stability of the structure, try to stick the balls of the second layer in between two balls of the first layer and so on for the third layer.

8. For the spun sugar: Cook the sugar with a bit of water and boil it to the hard crack stage (295°F/146°C). Remove from the heat and let it cool down until it starts to thicken (like the consistency of honey). Working over a large bowl, dip the tip of a fork into the caramel and make back-and-forth movements really fast to create nice and thin sugar threads. Use them to decorate—delightfully tacky.

Notes This is an excellent way to use cake trimmings.

The crème pâtissière is to be used as glue for the balls to stick to the cone, as well as a filling.

You'll need to make the Updated Financier (page 314) ahead of time before starting this recipe.

Updated Financier

Makes 8 playing card
financiers or 2 cups of crumble

━━━ ⌇ ━━━

You will need

Handheld mixer

Food processor

2½ ounces (96 g) egg whites
(3 to 4 large eggs)

½ cup (75 g) Bob's Red Mill Gluten Free
1-to-1 baking flour, or ¼ (40 g) each rice
flour and potato starch plus a pinch of
xanthan gum

⅔ cup (60 g) almond flour

⅔ cup (140 g) light brown sugar (packed)

1 teaspoon sea salt

½ cup plus 1 tablespoon (125 g)
brown butter (see Note)

We have a financier recipe in our first book. This one is gluten-free.

1. Preheat the oven to 350°F (180°C).

2. Using a handheld mixer, mix the egg whites (and xanthan gum if you're using rice and potato flours rather than GF flour) for 30 seconds until frothy.

3. Using a spatula, stir in the gluten-free flour (or rice flour and potato starch), almond flour, brown sugar, salt, and brown butter.

4. Spread the batter out onto a large parchment-lined sheet pan. Bake for 20 to 25 minutes, until golden brown.

5. Reduce the oven temperature to 250°F (120°C) and let the cake cook further until fairly dry, about 45 minutes. Remove from the oven and let cool.

6. When the cake has cooled, break it up into pieces with your hands, transfer to a food processor, and pulse until you have a fine crumb.

Note To make the brown butter, melt 1 cup (200 g) unsalted butter in a small saucepan and cook over medium heat until the butter has melted, and starts to smell nutty and take on a golden-brown caramel color.

Acknowledgments

⁓

DAVID McMILLAN

Thank you first and foremost to every member of our restaurant family team. As you may know, I've had a difficult couple of years and it's thanks to every member of our amazing family that I'm back in it, happy, and loving every moment. I hope you all know that I am always here for any and all of you and that there is no problem too small. The relationships we've cultivated mean everything to me and are the driving force behind why I still do this difficult, rewarding work.

I'd like to thank my children, Dylan, Lola, and Cecile—you are everything to me—as well as Julie Sanchez, for being a terrific mother, coparent, an exceptionally strong role model, and a pillar of strength for the girls; and for having never turned her back on me during my hardships through the years.

To Fred, Meredith, and Allison; I owe you a solid. Thank you for having my back, I'm here for you now and always.

Thank you to Vanya and Marco. Your drive, support, thirst for knowledge, and work ethic are inspiring to me and many. It's an honor to work with you, and the love I feel for you has no words.

Thank you Jenny May, for your devotion and great work.

Thank you to the 2491 team: Alexandra, Isabelle, Samia, Laura, Andy, Leo, Tristan, David, Terrell, Nelson, Ludo, and Antony.

Thank you to the 2501 team: James, Chris, Marius, Cecile, Carmelina, Dixon, and Tom.

Thank you to the 2519 team: Alex, Max, Zara, Fred, Florence, Steph, and Matt.

Thank you Ari and Zach; to continue to collaborate with you on a daily basis is too much fun. Levity and a big smile is long life in this business.

Thank you Derek R. and Gab D., kisses on the mouth.

J.C., happy to have you in my life. Eric Primeau same goes to you.

Thank you Ryan, Marley, and Emma, you're my pride.

Thank you Mom and Dad. Love.

In loving memory of John Bil. You're with me forever.

A full heart to Katie Worobeck, thank you for time spent. I think of you always.

Cass and Julian and of course Zaltos.

Thank you Hoffer and sons, Peter Doig, Parinaz and Gordon, Dorland family, Clint Roenisch and family. Mathieu Gaudet and Joe Lima. Bait and Schlang Tattoo.

Thank you Bobby Marier, you save lives. SOS home group.

Thank you Jeff B., David Lisbona, and Ronnie Steinberg.

Thank you Lesley Chesterman.

Thank you Lenny Lighter, Richard Hofmann, and the Chatsworth team, Hill family, the Battat family, and Mike Griffin and Co.

Thank you Barke Lake Kim and Charles, and the Deguire family.

Thank you to the Franks, I adore you guys. Riad, Lee, and Jorge, and the Vetri family. Billy Durney crew. Hill Farmstead family. Proud to count you as friends.

Thank you Charles-Antoine, the Toqué family, L'Express restaurant, Stevo, Jerkonee, Barb, Moose, Tuck

Index

Escoffier, Auguste, 42, 196
Everclear:
  Crab Apple Cordial, The Cellar, 3
  Melon Liqueur, The Cellar, 3
  Toasted Hazelnut Cordial, The Cellar, 3
  Wintergreen and Spearmint Cordial, The
    Cellar, 3

Faux Vin Rouge, 103
Fennel, Mirepoix Bolognese, 238
Ferent Branca, Spruce Cough Drops, 31–2
Fermented Chile Butter, 159
Fig Bars, 211–12
Filet de Veau P.E.T. (Pierre Elliott Trudeau),
    77–8
Filipovic, Momir, 177
First Nation Iroquois, 10, 277
First Nations peoples, 269, 287
  in Montreal, 267–73
Fish, smoked, "Beauty's Special" Saint
    Honoré, 169–70
Fish sauce, naturally fermented,
    Worcestershire Sauce, 106
Fish stock, QC Spring Seafood Pie, 83–4
Five Roses tea, 26
Flaherty, Sheila, 246
flaxseeds:
  Gâteau Renversé aux Truffes, 140
  Pemmican Sticks, 287
  Rye Crisps and Cottage Cheese, 193–4
Flour:
  Bee Pollen Gâteau Basque, Buckwheat
    Honey Parfait and Apricot Sauce,
    261–2
  bread, Lovage Croissants, 259–60
  chickpea, Brains over Matar, 51
  Crispy Frog Legs, 28
  gluten-free, Galettes au Sucre de
    Mammie, 213
  Kidneys à la Monique, 44–5
  Rye Crisps and Cottage Cheese, 193–4
  Smoked Meat Croquettes, 74
  see also Gluten-free flour
Flour, all-purpose:
  Brains over Matar, 51
  Bûche de Noël des Campeurs (Christmas
    in July Yule Log), 307–8
  Corn Doughnuts with Corn Custard, 305
  Jamaican Sturgeon Patties, 275–6
  Lobster Pelmeni, 173–4
  Rye Crisps and Cottage Cheese, 193–4
  Squash Sticky Buns, 179
  Tripes à la Mode de Caen (White Tripe
    with Cider), 95–6
Flowers, dried, Spruce Cough Drops, 31–2

Foie gras:
  Comté, Girolles, Foie Gras, and Vin
    Jaune (Famille Ganevat) (Dutch Baby
    variation), 36
  Foie gras terrine, Onion Soup Toast, aka
    Soupe au Sandwich, 49–50
  Microwaved Foie Gras, 136
  VGE Consommé, 25
Frank's RedHot sauce, Chips "All-Dressed"
    Butter, 60
Frappier, Marc-Olivier "Marco," 38, 57, 64,
    177, 237, 241, 246, 252, 292, 295
Fred & David Margarita, 293
French rub, 256
French-Smoked Rack of Lamb, Whole Duck,
    Blood Sausage, Beef Brisket, Rabbit,
    Chicken, and Whole Veal Shank, 256
Fricassée de Volaille aux Écrevisses, 68
Frog legs, Crispy Frog Legs, 28
Fruit:
  Cardinal Peaches, 9
  The John Bil Fruit du Jour Cocktail, 72
  see also specific fruits

Galettes:
  Galettes au Sucre de Mammie, 213
  Tater Tot Galette, 178
Garlic:
  Artichoke Bravas, 163–4
  Base Sausage, 89–90
  Bisque Rapide, 65
  Carbonnade of Deer Necks, 185
  Deer Beer Belly, 167–8
  Dulse Bagged Potatoes, 126–7
  Hot and Sauer Soup, 177
  Little Ghosts, 240
  Mirepoix Bolognese, 238
  Pickled Jalapeños, 165
  Porter Rabbit Stew, 18
  Pot-au-Feu D'hiver (Winter), 21
  Tripes à la Mode de Caen (White Tripe
    with Cider), 95–6
  Worcestershire Sauce, 106
Garlic chives, Egg Roll Salad Sausage
    Variation, 94
Garlic powder:
  Crispy Frog Legs, 28
  French rub, 256
Garlic scapes, Crispy Frog Legs, 28
Gâteau Renversé aux Truffes, 140
Gelatin, leaf:
  Bavarian Cream à la Doris, 145
  Bûche de Noël des Campeurs (Christmas
    in July Yule Log), 307–8
  Corn Doughnuts with Corn Custard, 305

Jambon Maquereau Persillé, 87–8
  Rum Ball Croquembouche, 311–12
  in Sauce Madère Rapide, 46
  Wine Gums, 233
Gelatin, powdered:
  in Igloo Mousse (or Winter Milk Jellies),
    38–9
  in Pot-au-Feu D'été (Summer), 22
Gherkins, Pot-au-Feu D'été (Summer), 22
Gin, 15
Ginger, fresh:
  Brains over Matar, 51
  Curried Bean Curd, 222
  Egg Roll Salad Sausage Variation, 94
  Halifax Lobster Curry and Marrow Pilaf,
    195–6
  Omar's Dungeness Crab Curry, 181–2
Ginger, wild, Spruce Cough Drops, 31–2
Gingerbread spices, Mouflet aux Mulberries,
    206
Giscard d'Estaing, Valerie, 25
Globe Restaurant, 201
Gluten-free diet, 190
Gluten-free flour:
  Bee Pollen Gâteau Basque, Buckwheat
    Honey Parfait and Apricot Sauce, 261–2
  Dutch Babies, 35–6
  Galettes au Sucre de Mammie, 213
  Updated Financier, 314
Good Ketchup, 214
Grasso, Jesse, 246
Grateful Dead, 224–5, 230–1
Gray, Nora, 135
Gray, Ryan, 153
Green onions, Worcestershire Sauce, 106
Greens Cheesecake, 248
Green tea:
  Cactus Pear Limeade, 221
  powder, Pemmican Sticks, 287
Grillades de Valleyfield, Épices à la Grillade,
    295
Gruyère:
  Onion Soup Toast, aka Soupe au
    Sandwich, 49–50
  Polentamales, 283
  A Very French Salade Composée, 252
Guillaume, 307

Habitant and Other French Canadian
    Poems, The, 5
Halifax Lobster Curry and Marrow Pilaf,
    195–6
Ham:
  ground white, Polentamales, 283
  Kidneys à la Monique, 44–5

ILLUSTRATION CREDITS

All photographs are by Jennifer May with the exception of those noted here: pages 3, 4–5 (photograph), 13 (center painting), 15 (bottom, second from left), 31, 33, 84 (bottom right), 188 (child with mushroom), 234 (bottom left), and The Cellar page 3 by David McMillan; pages xiv, 7 (photographs), 18 (left), 26 (top and bottom left), 61, 72, 79 (left), 88, 101, 108, 114, 133, 161, 166, 202, 214, 226–227, 230 (bottom left), 235 (top right), 236 (top), 237 (top), 290 (bottom left), 292 (bottom right) by Frédéric Morin; endpapers (front: "Chien Chaud," back: "Rue St Catherine E") and pages 57 ("Montreal Pool Room"), 251 ("Chez Paree"), and 302 ("Frites Doree") © Peter Doig. All Rights Reserved, DACS 2018 (all works 1988/89); pages 4–5 (painting), 7 (painting), 13 (top center), 138–139, 280, 293 by Peter Hoffer; pages 2, 19, 107 by Mickael Bandassak; page 12 (black-and-white photograph, left: MP-0000.1452.165), (colorized photo, right: MP-0000.158.86), 13 (black-and-white photograph, left: M2000.113.6.63), (black-and-white photograph, right: II-222292.0), 84 (top: M4824), 234 (black-and-white photograph: MP-1992.9.2.10) © McCord Museum; page 13 (flying canoe) by MNBAQ, Patrick Altman; pages 18 (magazine spread), 32 (map provided to *The Beaver* magazine by the British Museum [right]), 286 by *The Beaver*; page 32 by Dr. Karl Cernovitch (left); page 39 (bottom right) by France Décor Canada/ Vixit ltée; page 46 by Dylan McMillan; page 50 (bottom) by William Hereford; page 56 by John Bil; page 62 by Daniel Climan; page 77 by Genevieve Way; page 82 by Patrick Thibault; page 84 (bottom left) Rare Books and Special Collections, McGill University Library, Montreal, Canada; page 93 anonymously given by one of David McMillan's children; pages 152 (bottom) and 153 by Adam Scotti; page 164 by Kim Dorland; page 188 (top left) by Suzanne Semples; page 191 (bottom left) by Olivier Aubin Mercier; page 194 by La Presse; page 213 by ITT Nova; page 225 by Gabe Williams + Chanelle Sinclair; page 230 (top) by J. C. Rainville; page 230 (bottom right) by Doc Glatz; page 231 by Fairmont Hotel; pages 245, 246 (bottom), and 247 by Jonathan Castellino; page 246 (top) by Ryan Gray; page 269 (top) by 971.011 Chb/Champlain, Samuel de. Oeuvres de Champlain / publiées sous le patronage de l'Université Laval, par l'abbé C.-H. Laverdière / 2nd edition, vol. 4, facing page 25.Quebec: G.- É. Desbarats, 1870. Archives of Ontario Library; page 269 (bottom): 971.011 Chb/Champlain, Samuel de. Oeuvres de Champlain / publiées sous le patronage de l'Université Laval, par l'abbé C.-H. Laverdière / 2nd edition, vol. 4, facing page 81. Quebec: G.- É. Desbarats, 1870. Archives of Ontario Library; page 26 and The Cellar page 5 by Marc-Olivier Frappier.